"Reilly's energetic exposition of the hate crime hoax phenomenon indicts not just the perpetrators but the entire ideological complex devoted to propagating the lie that America is an incorrigibly racist, sexist, bigoted country. Reilly pulls no punches in his depiction of the hate crime inventors and the broader network of liberal college administrators and journalists who inadvertently egg them on, all to serve the narrative that virtually every American town, college, or white community is saturated in racial and ethnic hatred. This is a valuable book about an alarming new factor in American life, written with wisdom and courage."

—**Scott McConnell**, founding editor of *The American Conservative*

"Less than 1 percent of all calls for service from law enforcement require the use of any type of force. This means that the use of lethal force is a percentage of a percentage—and that there is no epidemic of police shootings. There is only a picture painted by a media that want the public to believe this to be something of major concern and out of control. Dr. Wilfred Reilly does us all a favor by illustrating the large number of misreported, misrepresented, and misunderstood incidents in our national media. In *Hoax*, Dr. Reilly dives into a number of well-known incidents that received massive media attention only to turn out to be false or completely misrepresented. *Hoax* is a good read for anyone interested in political science, criminal justice, and other social and behavioral sciences. Dr. Reilly touches on a subject familiar to myself and many readers: the so-called epidemic of police officers shooting persons of color. Through his examination, Dr. Reilly gives a number of examples related to recent events on this subject and helps to illustrate the realities of this controversial topic. *Hoax* is a great starting place to begin understanding these highly charged incidents."

—**Johnathon Sharp**, assistant professor of psychology at Kentucky State University and former sheriff's deputy

"*Hoax* is not simply a collection of data and testimony concerning faux hate crime, it speaks on a range of issues touching on the reality of leftist cultural bias at the heart of American politics. *Hoax* separates fact from fiction and drags many ugly things we often simply refuse to believe in squirming into the light. Dr. Reilly's logic and numbers-driven style of approaching a highly complex issue is incredibly valuable in our turbulent times. It is a refreshing change of pace from the hysterics and madness of the corporate news media. If you are looking to refine your worldview with reason and facts instead of reflexive empathy, there can be no better tool for honing those instincts than *Hoax*. I recommend this book for anyone who is serious about politics and social science."

—**Jimmy Cobb**, lead singer of The Snake Oil Salesmen

"Wilfred Reilly's book is a home run. After reading a few pages, it is genuinely hard to put it down. Reilly makes many points that are obvious, but taboo and rarely made. Most notably, he says that 'hate crimes' are rare—the exception and not the norm—and that many of those which are alleged are hoaxes. The mainstream media paint the picture that the U.S.A. is a racist hell-hole on the brink of civil war, but Reilly's research refutes this. The taboo topics Dr. Reilly discusses range from 'white privilege' to affirmative action. He discusses the bizarre claims of #BlackLivesMatter in some detail: the group actually says that only (1) immediate reparations for slavery and (2) the opening of all of our international borders can compensate minorities for the harms currently being done to them in the U.S.A. Black Lives Matter activists have demonstrated, with some justification, after one of their own has been shot, but they have also engaged in complete insanity. Reilly does not deny that real bigotry exists, but he points out where it does not. Both tasks are critical."

—**Darry Pinto**, weapons sergeant (ret.), United States Special Forces

"Using hard facts and a bit of witty humor, *Hoax* is able to provide a long overdue and much needed view of the realities of the hate crimes this country has been trying to overcome for decades. *Hoax* held my attention while opening my eyes to an epidemic of falsely reported hate crimes in the U.S.A. Dr. Reilly does a great job of dispelling the myth that we are a country of racists and bigots, all the while acknowledging that these behaviors do, to some degree, still exist. He doesn't diminish or take away from the victims of real hatred or turn a blind eye to the country's shortcomings when dealing with race and diversity. *Hoax* puts the current state of race relations and the idea of a forthcoming race war into a well thought-out, well researched perspective. Recounting in depth a number of falsely reported hate crimes, Dr. Reilly does a great job (albeit leaning slightly right) of dissecting each hoax and pointing out the disconcerting similarities in the way these instances are handled by society and the mainstream media. It is a well written, insightful read that will keep you smiling for the duration."

—**Tara Greaves**, personnel specialist, Carmel, Indiana, police department

"Will Reilly follows in the footsteps of Thomas Sowell with this iconoclastic, well-reasoned, and powerfully argued exposé of fabricated hate crimes. *Hoax* covers one of the most under-reported stories in America: the fabrication of hate crimes and the credulous role the media plays in promoting them. Will Reilly is a fresh new voice on race relations in America. By any measure, the United States is a less hate-filled nation than in the past. Reilly reminds us how far America has come in overcoming hatred and how the media perpetuates the pernicious myth that hate still rules the nation. With this blockbuster book, Will Reilly skewers the smelly little orthodoxies of our time: the blind acceptance of purported hate crimes as real (often they are not), the refusal to discuss the taboo of black-on-white crime, and the simplistic farce of "white privilege" as determining the success or failure of individuals."

—**Jonathan Bean**, author of *Race and Liberty in America: The Essential Reader*, *Beyond the Broker State*, and *Big Government and Affirmative Action*

HATE CRIME HOAX

HOW THE LEFT IS SELLING A FAKE RACE WAR

WILFRED REILLY

REGNERY
PUBLISHING
A Division of Salem Media Group

Regnery® is a registered trademark of Salem Communications Holding Corporation

Cataloging-in-Publication data on file with the Library of Congress

ISBN 978-1-62157-778-2
ebook ISBN 978-1-62157-893-2

Published in the United States by
Regnery Publishing
A Division of Salem Media Group
300 New Jersey Ave NW
Washington, DC 20001
www.Regnery.com

Manufactured in the United States of America

10 9 8 7 6 5 4 3 2 1

Books are available in quantity for promotional or premium use. For information on discounts and terms, please visit our website: www.Regnery.com.

To my beloved mother, Jean Marie Ward,
who helped inspire this work both before and after her death,
and no doubt is reading it somewhere. Also, to my Snoo,
my love and companion F. Jane Lingle; to the always striving
"Thorobred" students of Kentucky State University,
whose quest for the American Dream helps inspire my positive
view of American diversity; to my twin hometowns of Chicago
and Aurora, Illinois; and finally to the scholar Thomas Sowell,
who inspired me to look logically rather than emotionally at
questions of race, class, and success.

Mama, I made it. East Aurora, I made it!!

CONTENTS

INTRODUCTION
with Notes on Methodology

Authors of books that lean right are often accused of "hating" someone, or everyone. To the contrary! I am a proud Black man, and this book is both a pro-American and a *profoundly* pro-Black work of social science. I write it with the intention of lancing a boil. One major issue poisoning relations between whites and people of color (POC) in America today, and to a lesser extent relations between the two sexes and our nation's social classes, is an ongoing epidemic of patently false claims of oppression. Making outrageous claims of oppression—"Baseball is racist"; "The math SAT is culturally biased!"—is arguably the main thing the modern activist Left does, and the backlash against such patently absurd contentions is largely responsible for the rise of the even more god-awful alt-right, which is a sort of twisted doppelganger of the SJW identity politics movement for white dudes glued to computer screens in their parents' basements. Bigotry does exist. But that fact is no justification for false claims of oppressive violence, which are rife:

complete hoaxes make up a sizable percentage of *all* widely reported hate crimes.[1]

And false claims only undermine belief in actual hate crimes. Crying *Wolf!* didn't make people more likely to believe the boy. In fact, fake hate crimes give aid and comfort to the small minority of real racists who still blight America's national political discourse. They also give a big push in the wrong direction to the much larger number of white Americans—including Obama voters who switched their votes between 2008 and 2016 and helped elect Donald Trump—who are understandably concerned about identity politics, crime, and their own children's prospects in a country where schools teach that all white people are oppressors.

Although he deserves no blame or praise for its contents, my inspiration for writing this book is a sociologist named Barry Glassner, whose 1990s classic *The Culture of Fear* is perhaps the most important book I have ever read. Glassner demonstrates in painstaking detail that Americans are terrified of false threats that are not, in fact, going to kill us—and explains why. Discussing the frequent American epidemics of panic over risks such as airplane crashes and child kidnapping, Glassner pulls up hard data. As he points out, only a few hundred children nationwide are kidnapped each year, and flying in a plane is more than ten times safer than driving. We worry about these extremely rare dangers, shark attacks and the like, because people who profit from such fears— executives at broadcast TV networks and the makers of pharmaceutical drugs who advertise on them—put a great deal of effort into keeping us afraid. Though challenged by both liberal activists and right-wing academics, Glassner's main theses stood the test of time, and his bestseller remains relevant today.[2]

I am attempting to do for race relations what Glassner did for consumer advocacy: use hard data to penetrate an intentionally created fog of exaggerations and lies and expose a surprisingly positive reality. Many Americans today, especially on the activist left, seem to believe that the United States is a racist hell-hole on the brink of civil war. In the mainstream media we hear almost constant talk about scary new forms of racism: "white privilege," "cultural appropriation," and "subtle bigotry." The Black Lives Matter (BLM) movement argues that a near-genocide is underway in 2019 America, including police and vigilante murders of "tens of thousands" of Black men annually. The platform of The Movement for Black Lives, one of the founding documents of Black Lives Matter, claims that immediate reparations for slavery and the opening of America's borders are the only ways that minorities can be compensated for the harms currently being done to us.[3]

In reaction, the equally absurd alt-right claims that a "white genocide" is underway: whites are being murdered in job lots by people of color, who are also engaged in a well-organized attempt to breed whites out of existence. Some of the most potent pieces of evidence cited in support of these theories, especially by the Left but also to an increasing extent by the dissident Right, are ghastly examples of hate crime. Who can forget the torn hijab on the woman allegedly attacked by a mob of Trump supporters days after the 2016 election? Or the burnt Black church desecrated with the spray-painted words "Vote TRUMP"? Or the multiple death threats delivered to terrified students of color at Kean College?

It is taboo to say this, but it must be said: The novel theories of subtle but pervasive racial prejudice—"white privilege," "cultural appropriation," and so forth—are complete nonsense. And many of the hate crimes cited in support of those theories never happened.

No sane person denies that there are still racists in America. The results of my own research indicate that roughly one in ten whites and one in seven African Americans tests as a bigot. That figure for whites tracks fairly closely with the findings of past researchers, such as Sniderman and Carmines. I have never met a serious social scientist who contends that hostility on the basis of race and ethnicity does not exist; ethnic conflict is indeed the main subject that many of us study. But it should also be obvious that the United States has taken massive steps away from racism over the past one hundred years, both in our institutions and in individual attitudes. American schools were formally desegregated in 1954, the Civil Rights Act made institutional racism (and sexism) actually illegal in 1964, and affirmative action became the law of the land via the Philadelphia Plan back in 1967. It is simply bizarre to argue that these measures did not, generally speaking, succeed. Little more than half a century ago, in the fifties and sixties, white juries in states like Mississippi were refusing to convict the perpetrators of lynchings. The men who tortured Emmett Till to death for flirting with a white woman were acquitted in deliberations that lasted barely an hour—with one juror claiming that it took that long only because the jury took time out to drink soda. George Wallace was reelected on a platform of standing in the schoolhouse door to oppose equal education for Blacks. The constituency for "segregation now, segregation tomorrow, and segregation forever" has largely evaporated in the time between his day and our own. The last president of the United States, elected with roughly 45 percent of the white vote, was a Black man.

Given these undisputed facts, many of the specific examples cited by activists in support of what I call the "Continuing Oppression Narrative" are demonstrably false. There is no violent genocide against African Americans currently going on: both FBI and Bureau of Justice Statistics data indicate that interracial violent crime is fairly rare—and roughly 80 percent Black on white. The total number of people shot by police officers, a particular focus of Black

Lives Matter, was under 1,200 in the representative year of 2015, and 76 percent of the individuals shot were not black. The total number of African Americans killed by law enforcement officers during that year was 258, and the total number of unarmed Black men to die in such clashes was thirty-six. By my best estimate, the total number of unarmed black men shot by *white* cops was *seventeen*. The percentage of police shooting victims who were Black (23.5 percent) was slightly higher than the overall Black population percentage in the U.S. (13 to 14 percent), but this disparity is wholly explained by the fact that the Black violent crime rate is roughly 2.5 times the white rate.[4]

And, more specifically relevant to the topic of this book, a huge percentage of the horrific hate crimes cited as evidence of contemporary bigotry are fakes. Each of the notorious examples of hate crimes that I mentioned above was a hoax—although you probably have not heard that from the mainstream media. The woman who gained international fame by claiming that several boorish males ripped at her hijab on an NYC subway train simply made that up. The Black church was burnt by a Black parishioner who may have had an issue with the minister. The Albany "bus beating" of Black women; the burning of Velvet Ultra Lounge, the murder of Nabra Hassanen; the death threats made to Kean College students of color; and almost every damned noose found on an American university campus—all were fakes. That's the real story behind the "Whites Only" signs found posted over University at Buffalo water fountains and the claims on social media that smiling servers often find "nigger" or "faggot" written on their receipts in place of a tip.

You will read about almost one hundred fake hate crimes in this book. It is probable that *most* widely reported recent hate crimes have been hoaxes. While researching this book I put together a data set of 409 recent hate crime hoaxes. The Fake Hate Crimes

(FHC) website[5] lists 341, and still another researcher, Laird Wilcox, whose 1994 book *Crying Wolf* is well worth reading, compiled a list of at least 300 more cases in the mid-1990s.[6] Combined, the cases in these three large-N data sets represent a substantial percentage of all serious hate crimes alleged during the period under review.

As Glassner concluded, when millions of people are terrified of threats that do not even exist, there is strong evidence that someone is deliberately trying to scare them. In the case of U.S. race relations, and of majority-minority relations more broadly, it is not hard to figure out why multiple entities might attempt to do this. An astonishing edifice of power and profit rests upon the assumption that the United States is a racist nation: affirmative action, minority business set-asides, NGO donations, corporate diversity initiatives, and academic departments of post-colonial brother-man studies are all highly profitable for their beneficiaries. The large non-governmental organizations that promote hate scares, such as the Southern Poverty Law Center (SPLC); the NAACP, which does some good work but which also recently issued a racism-based "travel advisory warning" for the entire state of Missouri; Black Lives Matter and the Movement for Black Lives; the National Organization for Women (NOW); and the like owe their viability to this assumption. In many situations where a reasonable person might well conclude that there is no racism present—Hollywood's Oscars ceremony, for example—it has proven quite profitable and rewarding to invent some.

In and of itself, there is nothing remarkably wicked about organizations like BLM using scare tactics to increase their visibility or expand their donor base. Businesses and politicians play competitive social games like this on a daily basis, and I have enjoyed some of them myself. But *this* game has a dangerously negative effect on many real people. Having taught at colleges for many years, currently at a top-thirty historically Black university, I can testify that the primary thing holding Black students back is not racism but rather the heartfelt belief that the "white" world—defined to include everything from techno music to craft beer—is a pervasively racist place.

Many young Black men, including athletes, tell me that they do not wish to become police officers because "those are the murderers." Doing poorly on the SAT or GRE is not seen as a liability; those are the white man's tests. Substantive majors such as economics, which set their graduates up for lucrative employment, are often rejected in favor of activist ones such as post-colonial studies. Judging from at least a dozen in-class practice surveys, at least one quarter of my students—roughly the same percentage as that found among Blacks nationally—believe that the U.S. government is trying to exterminate the Black race by doing things like intentionally giving African Americans AIDS. Naturally, many of these incredibly impressive young people find it difficult to be traditionally patriotic. They would never consider military careers. America's opportunities are closed to them—not because of widespread racism, but because of their own erroneous belief in widespread racism.

These disturbing beliefs are important; they matter. The fact that a quarter of Black people think their government is attempting to kill them is not a harmless error or an amusing quirk.[7] If their belief were based in realty, I myself would be ready to take up arms against the United States of America. But it's *not* true. Police officers shoot very few unarmed citizens; the highest SAT scores in the country belong to Asians and Nigerians rather than whites; HIV first took root as a disease in Caucasian gay communities ... and so on down the line. For all its flaws, our great nation is not racked with hate crimes or run by Nazis, and the government is not putting deadly viruses or chemicals designed to sterilize brothers into the Snapple tea. When people in positions of power or visibility say such nonsense, they should be rebuked for it. Given that most of the divisive claims of the activist Left—and, it goes without saying, of the alt-right—are not true, it is difficult to think of a more compelling task for American scholars than to point out the lies.

I would describe this book as a work of social science, although the technique employed in gathering data for it was snowball sampling of the qualitative written record dealing with hate crime allegations, rather than quantitative techniques of linear, logistic, and time series regression. The process of research and analysis began with a few points of personal interest. When I was a graduate student several years ago, I became interested in two widely reported incidents near my hometown of Chicago. The first was the burning to the ground of the popular, gay-owned Velvet Rope Ultra Lounge in inner-suburban Oak Park. The second incident involved students at the University of Wisconsin-Parkside, where I once applied for an academic job, reporting death threats by apparent hate group members who put up hangman's nooses. Strong stuff!

I followed both cases intently and became aware of other Chicago and central Midwestern hate crime cases that occurred shortly after the original two. In November 2014 Derek Caquelin, a student who had previously criticized the University of Chicago administration for allowing "racist" Halloween costumes on campus, claimed that his Facebook page had been hacked by a reactionary group called the "UChicago Electronic Army." He alleged that the group used his page to post extraordinarily racist and violent messages targeting Caquelin and another student in retaliation for their activism. During the same year, up the road in Detroit, a female student at Grand Valley State University claimed that her dorm room door had been defaced with graffiti during Black history month. The graffiti included the phrases "Black Bitch," "Die, Nigger!", and "Fuck Black History Month." In 2015 Matthew Schultz, a student at nearby Michigan Tech, was expelled from the university after allegedly threatening to "shoot all Black people…tomorrow." Not long afterwards, serious hate crimes would be reported at Beloit College in Wisconsin and lovely little St. Olaf in Minnesota. Apparently, the pleasant American Midwest was awash with hate.

But I noticed something unexpected. Most of the hate crime allegations eventually turned out to be false. As we shall see, by 2016 the Velvet Rope Ultra Lounge fire had been exposed as an act of arson. The perpetrator, who was convicted on felony charges, had intentionally staged the fire to look like a hate crime. Similarly, almost all the incidents at Wisconsin-Parkside turned out to be the work of a disaffected student, Khalilah Ford, who claimed that she had wanted to test how seriously the university took racism. And Matthew Schultz had actually said that he wanted to shoot Black Michigan Tech students "a smile." His words were intentionally misquoted and reported to campus and police authorities by a fellow student.

This phenomenon of fake hate crimes did not appear to be small-scale or regionally isolated. While keeping an eye on my original Midwestern cases, I put together a fairly large database of hate crime allegations—346 of them—by searching for relevant terms such as "hate crime," "campus hate crime," "hate crime allegation," and "hate crime controversy" on Google, JSTOR, and Google Scholar. Over several years I was able to confirm that fewer than a third of these cases could even possibly have been genuine hate crimes. A genuine hate crime would require that the initial alleged crime was (1) never exposed as a hoax and (2) never discovered to have been committed by a person or group different from the person or group originally alleged to have committed it. The literal majority of these incidents, which were almost all initially reported with a great deal of fanfare and breast-beating, were later exposed as hoaxes. Well, in truth, "exposed" is a gross exaggeration. Evidence demonstrated that they were fake hate crimes. But that fact got very little exposure in the press—particularly in comparison with the initial publicity for the supposed hate crimes. The initial headlines that had touted each case as a horrific example of contemporary bigotry vanished from the internet, replaced by either nothing at all or by low-key rueful acknowledgements that a hoax had taken place. If you want to see an example, simply Google "Yasmin Seweid hate crime." A list of every single case in this first data set is available upon request; scrupulous honesty is a goal of this book.[8]

As I became more aware of the prevalence of hate crime hoaxes, the focus of my research shifted from hate crimes in a modern post-racial society to the phenomenon of fake hate crimes. In order to compile a topic-specific alternative to my initial data set of several hundred widely reported cases of alleged hate crimes, I spent roughly three weeks in 2017 searching specifically for "fake hate crimes" and "hate crime hoaxes," using the resources already mentioned, as well as topic-specific websites such as fakehatecrimes.org. By the conclusion of this research period, I had a data set of 409 confirmed cases of fake hate crimes, some but not all of which had also been a part of my earlier data set and all of which had at some point received substantial regional, national, or global media coverage. This second more specific data set provides the great majority of cases and statistics in this book. A final methodological note: I take no position on what exact percentage of all hate crimes are hoaxes. Such a conclusion would be nearly impossible to calculate. It would be necessary, just for starters, to determine the percentage of all cases of alleged interracial fist fights that were classified as hate crimes across every county-level police precinct in the United States, the conviction versus dismissal rate for those crimes, and the percentage of prosecutorial dismissals or *nolle prosequi* decisions that were motivated by a belief that the allegation in question was a false one.

In an analogous line of research, KC Johnson and Stuart Taylor's 2017 book *The Campus Rape Frenzy* points out that widely used estimates of what percentage of rape reports are false range from 2 to almost 50 percent. That number varies depending on whether the standard employed is an official determination that the allegation was false and hostilely motivated or that the allegation could or could not be successfully prosecuted.[9] Using Harvard data and an intermediate standard, the *Washington Examiner*'s Ashe Schow recently reached a third estimate: that 15.6 percent of rape allegations are false or baseless, and another 17.9 percent of cases are not substantial enough to be legally prosecuted.[10]

It must also be noted that my samples—like almost every sample used in the social sciences—have real and potential imperfections. Even my initial data set, which was not intentionally focused on fake hate crimes, may suffer from some form of selection bias: I found many of the early cases that I reviewed in articles discussing a handful of highly publicized Midwestern incidents that later turned out to be false. Not to mention the simple fact that a media search process focused on terms of interest to me could be more likely than, say, a simple scan of all reported hate crimes from the last six months to turn up controversial false allegations.

That said, what can be said with absolute confidence is that the actual number of hate crimes hoaxes is indisputably large. We are not speaking here of just a few bad apples. As we have seen, I was able to put together a data set of slightly more than 400 cases of fake hate crime, focusing primarily on allegations made between 2010 and 2017. Fake Hate Crimes was able to compile a substantially different database of 341 recent false allegations on their website. And Laird Wilcox put together a third distinct list of roughly 300 hate crime hoaxes in the pre-internet era, focusing only on cases contemporary to him. Given that official FBI records document only 5,850 hate crimes as having occurred during the most recent year on record (2015), and that probably fewer than one in every ten hate crimes is nationally reported and thus a candidate for these data sets, it seems indisputable that hoaxes make up a very large chunk of the pool of widely reported hate crimes, and quite possibly the pool of all reported hate crimes.[11]

Several serious studies substantiate this claim. In 2016, for example, a report released by the "Hate Response Team" at the left-leaning University of Wisconsin at LaCrosse had to concede that 28 of 192 recently reported bias incidents on campus were either hoaxes or had not occurred at all. This concession of a 15 percent rate of false reporting of hate incidents almost certainly represents a gross underestimate—given that the Hate Response Team's methodology treated such things as the "discover(y) of a Campus Crusade for Christ poster on campus" and "a blog post about life as a white student" as legitimate non-hoaxes.[12]

The benefits that the race-baiting Left and alt-right reap from fake hate crimes come at a heavy cost. People—even decent people, people of good will—cannot be completely unaffected when they are continually told that their fellow citizens are targeting their own race for crimes. The hoaxes are bound to increase hostility between Blacks and whites. The wonder is that, very much to the credit of the American people, these fake hate crimes have not (yet!) fomented more real hate crimes. But if the fake crimes continue unabated and unexposed, it is only a matter of time before the racial divisions they fuel will inspire actual violence.

It is my hope that this book will serve as a first step on the path back to a saner national discourse.

Chapter One

LANCING A BOIL

Why would anyone fake a hate crime? The basic answers would seem to be fame, profit, and the advancement of a political ideology.

It is no secret that there exists a large and well-entrenched grievance industry in the United States. The Southern Poverty Law Center (SPLC), which thrives on labeling organizations such as the Family Research Council and Jewish Political Action Committee "hate groups," pulls in $51,800,000 per year and has a well-invested endowment of $432,000,000.[1] The similar Anti-Defamation League (ADL) listed itself as possessing $144,158,994 in assets and $81,187,088 in post-liability net assets during fiscal year 2018 alone.[2] While perhaps a bit more cash-poor, the great Black advocacy organizations are no slouches when it comes to rallying the troops: the official Facebook page for Black Lives Matter boasted 326,993 likes and 332,368 followers when I accessed it in November 2018.[3]

Civil rights groups such as the NAACP, the Urban League, and indeed some of the very organizations mentioned above all did considerable good in the past, notably during the civil rights movement of the 1940s to 1960s. But it would be foolish to deny that today these organizations have a deep-rooted interest in presenting the sort of bigotry which they fight as a serious ongoing problem in the United States in order to continue receiving donations and funding. More broadly, it would not be wild speculation to say that one in every ten dollars spent in business interacts in some way with an affirmative action or minority set-aside program. These programs too have advocates, who welcome evidence of their own necessity in society. Especially in a liberal environment, such as a college campus, the false report of a hate crime brings both predictable notoriety and support from a preset group of allies and a chance to strike back at perceived oppressors.

Thus, when Yasmin Seweid falsely claimed that Donald Trump supporters had ripped off her hijab on a train, she received sympathetic national media coverage and a platform from which to speak out against racism and Islamophobia. After a Black graduate student hoaxed the University at Buffalo by placing "Blacks Only" signs above multiple water fountains around campus, the Black Student Union and major fraternities called a campus-wide meeting. In a few truly remarkable collegiate cases, such as a recent incident at Gustavus Adolphus College, representatives of organizations such as the Campus Diversity Council have themselves been caught placing racist or insensitive materials around campus in the hope that students would see them, recognize prejudice as a problem, and contact the Campus Diversity Council. Laird Wilcox describes hoaxes like these—all of which we will look at in more detail below—as the predictable results of a "market process." Where there exists a reward or payoff for victimization—such as media coverage, popularity, or the chance to punish enemies—the temptation to create it where none actually exists will be very strong.[4]

The fact that there *are* sizable payoffs for reported victimization, real or false, is the result of a quirk of historical memory. Simply put, the American activist Left often seems to have forgotten that the civil rights movement ever occurred, or at least that it was a success. Although most forms of institutional racism have been illegal since the passage of the Civil Rights Act in 1964, and anti-white affirmative action has arguably been the law of the land since the Philadelphia Plan in 1967, one of the most consistent themes of modern social justice activism is that the United States remains a "genocidally" racist nation. Allegedly the lives of Blacks, and to a slightly lesser extent other minorities, are nightmares of unstinting oppression.

This is no fringe opinion confined to the members of some witches' coven at Berkeley. The official manifesto of the Movement for Black Lives claims that Black people are "criminalized and dehumanized" across "all areas of (modern American) society," including—but not limited to—"justice and education systems, social service agencies …and the media and pop culture."[5] How the oppression is effected is not specified; it never is. But the ongoing genocidal oppression apparently terrorizing our society today is frequently alleged to start at the very top. President Donald Trump is called a racist and a white nationalist pretty much daily; a search for the phrase "Donald Trump white supremacist" turns up the headlines "How White Nationalists Learned to Love Donald Trump";[6] "Donald Trump, Pepe the Frog, and White Supremacists: A Primer";[7] "How Trump Took Hate Groups Mainstream";[8] and "Trump Promised White Supremacy. Now He's Delivering It";[9] among many others.

The activist Left's distrust for the United States goes well beyond even this kind of overheated political rhetoric. Although it is considered impolitic for whites or conservatives to mention this in mixed company, a substantial bloc of minority Americans sincerely believe that the U.S. government is attempting to exterminate them. According to a widely cited *Washington Post* article, roughly half of all African Americans believe that AIDS is man-made; 25 percent think that it was developed by the U.S. government "in a...laboratory"; and 15 percent believe that AIDS is a form of "genocide against Black people."[10]

The idea that civil rights laws and policies of affirmative action are toothless shams is quite common among both people of color and white social justice warriors. According to a well-designed study reported in the 2012 book *Mismatch: How Affirmative Action Hurts Students It's Intended to Help, and Why Universities Won't Admit It* by Richard Sander and Stuart Taylor Jr., after nearly fifty years of affirmative action programs 67 percent of African Americans believe that if a Black student and a white student were to apply to the same university with the same grades and the same SAT scores, the *white* student would be given an admissions preference and will be more likely to get into the school. Only five percent said that the Black student would have the advantage.[11]

And yet the latter is undoubtedly the more likely outcome under our current affirmative action regime. The representative University of Michigan affirmative action policy challenged in the famous *Grutter v. Bollinger* case awarded undergraduate applicants twenty full points for being Black or Hispanic, in contrast to twelve points for a perfect SAT score, four points for legacy status, and twenty points per one-unit increase in grade point average (GPA). Thus a Black applicant with a 3.0 GPA was as likely to get into Michigan as a white applicant with a perfect 4.0 average, and more likely to gain admission than a 3.0 white legacy student who also aced the SAT. Even after the Supreme Court's final decision in *Grutter* modified Michigan's affirmative action regime, very similar admissions preferences persist. In their 2009 book on race and higher education, *No Longer Separate*, Thomas Espenshade and Alexandria Radford point out that Black applicants to selective colleges generally receive "an admissions bonus equivalent to 310 ... points" on the now three-section SAT.[12]

Racial preferences this large have unintended consequences. As Sander and Taylor demonstrate in *Mismatch*, the boost that affirmative action gives to many Black and Hispanic students during the college admissions process results in huge gaps in preparedness between minority and white students at virtually every level of the American university system. Black students who might do very well on the local state campus or at a historically Black college find themselves struggling in the Ivy League or at their state's flagship university, where their GPAs and test scores are, on average, lower than those of their white classmates.[13] The resulting gap in success between white students and non-Asian minority students cries out for an explanation, at least within that huge majority of universities where the "sausage making" realities of racialized admissions are not honestly discussed. And gross exaggeration of racism in 2018 America is often a convenient one.

False hate crime allegations have value because they provide support for the meta-narrative of majority group bigotry. To quote Wilcox, "There's nothing like some (fake) racist graffiti to invigorate the militants. And, what the Hell, it's for a good cause. Right?"[14] Unfortunately, the hoaxers are playing with fire.

The mismatch problem is only one example of the general trend—which Thomas Sowell demonstrates using extensive research in his magisterial 2004 book, *Affirmative Action around the World: An Empirical Study*—for affirmative action to increase hostility between racial groups wherever it is implemented. Members of the races that are disfavored by the affirmative action policy (whites and especially Asians, in America) tend to resent the boost that is given to favored groups at their expense. And many members of favored races (Blacks and Latinos) naturally resent the fact that their accomplishments are called into question by that favoritism. One famous example of this latter trend is Clarence Thomas's affixing of a 15-cent price tag to his Yale Law diploma to express his frustration with prospective employers who assumed he had gotten into and through the Ivy League law school only because he was Black.

Both kinds of resentment increase hostility between the races and, as Sowell found in his research on affirmative action programs in countries from Sri Lanka to Sierra Leone, have even led to violence—up to and including race riots and civil war.[15] Thankfully, real interracial violence is a much, much smaller problem in the United States than in many less fortunate countries—and also a smaller problem in America today than was the case during America's past. More than three *thousand* Black Americans were lynched in the United States before the passage of the Civil Rights Act in 1964. Today, threats involving hangmen's nooses are likely to be hoaxes, as I will demonstrate in this book. But the perpetrators of those hoaxes are doing their best to exaggerate racial animosities—which may very well fuel real hate crimes in the future.

It is a tragic truth of human history that fake hate crimes have, on more than one occasion, been the precursor to real atrocities. The best-known example is probably the "blood libel" against the Jews. Throughout medieval Europe, Christians started rumors that Christian children were being killed and their blood used in Jewish religious rituals. These stories were, invariably, complete canards. But the false belief that the Jewish people were perpetrating violence against Christians became the inspiration and excuse for the Christians to commit real violence against the Jews—vicious pogroms in which whole Jewish communities were driven out of their homes, and many of them killed horribly.

So hate crime hoaxes are dangerous. Their perpetrators are playing with fire. While the current epidemic of hate-based violence in the United States is really an epidemic of hoaxes, and any "race war" going on today exists only in the minds of a few radicals, there are disturbing signs that the fakes are fostering real hostility between the races, which could lead to real violence in the future. Consider, for example, the fact that hate crime hoaxes are increasingly being perpetrated by white members of the alt-right, with the explicit goal of making Black people and leftist causes look bad.

Hate crime hoaxes take a variety of forms. College and university campuses were hotbeds of fake hate crime reporting throughout the duration of my study period (2013–17) and for some time before this research project began. Literally hundreds of major hate crime hoaxes have taken place on American university campuses during the past decade. Ninety-three of the 260 nationally reported hoaxes and sets of hoaxes to appear on the first eight pages of the Fake Hate Crimes website either took place on a college or senior high school campus or involved a student as the primary perpetrator—and FHC didn't get them all!

Many examples are truly outrageous, almost unbelievable. In 2016, at Kean University, the now-suspended Twitter account @keanuagainstblk was used to tweet out multiple disturbing messages such as "I will kill all the Blacks (who) go to Kean University," tauntingly tagging the campus police department in some of the tweets. This was taken as evidence that the university president, himself a minority activist named Dawood Farahi, had failed to "(do) enough to address racial tensions," and massive demonstrations swept the campus.[16] The state police and Department of Homeland Security were involved, and the total bill for restoring order and identifying the maker of the threats ran to $100,000. In the end, however, an IP-address trace by police showed that every one of the tweets came from the computer of one Kayla McKelvey, a leader of anti-administration protests with past grievances against Kean. McKelvey faced ninety days in jail and a fine of $82,000, and the long-suffering Kean University issued a statement noting that the institution continues to "wholeheartedly respect and support activism."[17]

As absurd as the Kean situation was, it was not especially unique. In late 2012, a remarkable and disturbing string of "hate incidents" swept the pleasant tree-lined campus of the University of Wisconsin-Parkside, about one hour's drive due north of Chicago. First an object resembling a hangman's noose, woven out of rubber bands, was found on campus by a group of students. The very next day, an honor student named Aubriana Banks was sent a second noose made of corded string in the mail. Later that night, students came across professionally made flyers posted around campus, reading "Niggers will DIE in two days," with the names of thirteen Black students written on the bottom of each. Finally, after a great deal of shouting and some detective work, most of the apparently anti-Black incidents were traced back to Black student Khalilah Ford. It is worth noting that Ford was initially identified as a suspect because her name was the only one on the double-digit list of Black targets to be spelled correctly. Incredibly, Ford defended her racist flyers and death threats by claiming that the Parkside administration had not responded quickly enough to the first "noose" found on campus—for which she rather implausibly denied responsibility—and needed to be prodded away from such unacceptable "racism."[18]

It would not be at all hard to fill a full-length book simply with campus incidents such as these. At the University at Buffalo in 2015, an anonymous vandal posted the classic "Whites Only" and "Blacks Only" signs associated with Southern segregation at the entrance to campus bathrooms and over several prominent water fountains on campus. The *New York Times, Daily News,* and other national mass media outlets reported breathlessly on the "surprise" and "outrage" of UB students. Then, during a formal campus-wide meeting hosted by the Black Student Union, a Black graduate student confessed that she had posted all of the offensive signs as part of an art thesis project called "Installations in Open Spaces." She did this to create dialogue about campus racism—of which none had previously been in evidence.[19]

The Diversity Leadership Council at Minnesota's well-regarded Gustavus Adolphus College went one remarkable step further than that, in 2017, by posting flyers across campus informing "all white Americans" that "America is a white nation" and that reporting illegal aliens to law enforcement is every white man's duty. Students who attempted to report the flyers *to* the Diversity Council or the college's Bias Response Team were informed that those entities had themselves posted the flyers to conduct "a social experiment educating students on issues of bias and racism."[20] Again, so far as I can tell, no incidents of actual racial bias have occurred at Gustavus Adolphus during the past decade.

Around the same time as the Gustavus Adolphus incident, and not too terribly far down the Midwestern roads, white student Matthew Schultz was both arrested and expelled from the Michigan Technical Institute for saying on the Yik Yak app that he planned to "shoot all Black people … a SMILE … tomorrow." His words were retweeted by a schoolmate with the words "a smile" removed, and described as a hate crime.[21] You literally cannot make this stuff up.

But as sophomoric as it may be, the recent epidemic of fake hate crimes is not a phenomenon confined to literal sophomores. Another common category of hate crime hoaxes is made up of what I will call "Klan Springs Eternal" (KSE) incidents, in which members of racial minority groups use fictional attacks by members of white hate groups to explain away their own crimes or struggles with mental illness. In one very widely publicized case, which drew the attention of the *New York Times* and then-presidential candidate Hillary Clinton, three Black women who claimed to have been attacked by a mob of white supremacists on an Albany bus were exposed on video as having actually been the aggressors in a very different sort of fight from the one they described. In reality, they violently attacked a young white woman, hitting her after a possible exchange of insults.[22] In another incident that received national media coverage, the individual responsible for torching a historic Black church in Greenville, South Carolina, and writing "Vote Trump!" on the blackened exterior turned out to be a Black parishioner with a lengthy history of legal troubles.[23]

Quite a few church burnings alleged to be hate crimes seem to be, in fact, hoaxes. A very similar case, involving the vandalism of the large and integrated St. David's Episcopal Church in Indiana with graffiti including a swastika, the words "Heil Trump," and multiple anti-gay slurs, wound down to a very similar conclusion in early 2017, when the church organist who had reported the vandalism confessed to being the culprit. Media outlets noted that his actions were not motivated by actual animus toward gays, Christians, or Blacks, but seemed to be an attempt to demonstrate the supposed consequences of the Trump presidency.[24] In a less political but equally bizarre case, a Black man in Florida was exposed by police as the individual responsible for faking a hate crime by battering his ex-girlfriend's car with bricks, writing the words "KKK" and "Trump" all over it, and then setting the vehicle on fire. The couple had apparently been clashing over issues of child custody.[25] In still another case that sparked a national media frenzy, a Black Louisiana woman who had claimed men in white hoods used lighter fluid to literally set her on fire was discovered to have actually set herself ablaze and simply made up her original story.[26] The list goes on.

As several of the cases immediately above illustrate, the election of Donald Trump as president seems to have inspired an entirely new category of hate crime hoaxes. In what we might call "Trump hate crimes," as in college campus hate incidents, the actual numerical majority of alleged crimes to have drawn recent national media attention seem to be straight-up total fakes. Perhaps most notably, Yasmin Seweid—the Muslim student who garnered headlines worldwide after claiming to have been accosted on New York City's Line 6 train by three drunken white men who called her a terrorist and yanked at her hijab—claimed that her assailants were yelling "Donald Trump." After being confronted by police about multiple inconsistencies in her story, however, Seweid broke down and admitted to making the whole thing up in order to avoid confessing to her strict Muslim parents that she had been out late enjoying a night of underage drinking with her boyfriend. The endgame of the Seweid case was simply bizarre, with Seweid appearing for court dates bald—apparently her unsympathetic parents had shaved her head—and the *Daily News* revealing that in 2012 her older brother had also falsely reported a potential hate attack.[27]

While obviously more troubled and imaginative than most people, Seweid is hardly alone in having tried to blame a made-up incident of racial terrorism on the tough-talking president. In Philadelphia's hard-scrabble South Philly neighborhood, a fifty-eight-year-old Black man named William Tucker was charged with vandalizing numerous cars and homes with slogans such as "Trump Rules!!!" just before Election Day. Back on campus, a bisexual student activist at North Park University claimed that she had repeatedly been sent pieces of hate mail with the hashtag #Trump containing messages like "Go back to HELL"—before she was exposed as a hoaxer by a campus-wide investigation.[28]

Bowling Green State University's Eleesha Long claimed to have been attacked the day after Election Day by three white men wearing "Trump" T-shirts who followed her for blocks and threw stones at her head. Perhaps unsurprisingly by this point, a police check of her Facebook and Verizon history showed that Long had been nowhere near the location where she claimed the incident occurred, apparently ever. Interestingly, Long appears to be quite the bigot herself; the same email search by law enforcement turned up such disparaging references to poor white Trump supporters as: "This is why you should take an IQ test to vote" and "I hope they all get AIDS and die."[29]

In still another notable case, Ann Arbor woman Halley Bass became one of the small number of people to actually receive a jail sentence for falsely reporting a hate crime after slashing herself across the face and claiming that a white conservative angered by her anti-Brexit pin was responsible for the injury. In a truly bizarre irony, Bass's false hate crime report appears to have been inspired at least partly by the story of a Muslim American woman who claimed to have been threatened with being beaten and set on fire if she did not take off her hijab in the "tense" post-election climate in Ann Arbor. That story was itself later exposed as a hoax; as far as anyone investigating the situation has been able to tell, no such thing ever happened.[30]

Extremely high rates of false reporting seem to be the norm for hate crime allegations of all varieties. As we shall see, judging from my own work as well as that of Fake Hate Crimes and Laird Wilcox, false allegations of anti-gay or anti-Jewish driven crime are substantially less frequent than fake hate crimes reported by campus SJWs or People of Color. But they are not infrequent. Mere blocks from my hometown of Chicago, Frank Elliott, the owner of the Oak Park suburb's well-known Velvet Ultra Lounge nightclub, was arrested in

November of 2013 and charged with arson and federal insurance fraud, after he burned down his own gay club, used spray paint to write anti-gay slurs throughout the fire-ravaged building, and blamed the fire on homophobes.[31]

It must be noted here that, especially given the small size of these populations, real hate crimes against LGBT Americans are all too common. According to the social scientists Caitlin Ryan and Ian Rivers, 80 percent of gay citizens report having experienced verbal abuse in the recent past, 44 percent report threats related to their orientation, and 30 percent report having been actually attacked or at least followed and chased. In contrast to collegiate "hate incidents," the majority of anti-gay hate crimes reported to police or other authorities are almost certainly real.[32] And yet this book contains multiple verified incidents of anti-gay hate crime hoaxes, and it cannot be ignored that the current climate of political orthodoxy makes false reporting of all varieties of hate crime extraordinarily common.

Elliott's crime came to light only as a result of multiple lawsuits against him by creditors holding past-due notes. By then he had already benefitted from a $20-per-head fundraiser at the city's trendy Hideaway Bar and opened a new venue (the Bonsai Bar) with the proceeds from his insurance settlement.[33] In a similar case, Joe Williams, the owner of the organic food store Healthy Thyme in Paris, Tennessee, claimed that three men came into Healthy Thyme near the close of business, beat him senseless, wrote a "three-letter homophobic slur" on his forehead, and set his little store on fire, causing him about $5,500 in damages and forcing him to file a claim with his insurance company. Inside a month Paris police had established that no such attack ever occurred; Williams was suspected of fraud and prosecuted for filing a false report.[34]

Some alleged attacks in this category go well beyond the banality of fraud, reaching a truly fabulous level of bizarre. In the spring of 2016, for example, Jordan Brown, the openly gay pastor of the Church of Open Doors in Austin, garnered national headlines after accusing a Whole Foods store of selling him a cake with "Love Wins … Faggot!" written on it in icing. Whole Foods responded by producing videos showing Brown doctoring the cake himself and pointing out that the chain does not normally sell customers profane cakes that cannot be viewed before purchase.[35] The story disappeared from the news. Around the same time a Baltimore woman raised $43,000 via GoFundMe after claiming to have received a threatening note telling her to tone down her "relentlessly gay yard"—before she was revealed almost certainly to be a hoaxer.[36]

A few years earlier, in yet another on-campus story, the student head of Vassar College's Bias Incident Response Team, Genesis Hernandez, was expelled from school for prominently 'tagging' multiple student residences with graffiti messages such as "Tranny Know Your Place," and reporting them, essentially to herself.[37] In a similar case, the man found responsible for making violent anti-Semitic threats to ten Jewish community centers—and Delta Airlines, for some reason—throughout 2017 was revealed to be not an anti-Semite but an Israeli Jew.[38]

One of the oddest things about the mainstream American media's coverage of fake hate crimes is just how long this pattern—massive coverage of an obviously questionable story followed by a well-hidden retraction if and when the story is exposed as a hoax—has been going on. In 1986, a young and mentally ill Black woman's claim that a group of white men had raped her, smeared her with dog feces, and written racial slurs on her body was reported globally as the "Tawana Brawley affair" and condemned as evidence of real racism. At one point, Brawley took on Al Sharpton as an advisor and accused police officers and a New York City district attorney of having participated in her abuse, before the entire nasty business was revealed to have been a complete hoax.[39]

In 2007, closer to our own shining era, a fight between white and Black teenagers, which initially led to felony charges against a Black brawler, became the "Jena Six" incident. After hangman's nooses in school colors were discovered on the campus of Jena High School following an unrelated teenage prank, frenzied accusations of hate and racism were levied against the sleepy integrated town of Jena, Louisiana. Jesse Jackson led a march of "40,000 freedom fighters" (his estimate) through the place. To this day, reports of what was almost certainly the real story appear only on obscure and sometimes genuinely racist right-wing websites such as American Renaissance and VDare.[40] The media climate responsible for the more recent national outcry over the shootings of Black teenagers Michael Brown and Trayvon Martin and the lack of a commensurate outcry over the shooting of white teenager Dylan Noble has apparently existed for some time.

In recent years, however, one new twist has been added to the fake hate crime game. Whites now seem to be as likely as any other group to perpetrate false hate attacks. Most recently, and most notably, New York City firefighter Jason Stokes was arrested for arson in 2016 for setting his own house on fire—with his family inside it—and attempting to blame the blaze on the Black Lives Matter movement. Stokes was found not guilty. But if he was guilty of the crime he was charged with, his plot was elaborate and bizarre. "Lie with pigs, fry like bacon," a popular BLM chant, was spray-painted across the exterior of his home, and multiple full canisters of gas were arranged around the building's back entrance as an apparent trap for officers arriving on the scene. Stokes attributed the fire to his family's decision to fly a "BLUE Lives Matter" flag outside their residence.[41] An apparently similar case occurred in Texas in 2015, when police supporter Scott Lattin claimed Black vandals nearly destroyed his white pickup: tearing out the glove box, ripping out all four seats, and spray-painting slogans including "Black Lives Matter" down both sides of the vehicle. Lattin raised nearly $6,000 via GoFundMe before being exposed as a hoaxer and arrested on misdemeanor charges.[42]

In 2014 in St. Louis, Bosnian immigrant Seherzada Dzanic garnered regional headlines after she claimed to have been attacked by three Black men who pulled a gun on her, pushed her to the ground, kicked her, and threatened to kill her. The specificity of Dzanic's story—she described three distinctive-looking Black men in their "late teens or early twenties"—led St. Louis police to focus on solving her case for "a good 7–10 days that could have been spent investigating real crimes," before she was finally revealed to have made the whole thing up.[43] Also falsely claiming that a Black assailant had attacked her was Bethany Storro, a woman from Portland, Oregon, who permanently disfigured her own face with sulfuric acid and received national attention after alleging that a Black man had done it. She also finally admitted to inventing the entire story. Media and scholarly analyses attribute her dangerously strange behavior to a combination of unresolved racial issues and "extreme narcissism."[44]

My research indicates that, although this has not always been the case, anti-white hate crimes reported by whites today are, like other hate crimes, very likely to be hoaxes. As a possible explanation, it is worth noting that the timing of my study period (2013–17) coincided with the rise of the white identity movement, including the formation of extremist Tea Party factions (2009–11), the publication of Jared Taylor's *White Identity* (2011), and the growth of the alt-right (2013–17). More whites have begun engaging in openly racialist in-group-promoting behavior such as falsely reporting hate crimes. And it bodes ill for the future of our country that the epidemic of hate crime hoaxes is already spreading from one race to another. The next danger is that, now that minority hate crime hoaxes have inspired white hate crime hoaxes, some of these hoaxes will inspire real retaliatory crimes.

Whatever the causes and the ultimate results, my research has established that a very large number of widely reported modern hate crime allegations are simply false. They are hoaxes. This statement holds true for allegations of white-on-Black and white-on-Hispanic violence, for alleged political hate crimes, and for almost all "hate incidents" reported to the media from inside the groves of academe—where the scholars still come and go, but now talk of "white privilege" and "cultural appropriation" more often than of Michelangelo. It holds true, though perhaps to a lesser extent, for allegations of anti-gay and anti-Jewish hate violence, and certainly seems to apply to the post-alt-right wave of Black-on-white hate crime allegations. This phenomenon is occurring within the context of the "Continuing Oppression" Narrative, which promotes racial discord via the argument that minorities are at constant risk of violent attack by whites.

There are ways we can address the problem of widespread false reporting of hate crimes. Prosecutors must put political correctness aside and enforce the law by seeking jail sentences for anyone convicted of falsely reporting a hate offense or similar serious crime. And we must begin to challenge the narrative with facts, pointing out as often as possible the actual rates of real hate crimes, fake hate crimes, interracial crime, and police violence against Blacks and others. Interestingly, success in removing the unjustified fears created by false perceptions of oppression would be the best possible thing for minority Americans. Until we succeed in dispelling that false narrative, the best defense against the epidemic of false hate crime stories is probably good old-fashioned skepticism. When some astonishingly unlikely-sounding event is reported—a giant swastika made of human feces being spotted on the wall of a mostly-Black dorm on a far-Left college campus, for example—normal Americans should take a pause for thought and ask some questions other than, "That's terrible; what can we do to make up for it?"

In this arena, solving the problem must begin with the acknowledgement of its existence.

Chapter Two

A CONFLICT OF VISIONS: THE "CONTINUING OPPRESSION" NARRATIVE VERSUS REALITY

Today's epidemic of fake hate crimes is happening within the context of a larger false story: the left-wing narrative that dominates "discourse" in the United States. American pundits and scholars claim that the America of 2018 is a genocidally racist country, where minorities live at constant and terrifying risk of violence from the white majority. The Platform of the Movement for Black Lives spells out this argument in detail, contending that policemen and vigilantes annually attack thousands of Black men for sport, the criminal justice system has intentionally created "a pipeline from schools to prisons for Black and Brown communities," and state targeting of slum communities has caused millions of minority citizens to "become political prisoners." Other scholars and activists invoke new forms of "invisible racism," such as "white privilege" and "cultural appropriation," that are alleged to limit the opportunities and hopes of Black Americans and other POC (the currently popular shorthand for "people of color," which must never be confused with the almost identical phrase "colored people," which is horribly offensive). Structural problems in minority communities—such as an annual illegitimacy rate of 72 to 75 percent for American Blacks during the past decade—are almost universally attributed to racism and invoked as evidence that the alleged regime of ongoing horrific bigotry is a reality.

Despite lack of evidence for it, the Continuing Oppression Narrative dominates contemporary academia and the media, and it has helped create the zeitgeist within which the epidemic of fake hate crime allegations is occurring. It is thus worth examining that zeitgeist in some depth. Here, again, the Platform of the Movement for Black Lives—a document of the mainstream Left, hosted on a major website and regularly discussed by Black Lives Matter's allies in the Democratic Party—is a great place to start. The platform is doom-laden, almost apocalyptic, in its analysis of the United States. A section called "End the War on Black People" argues that Blacks are criminalized and dehumanized in "all areas of society," including "justice and education systems," "social service agencies," and even "pop culture."

In schools, Black children are intentionally pushed off the academic and honors track and onto "a track to prison." They make up 35.6 percent of students subjected to paddling or other serious discipline, although they make up only 17.1 percent of the students, and the reason for this must be racism rather than behavior. Outside the classroom, young Black Americans similarly make up 17 percent of all juveniles but 31 percent of arrests, and the reason for this is racism rather than behavior. Even stable neighborhoods of adult African American (and Hispanic) citizens cannot escape the strong hand of Big Brother. Minority communities have been "disproportionately targeted by the state" and so "remain under surveillance by all levels of law enforcement." The reason for this is, of course, racism rather than behavior: "The intention is preventing the growth of another nationwide (civil rights) movement." And so on.

The Black Lives movement proposes drastic solutions to the alleged nightmare of current oppression in America. These solutions take up a full section of the platform called "Reparations," which opens with a demand for fiscal reparations to Blacks for all "past and continuing harms" endured by African Americans as a group. Among other items, this list of benefits would include "full and free access for all Black people ... to lifetime education including open admissions to public colleges and universities"; a substantial guaranteed "minimum livable income for all Black people"; and repayment of all wealth ever extracted from a majority-Black community via "racism, slavery, food apartheid, housing discrimination, and ... capitalism."

The pool of individuals eligible to receive these benefits seems to stretch beyond American citizens to everybody in the world with a nice tan. One major prong of the "Reparations" section specifically demands that the U.S. government "provide full access for all undocumented people to state and federal programs that provide aid and cover the full costs, including living costs, to attend public universities, and colleges, and technical education programs, and lifelong learning programs." It is worth pointing out that none of these suggestions are made to any degree in jest, and that a quick glance at the comments about and reviews of the BLM Platform posted online indicates that tens of thousands of people agree with them. An intellectually serious, culturally dominant movement believes that Black Americans today are so injured by racism that only a lifetime's worth of free education and guaranteed income can compensate for this harm.[1]

What could possibly justify this claim? Allegedly, institutionalized legal murder. The claim of extreme and prevalent police violence against minorities is probably the most frequent example of contemporary "oppression" cited by BLM and its allies. The idea that police officers—and to a lesser extent, "vigilantes" and other whites—have been killing Blacks essentially at will for sport has gained astonishingly widespread credence in our nation. The *Washington Post,* in addition to setting up a comprehensive database of every police shooting in the United States over the past several years, broken down by the race of the victim, ran literally dozens of features during 2015 and 2016 bemoaning the "racially disparate" nature of cop shootings.

According to the *Post*'s Wesley Lowery, police shootings of Black men by law enforcement officers are something of an epidemic. While white people make up 62 percent of the U.S. population, they account for "only about 49 percent of those who are killed by police officers," 13 percent less than what might be expected. Blacks account for roughly 24 percent of those fatally shot by cops despite making up "just 13 percent" of the population. Lowery points out that, "as the Post noted in a new analysis last week"—that piece being completely distinct from the feature story being quoted here—these figures mean that African Americans are at least 2.5 times as likely as whites to be killed by police officers.[2]

The crisis of police violence against Black Americans, is, allegedly, even worse in specific regions of the United States and among niche categories of Black victims. In Florida, according to the *Post* (in a third major article), whites outnumber Blacks nearly three to one but "cops shot more Black people than white people" in 2015. Moving back to the national stage, unarmed Black people were five times as likely as unarmed white people to be shot and killed by a law enforcement official during roughly the same period. The *Post* notes that of all the unarmed people shot by police in 2015, "Black men accounted for about 40 percent of them," even though Black men make up just 6 percent of the nation's population.[3] It is worth noting that this is a transparently dishonest way of presenting a statistic. The huge (95 percent plus) majority of violent crimes and violent encounters with police officers involve men, and it would be more appropriate to say that Black males make up 13 percent of the male population and 40 percent of the almost entirely male pool of unarmed individuals who physically engage the police and get shot.

Washington Post writer Justin Hansford, scribing a fourth distinct major article on this topic, offers up a theory for why excessive rates of police-on-Black shooting continue to occur: blasé intentional murder. "In an environment where state excessive force laws make criminal conviction of police officers almost impossible, a police officer literally has nothing to lose by killing unarmed Black men." Morality, logic, and fellow feeling apparently place no checks on human behavior in a society as prejudiced as ours.[4]

According to Black Lives Matter and the rest of the activist Left, the widely cited "wave" of white-on-Black police and vigilante homicides is merely the tip of the iceberg of American racism. An even more pervasive and wide-reaching problem than wanton murders of Blacks is "white privilege," which many radical authors argue has replaced the old U.S. system of legal segregation as a guarantor of dominant-group status for whites. Essentially, the theory of white privilege is that being white or seen as white carries with it an extremely high level of societal advantage in America, and that this advantage has changed hardly at all over the years. According to the activist writer Jennifer Halladay, the "transparent preference for whiteness that saturates our society" confers "white skin privilege" on all or almost all Caucasians.

This privilege carries with it dozens of minor perks, from Band-Aids matching one's skin tone to "the complementary shampoo in the hotels" working well with the texture of a guest's hair. There are also more serious claimed advantages to whiteness, such as skin color rarely working against one during a job hunt or performance review, freedom from harassment by the police, and the pleasure of consistently being told that people of one's own color are good and made modern America what it is.[5] This set of benefits has great value. Queens College's Andrew Hacker once speculated that the average young white American would have to be paid $50,000,000 to change his race and become Black.[6]

Truth be told, there very likely is some benefit, during an upper-end job hunt, to being white—or tall, or handsome, or a child of wealth with perfect teeth. But according to the Continuing Oppression Narrative, white privilege is supposed to outweigh *all* other potential privileges in its impact. In a famous article titled "Explaining White Privilege to A Broke White Person," feminist author Gina Crosley-Corcoran argues that lower-class status does not obviate or lessen white privilege, and she implies that whiteness outweighs class as a predictor of success in America. Despite a genuinely hardscrabble childhood that is sometimes difficult to read about—including living through a northern Illinois winter without heat or running water, making ramen noodles in a coffee pot with water taken from public bathrooms, and setting up house in a camper for a year—Crosley-Corcoran unironically describes herself as privileged. Because of her white skin, even while dirt poor she could "turn on the television ... and see people of my race," avoid police harassment or racially motivated IRS auditing, "arrange to be in the company of people of my race most of the time," and so on. Crosley-Corcoran doesn't ask whether most people might trade these benefits for the chance to be warm in the winter and eat decent food.[7]

A slam poem performed by fourteen-year-old Royce Mann, who won first honors at a prestigious poetry competition hosted by the Padelia School in Atlanta, Georgia, sums up how right-thinking whites are supposed to feel about white privilege. It opens:

Dear women, I'm sorry.
Dear black people, I'm sorry.

Dear Asian-Americans, dear Native Americans, dear immigrants who came here seeking a better life, I'm sorry. Dear everyone who isn't a middle- or upper-class white boy, I'm sorry.

I have started life on the top of the ladder while you were born on the first rung.[8]

Apparently, you can never stop or overcome white privilege, but only hope to contain it—while apologizing as often as possible for existing.

Another idea that is often linked with white privilege in scholarly articles that is gaining currency in contemporary activist circles is "cultural appropriation"—that is, whites' abusing POC by "stealing" things from our cultures and using them for personal enjoyment or (gasp!) profit. Probably the best definition of cultural appropriation is provided by Fordham law professor Susan Scarfidi, who, in her entertainingly titled *Who Owns Culture?*, defines the practice as "taking intellectual property, traditional knowledge, cultural expressions, or artifacts from someone's culture without permission." Cultural appropriation can include using another culture's "dance, dress, music, language, folklore, cuisine, traditional medicine, (or) religious symbols."[9] Theorists of cultural appropriation almost all agree that borrowing of this kind has gotten worse, and thus more oppressive, in the era of modern global pop culture. Commonly cited examples of the practice, as reported by cultural critic Nadra Kareem Nittle, include Elvis Presley's employing the vocal stylings of Black blues musicians in the late 1950s, Madonna' popularizing the "voguing" style of dance which began in "Black and Latino sectors of the gay community," and pop star Miley Cyrus's "twerking" in rock and rap videos.[10]

One interesting recent hipster-Left twist to cultural appropriation theory, which should surprise no one familiar with recent academic debates about racism, is the idea that only white people (sorry: "national majorities in globally hegemonic states staggering under the effects of late capitalism") can be guilty of cultural appropriation. Scarfidi claims that appropriation is harmful mostly or only when the "source community" is a minority group. In that case, they have already "been oppressed or exploited in other ways," and the thing being borrowed from them is probably "a sacred object."[11]

Writer Maisha Z. Johnson makes a similar argument, describing cultural appropriation as "the power dynamic in which members of a dominant culture take elements from a culture of people who have been systematically oppressed by that group."[12] Left-wing authors argue that cultural appropriation in the United States almost always involves "members of the dominant group" (or those who identify with it) borrowing from the cultures of minority groups.[13] Black music and dance, Native American costumes and rituals, and even "Asian martial arts" have all been shamefully appropriated by Westerners in recent years.[14] A race-neutral concept of cultural appropriation would include Black people wearing pants and hoodies or Asian salarymen in suits as some of the world's biggest appropriators. But the docents of cultural appropriation theory choose not to criticize POC.

Debates over cultural appropriation have recently outgrown the leafy (and organic!) groves of academe to assume a prominent place on the national and even global stage. In Canada, during May and June of 2017, at least three editors of major journals and reviews were fired for defending cultural cross-fertilization. First *Write* magazine's Hal Niedzviecki, editor of the official magazine of the Canadian Writers' Union (and judging by his last name, clearly a member of the privileged Anglo-Saxon elite), was sacked after penning a well-received column defending the right of white authors to simply *create characters* of indigenous or other minority backgrounds. When Jonathan Kay, editor of *The Walrus*, tweeted out support for Niedzviecki, he too was forced to resign by a social media frenzy. The ideological bloodbath was not yet done. Steve Ladurantaye, broadcaster and managing editor of the Canadian Broadcasting Company's flagship news program *The National*, tweeted about both firings and was let go and shunted into a lesser post.

In the context of risks like these, notable artists accused of cultural appropriation have responded by destroying significant works. After Native American activists protested that his work *Scaffold* was "appropriating their history," sculptor Sam Durant ceased construction of the sculpture—a large piece depicting thirty-eight Native warriors that was to have held a place of pride in the Minneapolis Sculpture Garden. The obviously traumatized artist eventually dismantled his own work and made its wood available to be burned in a Dakota Sioux ceremony. It apparently does not matter whether or not the intent of the artist was in fact racist, in any real sense of that word. *Scaffold* was designed to honor a respected group of Indian braves executed under questionable circumstances in 1862. Commenting on the extreme results of cases such as this one, the *New York Times*'s Kenan Malik calls an accusation of cultural appropriation "a secular version of the charge of blasphemy."[15]

The activist Left's argument that the United States of 2018 is a racist hellhole full of killer cops and anti-Black vigilantes, white privilege, cultural appropriation, and subtle bigotry may be implausible, but it does not arise from a vacuum. The key reality that underlies the widespread belief in the power of subtle but insidious racism is the very real prevalence of a great many social problems in minority and, in particular, Black communities today, for which racism has long been the sole socially acceptable explanation. The logic here is causal: if the problems of Black or ethnic underclasses still exist after the triumph of the civil rights movement and fifty-odd years of affirmative action, then the racism that is believed to cause those problems must still exist as well.

And the problems themselves are hard to ignore. According to *National Review*'s Roger Clegg, the illegitimacy rate for non-Hispanic Black Americans is 72.3 percent. Rates for Native Americans and Hispanic citizens come quite close, at 66.2 and 53.3 percent, respectively. White Americans, admittedly, should not feel too superior on this count. The 2012 illegitimacy rate for whites, sourced from the same data set as Clegg's figures, was 29.1 percent and the illegitimacy rate for many younger and lower-income white cohorts was over 40 percent. Even Asian-Americans have an officially recorded illegitimacy rate of 17.2 percent. The United States of America, as a whole, suffers from a bad case of "Late Roman Empire."[16] That said, Black and Latino fatherlessness rates remain the worst of a troubling lot.

Largely as a result of the Black illegitimacy rate, only 16 percent of Black households consist of a married couple (gay or straight, of any age) with children, while fully 20 percent are female-headed households with children. Fifty-four percent of all Black children live with only their mother.

The problems currently bedeviling African Americans, and to a lesser extent other minorities, extend well beyond the home. The *Wall Street Journal*'s invaluable Jason Riley points out that the Black unemployment rate is generally about twice the unemployment rate for whites, and that this holds true "irrespective of the economic climate." In December 2012, unemployment rates were 14 percent for Blacks, 9.8 percent for Hispanics and at least 10 percent for Native Americans, but only 6.3 percent for whites. (Interestingly, by the early spring of 2018 the Black unemployment rate had fallen to an all-time recent low of 6.8 percent under the tough-talking Republican President Trump. The white rate, however, remained even lower.) The unemployment rate for Black teens was 40.7 percent, compared to 24.2 percent for all teens.[17] Racism probably plays some role here, but a major root cause of this gap is extremely low academic performance on the part of Black Americans and many other non-Asian minorities.

In 2004, when one of the most comprehensive recent studies of racial learning gaps was conducted, Black seventeen-year-olds scored at the same mean level of reading and math proficiency as white thirteen-year-olds, who also significantly out-performed the Black high school juniors and seniors in a third field, science. The differences in preparation and performance carry over to examinations of scholastic aptitude, such as the SAT. A study in 1995 concluded that less than two percent of Blacks, versus 9.6 percent of whites, post a score higher than 600 on the (easier) verbal section of the SAT. Almost two decades later, in 2012, virtually nothing had changed. The average Black SAT-taker's score trailed the average white test-taker's score by 99 points on the reading portion of the exam, 108 points on the math section, and 98 points on the written essay portion.[18]

As a result of both high rates of unemployment and low levels of academic performance, African Americans' incomes tend to be low. In 2015, according to *Forbes*'s Niall McCarthy, employed white Americans earned an average hourly real wage of $25.22, compared to $18.49 for Black Americans. The "racial wage gap" between Black and white Americans was actually greater in 2015 than it was in 1979, when white workers brought home an average wage of $19.62 in inflation-adjusted constant dollars versus $16.07 for African Americans (who thus earn 18.1 percent less). The discrepancy between Black and white household earnings is even worse. The median household income in 2011 was $67,175 for whites and $40,007 for Blacks (40 percent less).[19] The discrepancy in household income is due in very large part to the proportion of Black families headed by a single mother rather than two parents. Recall that the illegitimacy rate is currently 70–75 percent for Blacks in a typical year, versus roughly 30 percent for whites. The $3.55 discrepancy between average wage rates for whites and Blacks, while troubling, would not correlate to a household income gap of $27,118.

And there are worse things than working a low-paying job. In part because of the struggles predictably faced by badly educated, unemployed men, the incarceration rate for Black men in 2010–2011 was roughly six times the rate for white men, at 4,347 per 100,000 versus 678 per 100,000.[20] It is easily to understand how someone hearing these arguments and viewing these troubling statistics could come to the conclusion that the Black community is under brutal and sustained assault from powerful racist forces.

But this is simply not the case.

Let's look first at the "new racism" invoked by the activist Left. White privilege theory and its ilk simply collapse when they are subjected to empirical scrutiny.

There is literally no evidence that white status confers more "privilege" (measured as income, happiness, or perceived agency) on individuals in modern America than does social class, high IQ, male sex, growing up in a two-parent home, or a dozen other factors. The argument that Black Americans' real problems, such as a high rate of illegitimacy, are due to contemporary racism also fails. These same problems did not exist for Black Americans when racism was much worse (the Black illegitimacy rate was 14 percent in 1940),[21] and almost none of them exist for African and West Indian immigrants to the United States today.[22] Besides, many social pathologies have increased among whites as rapidly as they have among Blacks between the 1960s and today. The white illegitimacy rate has quadrupled just since 1975, and it stands at roughly 30 percent today. Remarkably, the illegitimacy rate among whites today is significantly higher than the rate among Blacks (23 percent) that triggered the famous Moynihan Report warning about the coming collapse of our inner cities.[23] Surely this new epidemic of fatherlessness among *whites* cannot be explained by racism.

For all the shrieking in academia about the trendy new varieties of alleged racism—and despite the fact that the mainstream media increasingly operates under the assumption that these explain all of Blacks' problems—there is shockingly little evidence that this "New Racism" even exists. Multiple well-done empirical studies demonstrate that being white in the United States today is simply one of dozens of factors that sometimes correlate with increased income and success at various life outcomes, and it is by no means the most significant among them.

In a piece published by *National Review*, Dennis Prager concedes that there may indeed be some advantage to being white in a variety of situations, but he argues convincingly that "a host" of other factors "dwarf white privilege" as competitive advantages. To give a simple and hugely relevant example, having two married parents—call it "traditional family privilege"—is probably the single largest predictor of later success in mainstream American life, especially for males. The poverty rate for two-parent Black families is only seven percent, versus 22 percent "among whites in single-parent homes." That is a 314 percent difference, in favor of married Blacks. For purposes of comparison, the Black-white wage gap given above—a common measure of white privilege—is only 26 percent before education, region of residency, tested IQ, sex of the person working, and other factors are adjusted for.

It might make just as much sense to speak of "Christian privilege" or "Gentile privilege." As Prager points out, "For most of American history, it was a lot easier being a Christian than a Jew in the United States." And, given available data on religiously motivated violence sourced by, for example, the Anti-Defamation League, there is reason to conclude that this is still the case in our era of increasing hostility to Israel. An argument for "Asian privilege" could also be made. Asians are often beneficiaries of both upper middle-class culture and affirmative action protections, and they outperform Western *guei lo fan* "in school, on IQ tests, in credit scores," and frankly on almost all other "positive social measures." Looking at the full range of privileges that might, theoretically, benefit a random person in a competitive situation, Prager calls assertions of universal white privilege "largely meaningless."[24]

My own research supports similar conclusions. Early on in my academic career, I conducted a large-N study of several hundred college undergraduates in an attempt to empirically analyze the effect of various characteristics on success in life. The dependent variable in the study was a one-hundred-unit measure of privilege, designed by a small team of social scientists, and the respondents' Yes or No replies to questions such as "I have never felt poor" and "I have never gone to bed hungry." Independent variables in my model, tested directly against the dependent variable using modern regression methods, included the race, sex, age, sexual orientation, social class (measured as reported income), religious faith tradition, height and weight, self-reported level of attractiveness, Southern or non-Southern and urban or rural background, and the political ideology of each respondent.

Unsurprisingly, I did find that being Black or Latino had a statistically significant 2- to 3-point negative impact on median privilege on my 100-point scale. This result means that some racism still exists, and the average Black guy is two or three percent less privileged than the average white guy when all variables besides race are held steady at their median—that is, when the Black and white respondent's backgrounds have the same characteristics. This small but real amount of racism is unfair and unfortunate. However, I found that numerous other factors, including LGBT sexual orientation, religious minority status, female sex, and even a rural background come with decreased privilege far more than minority race does.

By far the most influential factor was social class, measured as income, which had about six times as much impact on "privilege" as racial minority status. Simply put, how much money you earn is by far the biggest predictor of how privileged a life you will lead. There may be a few exceptions to this rule involving genuine bigots, but steakhouses and jewelry stores and greedy politicians will almost always treat a rich Black guy better than a broke white guy. Using empirical methods, I found virtually no evidence that whites enjoy massive unearned privilege simply as a result of being white. Obviously, even less evidence exists that this largely non-existent privilege causes actually existent problems, such as Blacks' low SAT scores.

Cultural appropriation theory is also debunked by investigation. Under the broadest academic definition of cultural appropriation—Scarfidi's simple standard of "taking something ... from another culture without permission"—almost literally everything human beings do qualifies as appropriation of some kind. In an appropriation-free world, whites could not use gunpowder or study kung fu (both Chinese inventions), and they would be reduced to attempting mark-to-market accounting with Roman numerals rather than the less clunky Arabic ones we use today. Blacks would have iron and some sophisticated architecture, but no access to pants or printed books or glass windows. And pity the poor American Indians! They would have to give up spoked wheels, the alphabet, and any recipes involving meat from domesticated animals.

Even more sophisticated definitions of cultural appropriation, such as Maisha Johnson's claim that it occurs only when a powerful group takes something from a group they themselves have oppressed or warred with, face crippling problems. First, the Johnson standard would still preclude probably half of all civilized exchange. No Mongol could drink Russian vodka or play Chinese checkers. No Turk could eat gyros, which originated in Greece. The United States and Japan, nations which fought a war of extermination less than a century ago and treated each other's majority race terribly for some time after that, could trade almost nothing. We would have to shutter our sushi bars, and their salarymen would have to give up their beloved Brooks Brothers suits and go back to silk kimonos and Masamune swords.

In fact, a real campaign to eradicate cultural appropriation under the Johnson standard would not stop there. Oppression is not only racial in nature, as Malcolm X pointed out! In 2017, gays and the poor are more oppressed than upper middle-class Black Americans, not to mention visiting Japanese. So, logically, no individual outside those particular disadvantaged groups should be allowed to experiment with any of their art forms, such as the country and Western music of the white lower classes and the electronic dance beats and drag culture of the LGBT community.

The Johnson standard—at first glimpse more practicable than Scarfidi's broader definition of cultural appropriation—is also ultimately unworkable. Though the activist Left often seems to forget this, there is no rule that the loser of every long-ago racial or ethnic quarrel will be the winner's bitch for the rest of time. Assertions that only whites can be racist, or only men sexist, or that only majority group members can engage in intellectual theft all seem to rest upon this premise—that the victims of any harm done in the past will forever be victims, and the descendants of the group that perpetrated the ancient injury need to make amends by embracing double standards essentially forever. But conquerors and oppressors regularly find themselves conquered and oppressed in their turn.

History is replete with examples of this kind of reversal of fortune, from the Old Testament—where the Israelites first took over the Canaanites' land, conquered and even eradicated Jebusites and other native peoples along the way, and then were themselves conquered by the Babylonians—to the conquest of the New World, when Europeans took over the American West just in time to save the Hopi Indians from genocide at the hands of the Navajo (a fact that explains why maps of Arizona show the Hopi reservation as a tiny dot in the middle of the vast Navajo reservation). The oppression that is supposedly addressed by solutions such as eternal bans on "cultural appropriation" has generally ceased to exist within a generation or two of any particular conflict.

But most significantly, the solution proposed by Johnson and others to (the non-problem of) eternal oppression in the U.S. runs directly counter to the letter and spirit of American law, which is grounded in the principle—stated explicitly in the Fourteenth Amendment, added to our Constitution in the wake of the Civil War that ended slavery in the United States and made Blacks equal citizens—that all citizens have the right to equal protection of the law.

Our legal system is imperfect, and surely it sometimes privileges the wealthy over the poor. But there is not one single county in this nation where the official sentence for robbing a house is "one year for whites, two for Blacks, and five for Hispanics." Yet the proponents of the Continuing Oppression Narrative would justify the mirror image of that non-existent regime: actual social and legal advantages for some groups and formal disadvantages for others. It is difficult to imagine any sort of free modern society thriving where such laws did exist.

Abandoning equal protection under the law would be immoral— and it would inevitably produce more racial tension and strife.

Leftists in general need to remember that human beings are individuals, not simply members of groups—though collectivists recoil from that fact like vampires reacting to garlic-flavored holy water. To someone looking at people in the proper light—as individual free-willed agents—it is deeply silly to contend that a Black or Asian may borrow from a white but not vice versa simply because whites as a group "outweigh" Blacks or Asians as a group. That point is profoundly irrelevant to the question of whether an Irish guy jacking a move from a friendly POC rival during a dance match or cooking contest is acting unethically.

As we have seen, any individual person is not necessarily in a position of power relative to his opponent. A white American may have 3 to 5 percent more "privilege" than a Black American on average—although probably less than an Asian American. But that's just on average. Individuals vary significantly from the averages for their groups—there are plenty of white orphans and pampered Black suburban teens. The white guy's Black rival in the aforementioned dance or cooking competition has an equal chance to borrow from him, something that surely happens as often as the reverse. In neither of these scenarios is anyone hurt or even disadvantaged—except perhaps in the day's competitive standings—by the borrowing we are talking about. And society as a whole is undoubtedly improved by it.

In summary: "Cultural appropriation" is impossible to define in any way that distinguishes it from, basically, life in general. It fails even as a logical construct, not to mention as a real-life explanation for ongoing problems in the Black community. And it would be both completely impractical and entirely unethical to punish it.

If phenomena such as white privilege and especially cultural appropriation are not real, they clearly cannot explain real-world problems in minority communities. The broadest claim of the Continuing Oppression Narrative—that contemporary racism of both new and old varieties causes essentially all minority problems—thus fails. While some actual traditional racism certainly does still exist, and likely always will given flawed human nature, it cannot explain contemporary problems facing the Black community or *el barrio*, such as illegitimacy and the myriad dysfunctions attendant on unwanted single parenthood. First, those problems did not exist in the past when racism was much worse. Second, they do not exist among Black immigrant minorities to this day. If racism is responsible for the contemporary problems of Black Americans, why do African, West Indian, and South Asian immigrants to the United States, who are often more dark-skinned than African Americans, enjoy such success? And why have the rates of Black illegitimacy, family dysfunction, and child-rearing failure only gone up since the Jim Crow era?

The fact is that many of the very real disadvantages under which Blacks in America labor today are the result of a relatively recent collapse of the American family, not of prejudice. The discrepancy in household income between whites and blacks, for example, is due in very large part to the proportion of Black families headed by a single mother rather than two parents. Recall that the illegitimacy rate is currently 70 to 75 percent for Blacks in a typical year, versus roughly 30 percent for whites. The $3.55 discrepancy between average wage rates for whites and Blacks, while troubling, would not correlate to a household income gap of $27,118. Marriage is one of the surest routes to household financial stability. And tragically, in the very time period when the success of the civil rights movement should have allowed Blacks to benefit from equal treatment under the law and the drastic diminishment of racism in the U.S., Blacks as a community moved away from marriage, which not only bolsters financial stability of a household but is also key to the success of the children raised in that household.

Few of the problems that plague the Black population today existed in 1960, when segregation was still the law across large chunks of the United States. The African American illegitimacy rate in 1960 was 21 percent, and that illegitimacy rate represented a significant and commented-upon increase from 18 to 19 percent in 1940. Jason Riley points to a plentitude of numerical evidence demonstrating that African Americans' rates of unemployment were lower and their marriage rates higher than the rates for whites until the end of the 1940s. In 1925 in New York, 85 percent of Black households consisted of a married mother and father with their children, and the huge majority of these fathers were employed working men.[25]

Even high rates of Black incarceration are a surprisingly recent phenomenon. In 1960 only 1,313 Black men per 100,000 were incarcerated in a prison or jail, while in 2010 the number was 4,347 Black men per 100,000 (versus 678 white men). In percentage terms, the Black incarceration rate grew from less than five times the white rate under segregation to six-plus times the white rate in 2010.[26] The increase of the Black incarceration rate, almost entirely caused by recent surges in the Black crime rate, becomes even more dramatic if we pick a starting date earlier than the 1960s for comparisons. In 1931, during the Al Capone era, the heyday of white American crime, 77 percent of all inmate admissions to state and federal prisons (combined) involved whites, while only 22 percent involved Blacks. Of the more than 10,000 admissions specifically to the federal graybar hotel that year, 87 percent were white and only 11 percent were Black. In fact, it was not until 1978, following the period of social upheaval often mislabeled "the Sixties," that the percentage of newly admitted federal prison inmates who were Caucasian dropped below 70 percent.[27]

It is indisputable that African Americans were the victims of horrific racism in the United States, with Black men and women used as human cattle for the enrichment of enterprises like the South's great cotton and tobacco plantations. The peculiar institution of slavery was the law of our "land of the free" from 1776 to 1865. It *is* worth noting that, while horrible, slavery in the United States did not endure "for four hundred years," as activists often claim. This number seems to be based upon the fact that Europeans living in various parts of the vast Americas very distinct from our own thirteen colonies— Spaniards, Portuguese, and French—owned slaves from the time of the European discovery of the New World in 1492. That's true enough. But this has literally nothing to do with the United States, which was not established until the Declaration of Independence in 1776. The first successful English colony in the new world, for that matter, dates to 1607 at the earliest. And we all know that slavery in the United States was abolished in 1865, not 2007. Human beings owned slaves well before any human beings were Americans, and that unfortunate fact is not America's fault.

That said, the horrors of chattel slavery are difficult for any human being alive today even to conceive of. And the end of slavery in the United States was followed, at least in the South, by another ninety-odd years of American apartheid: legally enforced policies of "separate but equal" Jim Crow segregation. Racially motivated atrocities were common during both of these eras. Tuskegee Institute records indicate that 3,446 Black Americans (and 1,297 whites) were lynched just during the period between 1882 and 1968, many by members of organized terrorist hate groups such as the original Knights of the Ku Klux Klan.[28] School desegregation did not come to the former Confederate states until 1954; the Civil Rights Act was not passed until 1964; and the first affirmative action program, the Philadelphia Plan, did not begin until 1967. None of this is contested by serious people. Portions of American history are written in blood and can be difficult for modern eyes to read.

But two things can be true at once. Looking at the numbers, it seems to be a plain empirical fact that the changes following the American cultural revolution that began in the 1960s—pay-per-child welfare, no-fault divorce, the legitimization of illegitimacy, the temporary abandonment of proactive "broken windows policing" (as it would come to be called), and the globalist outsourcing of blue-collar jobs—have had a greater effect on markers of cultural dysfunction among the African American population, such as the incarceration rate, than even the horrific racism of the past. In 1940, the African American illegitimacy rate was 18 percent; in 1960 it was 21 percent, and today it is 75 percent. The total number of Black men murdered, mostly by other Black men, in the single year of 2015—7,039—is 205 percent greater than the number of African Americans lynched in the entire history of the United States.

It is especially notable that these same negative metrics are increasing dramatically for whites, who surely cannot claim to be the victims of any sort of broad-based systemic oppression in America. The illegitimacy rate for American whites long since passed the 25 percent marker and now hovers at around 30 percent for all whites and 50 percent for younger and lower-income white groups. There were 5,854 white murder victims in 2015, an increase of more than 8 percent over the previous year.[29]

Clearly racism is not the primary cause of the struggles that affect both Black and poor white communities. That is confirmed by the remarkable success of recent immigrant groups made up of dark-skinned Africans, East Asians, and South Asians. The 2015 U.S. government data on incomes by racial and ethnic group, which was striking to enough Americans to become a trending Internet meme, shows that the wealthiest single ethnic group in the U.S. is not Anglo-Saxon whites but rather Indian Americans, with an average family income of $103,821. Taiwanese Americans ($91,000), dark-skinned

Filipinos ($82,000), and Lebanese Arabs ($75,000) finish second, third, and fifth respectively. The highest-earning Black African group was Nigerians ($62,000), followed closely by Egyptians ($61,344). Most white ethnic groups finished squarely in the middle of the statistical pack, well behind every Black or Asian group just mentioned. West Indians apparently had a bad year in 2015, but scholars including Dinesh D'Souza[30] and John McWhorter have pointed out that these Black islanders also generally outperform whites in terms of academics and income.[31]

Nigerians and Black West Indians look exactly like Black Americans, most of whom have ancestors from West Africa. Many or most of these high-performing Black immigrants are not especially exotic in appearance and behavior: the official language of Jamaica, Bermuda, and the Bahamas is English, and the national anthem of Bermuda is "God Save the Queen." In short, bigots who dislike Black Americans are not likely to set their prejudices aside when they meet a West Indian or an African immigrant—or, for that matter, a dark-skinned Pakistani Muslim. Members of these groups are so successful in the U.S. not because they never experience racism but because they successfully utilize resources—free public education, affirmative action programs, small business loans—that are at least equally available to native-born Americans of any race. Their success is proof that a group's own healthy culture can, generally speaking, trump any obstacle that racism in America throws at its members.

Most people understand, at some level, that white privilege, cultural appropriation, and so forth are not real things—much less viable explanations for low Black SAT scores or crime rates in *el barrio*. In contrast, the allegation that there is an ongoing epidemic of police and white vigilante murders of Blacks has garnered massive, supportive public attention from both the leftist mainstream media and the gullible public. This claim is the true cornerstone of the argument for New Racism. It inspired the Black Lives Matter movement, which has made international heroes of such upstanding young men as Trayvon Martin, Michael Brown, and Alton Sterling, and it is the cited inspiration for the *Washington Post*'s globally praised "The Counted" project, which focuses on police and anti-Black violence. This claim is also false.

The assertion that Black Americans are being disproportionately killed by police, which would appear at first glance to be supported by the numbers, does not withstand serious statistical scrutiny. Blacks and other minorities are not at special risk of violent attacks from law enforcement officers. In 2015, the year Black Lives Matter reached national prominence, fewer than 1,200 people nationally were shot by police and exactly 258 of them were Black. In fact, interracial crime of any variety is rare, with the overwhelming majority of both white and Black murder victims being killed by members of their own race during any given year. The inconvenient fact, almost never discussed by the mainstream media, is that the relatively small amount of interracial crime that does occur in the United States is almost entirely POC-on-white, and especially Black-on-white.

Fatal police violence targeting African Americans, especially unarmed or non-violent African Americans, is a vanishingly small phenomenon in the United States. During 2015, fewer than 1,200 people of all races were shot by police officers, and exactly 258 of them were Black. Fewer than 100 of these police shooting "victims" were unarmed, and of those 36 were Black. According to the most comprehensive survey of the data conducted by myself and a research assistant, utilizing internet resources such as killedbypolice.net, exactly 17 unarmed Black men were shot exclusively by white officers in 2015. Even taking the highest available figure for Black deaths at the hands of police (258), and counting each of those deaths as a homicide, less than 4 percent of all Black homicide victims during 2015 were killed by a police officer.

It is true that 23.5 percent of all persons shot by police during this typical year were Black, while only 13 percent of Americans identify as Black. This disparity represents a roughly 10 percent divergence from expectations—or, as mainstream media hyping the danger police pose to Blacks might choose to call it, "a disgraceful 81 percent over-representation!" However, there is almost literally no evidence that this over-representation is due to racism. The rate at which individuals and groups are involved in violent encounters with police is directly correlated with the rate at which those same individuals and groups are involved in all encounters with police. As of 2016, the overall crime rate, violent crime rate, police encounter rate, and incarceration rate were all at least 2 to 3 times higher for African Americans than for whites. The Black violent crime rate was almost 2.5 times the white rate, precisely matching African Americans' 250 percent higher chance of being shot by police officers of all races.[32]

Thus the disproportion between the Black percentage of the U.S. population (13 percent) and the Black percentage of those shot by the police (23.5 percent) is wholly explained by the fact that the Black crime rate, violent crime rate, police encounter rate, and arrest rate are all at least two to three times the equivalent rates for whites. Adjusting for any single one of these rates—which essentially predict an individual's chance of a hostile encounter with police—eliminates any apparent racial disparity in the rates of police shootings.

Some scholars contend, of course, that Blacks are more likely to encounter the police than whites in the first place wholly or partly because of racial animus. Van Jones correctly points out that Black youths are substantially more likely to be harassed or arrested than young white men for minor offenses, such as using drugs or carrying a penknife.[33] But that heightened police attention is more reasonably explained by higher rates of crime—causing officers to be more aware of individuals in particular categories, such as young, urban, minority men—than by racial animus on the part of police. Black arrest rates for violent crime track the rate at which victims accuse African Americans of committing that crime very closely—as per both nationwide FBI crime data (the Uniform Crime Report)[34] and a massive annual randomized study of self-reported crime victims conducted by the Department of Justice's Bureau of Justice Statistics.[35] Any competently constructed statistical model, which simply adjusts for the rate at which African Americans commit crimes and encounter the police, completely eliminates racial disparities in rates of police shooting.

The real data on police violence and the fallacies of Black Lives Matter's argument, while not widely known, are hardly my own discovery. Heather Mac Donald makes this exact argument much more eloquently, in her excellent 2016 book *The War on Cops*.[36] And, perhaps surprisingly, Milo Yiannopoulos gives a sober summary of the same evidence in *Dangerous*.[37] The data is not in serious dispute. But whenever I make this argument at a Chicago or Louisville cocktail party, it draws the same response: *That can't be true! Every time I turn on the news, I see another dead person of color!* The simple but true answer is that the mainstream American mass media is astonishingly ideologically biased. According to Pew Research Center's 2004 nationwide study of "547 local and national reporters, editors, and executives," only 7 percent of reporters identify as conservatives.[38] Veteran media researcher Robert Lichter has found that 81 to 94 percent of the "U.S. media elite" voted for the Democratic Party in every election from 1964 until the start of the 1980s.[39]

Thus the storyline about killer cops shooting innocent and unarmed Black men appeals to the media's left-wing sensibilities in a way that the mundane truth never could. We can debate percentages, but it is absolutely undisputed that the large numerical majority of American men shot by police are white and Hispanic. Yet media coverage of police violence in the United States is not just 23.5 percent, 51 percent, or even 75 percent focused on cases involving a Black victim. It is focused on those cases almost exclusively. It is a good bet that we won't be hearing the story of Dylan Noble—a young white man shot by the police—on MSNBC anytime soon. The word "bias" means "slant," and coverage this slanted must be, at least in part, the result of strong ideological bias.

However many people may think and say otherwise, there is no epidemic of killer cops, or at least of killer cops targeting Black people. (For good or ill, American police do kill quite a few people; they just don't seem to be racist about it. Law enforcement officers in the United States fatally shoot or otherwise kill 1,000–1,200 people in a typical year. In contrast, a quick look at the official INQUEST website breaking down all officer-involved fatal shootings in England and Wales between 2007 and 2016 reveals figures such as "2016: five deaths.")[40]

Moving beyond sworn officers, the idea that white civilian vigilantes are engaged in epidemic violence against African Americans is simply absurd. As we have seen, there is relatively little interracial crime of any kind in the contemporary United States. According to everyone from Tim Wise on the activist left to Jared Taylor on the extreme right, Black criminals target whites only 43 to 45 percent of the time, although white Americans make up nearly 70 percent of the U.S. population. White criminals return the favor, targeting Blacks 4 percent of the time despite the fact that Blacks make up 13 percent of Americans.[41] Both rates are substantial underrepresentations: 65 percent of what would logically be expected in the case of Black-on-white crime and only 31 percent of what would be expected in the case of white-on-Black crime. For all the discussion of racial tensions in America, both white and POC criminals commit interracial crimes substantially less often than random chance would predict.

The rarity of interracial crime is especially notable in the case of homicide. If you ever turn up murdered, the culprit will almost certainly be someone of your own race whom you know well—think your ex-wife—rather than five unknown males of a rival ethnic group who chose at random to jump out of an Econoline van and do you in. Interracial homicides such as the "white"-on-Black Trayvon Martin killing (by "white Hispanic" George Zimmerman) receive a great deal of national attention in part because they are such atypical man-bites-dog cases. Overall, 84 percent of white homicide victims are murdered by other whites, and an astonishing 93 percent of Black homicide victims are murdered by other Blacks.

There is an astonishing level of consensus, at least among scholars, on the fact that almost all of the interracial crime that does occur in the United States is POC-on-white. In the representative year of 2008, 429,000 Black-on-white violent crimes and only 91,000 white-on-Black violent crimes were recorded by the FBI, and the proportional breakdown of interracial offenses by race was nearly identical during 2012 and 2015. Anti-racist activist Tim Wise, who provided the figures just given, thus estimates that 82.5 percent of interracial crime involving Blacks and whites is Black-on-white crime.[42] At the exact opposite extreme of the political spectrum, Jared Taylor of American Renaissance has given a figure of 84.5 percent.[43]

The average Black American is five times as likely to attack an individual white American as vice versa. It should be noted that social scientist John Dilulio, from whom I derive this figure, has estimated the likelihood of Black-on-white crime at twenty-five times that of white-on-Black crime. But that statistic is flawed. Dilulio derived it from the fact that there are roughly five times as many Black-on-white crimes as white-on-Black crimes despite the fact that there are only one fifth as many Blacks as whites, and 5 x 5 = 25.[44] True enough. But the proper final step in that equation is to divide the 25x figure by 5 to reflect the fact that there are only 1/5 as many potential Black targets as there are white ones. So Blacks are 5—not 25—times more likely to commit crimes against whites than whites are to commit them against Blacks. Nonetheless, even the lowest-bound figure that can be extracted from the available data completely debunks the Movement for Black Lives' absurd claim that there is an ongoing epidemic of interracial violence directed at Black Americans.

None of this data necessarily implies racism on the part of African Americans. There are five times as many whites as Blacks in America, and Blacks have a crime rate at least twice as high as that of whites. Given the composition of the American population, there would logically be more Black-on-white crimes than white-on-Black crimes, even in a society entirely free of racism.

But the widespread false belief that racism is fueling police murders of Blacks is itself responsible for many problems. First, any amount of time that serious people spend chasing ghosts takes away from their ability to solve real problems. The obsessive focus of scholars and the media on white-on-Black and police-on-Black violence diverts attention from the much more serious issues of Black-on-Black violence. Second, and more important, many of the solutions to nonexistent problems that activists on the Left push have deeply harmful real-world results. Black Lives Matter's demand that police stand down from active policing in minority communities, for example, has already increased crime in the United States.

The demoralization of police officers working in crime-plagued Black neighborhoods has been a significant effect of the Continuing Oppression Narrative. After the nationally televised riots that followed the death of Michael Brown, police in major cities such as

Chicago cut back their rate of discretionary drug-and-gun stops by as much as 90 percent—with sadly predictable results.[45] Homicides in the country's fifty largest metropolitan areas rose by nearly 20 percent in 2015, which the Manhattan Institute's Heather Mac Donald has called "the greatest surge in fatal violence in a quarter-century."[46] The surge in murders continued through the next calendar year, with nine hundred more Black men murdered in 2016 than in 2015. In 2016, roughly a thousand more Black men were murdered than white and Hispanic men combined, despite the second population being roughly five times as large as the first.[47] The focus on the fake problems of police genocide exacerbated the real problem of epidemic urban crime, especially urban Black crime, and real people died as a result.

If Black Lives Matter succeeds in persuading all of America to acquiesce to the police stand-down they are promoting, then "the Ferguson Effect" will cause many thousands of deaths annually. Meanwhile, a focus on the elimination of "racism" as the sole solution to the problems of the hood prevents a true national focus on initiatives—proactive policing, educational competence, and involved fatherhood—that would actually fix these problems.

Although interracial crime of any kind is rare, the almost obsessive focus of many activists and media personalities on atypical incidents of white-on-Black violence certainly distracts from the fact that whites should logically be more worried about it than Blacks or other minorities. Truly shocking racially charged incidents targeting whites receive a tiny fraction of the coverage that white-on-Black hate incidents do, and often they are not effectively punished. In 2007, for example, a white Knoxville couple were kidnapped, tortured, and raped by an all-Black group of men and women. At the end of a night of genuine horror, Hugh Newson was shot in the head execution-style and burned as he began to die, while girlfriend Channon Christian had her genitals "washed" with bleach before she was suffocated in a trash bag. Coverage of that case was essentially local, and the only major-media result of a contemporary search for it is the alt-right website American Renaissance.[48]

In an even more shocking 2009 case, a white seventeen-year-old spring breaker named Brittanee Drexel was kidnapped by a group of Black men, raped over a period of several days, made into a sex slave and prostitute, and eventually fed to alligators. Law enforcement's pursuit of Drexel's abusers was in fact quite dogged, spanning a period of nearly a decade and resulting in criminal convictions at least tangential to her case.[49] But a Google search for the Drexel matter again turns up mostly niche right-leaning websites such as WorldNetDaily and The Daily Caller.

The disparity in mainstream media coverage of racially motivated attacks on whites, versus on minorities, has been clear for some time. Almost certainly the bloodiest race-inspired murders ever to take place in the United States were the Zebra Killings, which occurred in San Francisco between October 1973 and May 1974. These murders were very explicitly racial: a group of male Black Muslims gave themselves the *nom de guerre* "Death Angels," and murdered, by several accounts, seventy-three white women and men because "they were devils." According to the well-known criminologist Anthony Walsh, the Death Angels killed more people than all other known serial killers operating during that year, and perhaps during the decade, put together.

After a lengthy investigation into these mass murders, four Death Angels were convicted and sentenced to life imprisonment. But observers of the case complained that those accused and charged were probably only a small sub-group of the Death Angels gang and that prosecutors did not pursue the death penalty. The only book describing this extraordinary crime wave, which held San Francisco

in terror for a year, seems to be Clark Howard's excellent little
Zebra, published in 1979, whose account I have been following here.
It has been out of print for three decades.[50] Had a group of Klansmen killed dozens of Black Americans in a major world city during
the modern era, the level and tone of the coverage might have been
a wee bit different.

The Continuing Oppression Narrative—"white vigilantes" and
all the rest of it—serves to deflect attention from cultural issues within
the Black community. Once this is realized, one obvious question is
why the white Left is so desperate to avoid honestly looking at these
problems. I sincerely suspect that many activist liberals are reluctant
to do so because they are as racist, in the literal sense, as their opposite numbers on the alt-right. Both blocs seem to believe, deep down,
that Blacks are intrinsically inferior to whites. What could possibly
explain the Left's near-taboo against even discussing IQ statistics,
other than the belief that Black and Hispanic Americans have lower
genetically-determined intelligence than whites and East Asians?

Only this belief would seem to explain the hostility of the Left to
any research whatsoever into questions of race and IQ—not only
toward the work of right-wing scholars like Arthur Jensen but also
to skillful studies done by social scientists like Thomas Sowell. The
respected linguist John McWhorter famously penned a feature article
arguing that discussing race and IQ "serves no purpose,"[51] and genetics blogger "Human Biological Diversity (HBD) Chick" was recently
suspended from Twitter as if she were a neo-Nazi or white-robed
Klansman.[52] The self-described champions of human equality seem
more than a little leery of what scholars peering inside the braincase
and the genetic code might actually find.

However, what serious anti-racist scholars of race and IQ have
actually discovered is profoundly heartening, rather than horrifying.
The maximal potential g-factor IQs of individuals—that is, how

smart people can be if all were properly trained—seem to vary little, if at all, across the major races. It is cultural practices that explain racial differences in test scores. Scholars Christopher Jencks and Meredith Phillips, after conducting and reviewing a number of large-N studies, conclude that roughly two-thirds of the Black-white test score gap disappears when differences in a small number of parenting practices and other socio-cultural variables are adjusted for.[53] Roland Fryer and Steven Leavitt go even further, concluding that "nearly all" test score differences among Blacks, whites, and Hispanics disappear when "half a dozen characteristics" are controlled for. These include "the age of the mother, the birth weight of the baby, [family income], and the number of books in home."[54]

My own conclusion, after years of examining the empirical record and some—admittedly small-N and limited—quantitative work of my own with college students and social media users is that adjusting for only four variables appears to equalize IQ scores across racial groups. Those factors are: (1) the presence of a father in the home growing up, (2) the number of books in the home, (3) the number of hours spent watching television and studying per night, and (4) the high school grades expected by a student's parents. I will note that McWhorter also mentions all of these specific factors as affecting classroom performance and presumably IQ among college students, and he analyzes the effect of each from a qualitative perspective in his 2000 book *Losing the Race*.[55]

These results strongly suggest that there are a number of things activist NGOs and regional governments can do that would actually have a dramatically positive effect on the performance of Black—and poor white—Americans. To suggest just six: (1) give or cheaply sell books to poor families; (2) financially reward students who obtain a library card or finish a certain number of books from a set canon; (3) promote prenatal and early post-natal health for infants and mothers, as well as sexual responsibility; (4) work toward solving the problem of "food deserts" in poor urban areas; (5) aggressively support pro-active policing and engage in citizen patrolling to fight inner-city crime (which causes the food deserts in the first place); and most importantly (6) promote fatherhood using all available tools including social media and actual enforcement of child-support laws.

The NAACP, the Urban League, and even major African American fraternities such as Alpha Phi Alpha—which are male-dominated Black networking organizations—could do an almost inexpressible amount of good by focusing on this last initiative. But progress toward enacting this actually effective agenda would require abandoning the activist Left's laser-like focus on fighting the imaginary epidemics of continuing oppression. A march promoting responsible fatherhood and taking a stand against violent gangs would do unimaginably more good for struggling minority communities than one protesting white-on-Black vigilante violence, but serious people would have to divert their time and money away from the second of those in order for the first to be held.

Michael Bown, Freddie Gray, Alton Sterling, Philando Castile, and Sandra Bland have become household names, while few outside the law enforcement community and genuinely racist alt-right circles have ever heard of Dylan Noble or Jeremy Mardis. Stories such as "Chicago Racist Yells at Black Woman"—an actual headline on my Facebook news feed the morning I wrote this paragraph—regularly make the national news, while, as we have seen, the only book on the Black-on-white Zebra killings of seventy-three people was published in 1979.

The alleged epidemic of hate crimes in America provides the most potent imaginable support for the Continuing Oppression Narrative, and it is regularly cited by the activist Left as evidence that their perspective on American race and inter-group relations is true. But the narrative is in fact false, and so are most of the "hate crimes" invoked to support it. As the next chapters will detail, many or most widely publicized hate allegations made in recent years have proven to be hoaxes. Debunking the best-known of these, one by one, is a great first step toward debunking the narrative that rests upon them and that, a century and a half after the last slave was freed, holds more than a few minority Americans in bondage.

Chapter Three

BIG FAKE ON CAMPUS: FAKE HATE CRIMES IN AMERICAN ACADEMIA

I ndisputably, the most common host environment for recent hate crime hoaxes has been the American collegiate campus. As of January 2018, at least 80 of the 269 nationally reported hoaxes featured on the first nine pages of the Fake Hate Crimes website were incidents that took place on a college, university, or high school campus. This might initially appear counterintuitive: a logical person might wonder why students enrolled in liberal academic institutions, where any deviation from the prevailing center-Left orthodoxy is policed with remarkable vigor, would be more likely to report that they were the victims of ugly bigoted attacks. The truth is that certain aspects of the politically correct culture on many campuses—including mostly radical faculties, formal speech codes, and activist mobs on the quad—create a perfect environment for (1) normal words and actions to be redefined as hate speech and violent attacks and (2) actual hoaxers to receive support from a predictable contingent of allies.

The liberal, if not radical-Left, composition of most college faculties is well-documented. Pointing this out should be no more controversial than saying "Most military men are conservatives." The most
recent major study of this topic, conducted by Brooklyn College's
Tony Quain and George Mason University's Daniel Klein for the
September 2016 edition of *Econ Journal Watch,* concludes that Democrats outnumber Republicans on college faculties by roughly a dozen
to one. Out of 7,243 professors at 40 highly representative universities
interviewed or documented by the scholarly pair, 3,623 were Democrats, while only 314 preferred the pachyderm option on the ballot.

Reviewing Quain and Klein's data, the *Washington Times* drily
noted, "The field friendliest to conservative scholars is economics,
where there are only 4.5 liberal professors for every [Republican]."
Conversely, history and sociology are the least welcoming departments for traditionalists, with liberal historians outnumbering
conservative ones 33.5 to 1. Should party identification strike you
as a poor proxy for personal ideology, another high-quality data
set, put together by UCLA's Higher Education Research Institute
(HERI) in 2014, reveals that 60 percent of professors describe
themselves as liberal or "far left," outnumbering all varieties of
campus conservatives, who make up less than 12 percent of professors, by at least 5 to 1.

The Quain/Klein and HERI data reveals several other interesting, and mostly disturbing, trends. First, the disparity between liberals and conservatives in faculty representation is the most pronounced
on the most elite American campuses. Quain and Klein found that
large Midwestern state institutions have Democrat-to-Republican
staff ratios of 6 to 1. In contrast, however, Ivy League pillars Princeton
and Columbia "both weigh in at 30 to 1." Further, across all institutions
of higher learning, these extreme disparities are getting worse. As the
Times notes, "While there are 10 Democrats for every Republican

among professors over the age of 65, the ratio balloons to 22.7 to one among scholars under the age of 36." This trend means that "ideological disparities could continue to grow," as "more senior professors are pushed out and replaced by a new generation of scholars."[1]

The mere fact that professors almost invariably lean left would not, by itself, necessarily be cause for great concern. As noted above, the U.S. Army leans right, and by all accounts runs ethically and well. Simply having a certain political perspective does not disqualify anyone from doing a serious job. But there is considerable evidence that the "politically correct" ideological preferences of many academics do not remain a private affair. Instead, the faculty imposes those views on their students. Speech codes are perhaps the best example.

The Foundation for Individual Rights in Education (FIRE), an organization that opposes campus speech codes, notes that "more than 400 of the largest and most prestigious American universities" have speech-restriction codes in place. The organization defines a 'speech code' as "any university ... policy that prohibits expression that would be protected by the First Amendment in society at large," and points out that a majority of U.S. colleges probably use the campus legal system to stringently restrict speech. Speech codes profiled by FIRE over the years have banned such "offensive" material as (1) flyers advertising a speech by an opponent of illegal immigration at Central Washington University, (2) a recruitment flyer for the Young Conservatives of Texas that contained a series of half-joking gun safety tips, and (3) brochures passed out by Montclair State University's Students for Justice in Palestine chapter that were "harshly critical" of Israeli foreign policy.

In its written materials, FIRE accurately criticizes speech codes: "These codes lead students to believe they have an absolute right to be free from offense, embarrassment, or discomfort." This has real-world consequences. If those Americans enrolled in our nation's top colleges "learn that jokes, remarks, or visual displays that offend someone may rightly be banned, they will not find it odd or dangerous when the government itself seeks to censor [citizens]."[2] How true.

And censorship on the modern campus, particularly of right-wing ideas, unfortunately often goes well beyond speech codes. During the past two years, open riots—one famously labeled the "Battle of Berkeley"—have greeted the arrival on campus of quite mainstream conservative speakers, such as Ben Shapiro and the team of Christina Hoff-Sommers and Milo Yiannopoulos. As *The Hill* notes, "With the election of Donald Trump, protesters have taken their opposition to an unprecedented level. Petitioning, disruptions, and general harassment were common tactics at first—but now that arsenal has expanded to include rioting, looting, and lobbing Molotov cocktails at police officers."

Some universities have responded to this threat with the craven expedient of simply banning conservative and Libertarian speakers from campus. Chicago's DePaul University recently threatened to arrest Shapiro—a five foot nine, yarmulke-wearing conservative Jew—and have him sent to the Cook County Men's Jail "if he set foot on campus again."[3]

On more than a few campuses, students who claim to have been hate-crime victims are essentially guaranteed thousands of supportive ears. In contrast, those who espouse mainstream conservative ideas may well be guaranteed a beating. Intentionally or not, many—though thankfully not all—contemporary universities have created ideal "greenhouse" environments for hate crime hoaxes. When a student makes a false claim of bias at a typical elite American university, the faculty will be supportive; the student body will have been conditioned to see "hate" everywhere; hundreds of willing and aggressive radical allies will spring from the ground like soldiers from dragon's teeth; and the risk of punishment from on-campus judicial procedures (assuming the hoaxer is ever exposed) will be low. Any competent strategic analyst would expect dubious claims of bigotry to flourish like hot-house flowers in such a context.

And flourish they do.

NOOSES, NOTES, AND A HIT LIST AT PARKSIDE

One of the most complex and bizarre hate crime hoaxes in recent history, the one that actually sparked my interest in the phenomenon of hoax hate crimes, took place during the winter of 2012 on the Chicago campus of the University of Wisconsin-Parkside.

The whole situation began on a cold Wednesday in February, when several Black History Month events were being celebrated. On that day, several students walking across Parkside's pleasant tree-lined campus—where I once applied for an academic job—found a crude "noose" made of rubber bands lying on the ground. This incident sparked some comment, and the noose was apparently reported to campus authorities, but nothing much appears to have been done about it. The next day, things escalated dramatically. Popular Black student Aubriana Banks had a second noose made of plastic string placed on her dorm room door. She then received a profane and threatening note containing several racial epithets. Finally, later that evening, multiple students on the Parkside campus came across flyers reading, "Niggers will die in 12 days! No niggers wanted!" At the bottom of the flyers, someone had written the full names of thirteen Black Parkside students.

In response to what seemed to be a sudden explosion of hate crimes, the University of Wisconsin-Parkside descended into near-chaos. Terrified, many students temporarily left campus, returning to the presumed safety of Chicago and Detroit. All probably agreed with a spokesman who described the situation as "embarrassing and unfortunate." A campus-wide meeting was held on Thursday night—the late evening of the day when the racist note and the so-called hit list were found—to "bring the student body together" and let students vent. The room was packed, and many young people were in tears, with one saying: "This saddens me. I can't think. I've been crying since I got up this morning." The chancellor of the university issued what would be the first of several statements, stating firmly, "Hate cannot and will not be part of UW-Parkside." Inevitably, of course, both university and area police did everything they could to find the hate culprit, with the Kenosha County Sheriff's Department assigning seven detectives to work the case, eventually creating a forty-one-page incident report.

Then the unexpected happened. Black Parkside student Khalilah Ford admitted to committing most if not all of the terrifying hate crimes, shortly after the investigation began. By February 6, 2012, Ford had confessed both to sending Banks the racist note and to putting her own name and those of twelve other African American students on the "hit list discovered in the dorm Thursday night." Initially Ford did not admit to making the nooses, but Wisconsin's *Badger Herald* newspaper states unequivocally that by March 18, 2012, she had confessed to creating "the death list and nooses," and had possibly worked with another student to do so. Eventually Ford ended up being charged with a pair of fairly minor misdemeanors: disorderly conduct and obstruction of a police officer.

Ford does not seem to have been the world's highest-IQ criminal. Kenosha County Sheriff Bill Beth has said that it was so easy to catch Ford and obtain a confession because her name was "the *only* name to appear spelled correctly" on the thirteen-name hit list. But even more intriguing was Ford's explanation for why she concocted a wave of fake hate crimes: because the University of Wisconsin-Parkside was racist. She explained in some detail that she created the hit list and threatening note because she did not feel "that the original noose incidents were being taken seriously enough."[4]

Now recall that, according to the *Badger Herald*, Ford herself was responsible for the original noose incidents. In other words, Ford probably created the original noose scare to convince other students that Parkside was racist, and then she definitely dreamed up a whole series of other disturbing hoaxes because she was not pleased with the university's response to the nooses and wanted to punish the place ... for being racist. Given that Ford's final two pranks took place the same day as a campus-wide rally against hate, it is difficult to imagine what more Wisconsin-Parkside could have done to please this passionate and well-meaning activist.

Even more astonishing than Ford's justification for her felony-level hoaxes (punished as misdemeanor-level hoaxes) was the university's reaction to her unique logic. The University of Wisconsin-Parkside responded to Ford's hate crime hoax by behaving as though a wave of real hate crimes had taken place and university authorities had indeed not responded to them sternly enough. Following the incidents, Parkside's dean of students committed the school to completely re-evaluating "how it handles racist incidents in the future." According to the local Fox 6 affiliate, students and faculty wore "No Hate" stickers around campus for months after "the incidents." In another final statement, Wisconsin-Parkside's chancellor declared herself to be "so proud" of her students' hostile reaction to "any intolerance of diversity." In a ringing passage she asked the campus community to continue "support of and respect for one another as we begin the healing process."

Even the police got into the act, telling the Fox affiliate that their focus had shifted from "finding the perpetrator to protecting the perpetrator" immediately after the discovery of Ford's lies. Ford did face minor criminal charges, but even her name was not initially released to the press, presumably in order to give her the chance to leave campus safely and perhaps seek education elsewhere.

To recap: an African-American student created an entire wave of hoax hate crimes that kept one of the major campuses in the University of Wisconsin system paralyzed for a week. She then explained that she did this because the college was racist and had not responded seriously enough to earlier (likely fake) hate crimes—for which she was probably also responsible. The university essentially agreed, making major changes to its policies dealing with racial incidents despite the fact that no real ones seem to have occurred at Parkside at this time. Numerous students and faculty members condemned "racism," and several apologized for it.[5]

KEAN U AGAINST COMMON SENSE: THE MOST EXPENSIVE HOAX SO FAR

The story just told is not unique to the University of Wisconsin-Parkside; this sort of thing happens all the time. One of the most costly and ingeniously manipulative hate crime hoaxes in recent memory took place during the fall 2015 semester at New Jersey's Kean University.

On November 17, 2015, an anonymous Twitter account with the handle @keanuagainstblk ("Kean University against Blacks") went live and began posting from the Kean campus. Within hours, the account had tweeted out multiple serious threats, including promises to murder a large number of Black college students. One tweet read, "Kean University twitter against Blacks is for everyone who hates Black people." Another stated, "I will kill all the Blacks today, tomorrow, and any other day if they go to Kean University." The anonymous account also displayed contempt for the police, tagging Kean

University law enforcement in its most threatening messages, and openly mocking the campus police. Panic followed the discovery of the tweets, with the student body president Nigel Donald telling students to "stay in their residence hall[s]" all day and not travel through campus, and a group of local Black ministers demanding the resignation of the KU president—himself a minority activist named Dawood Farahi.[6]

You have probably guessed, by this point in the book, that the mastermind behind @keanuagainstblk was, inevitably, a POC activist or other campus radical. Indeed. But three things rescue the Kean University case from mundanity and make it stand out as an example of a hate crime hoax: (1) the elaborate orchestration of the hoax, (2) its extraordinary success, and (3) the remarkable cost of pursuing and catching its perpetrator. As it eventually turned out, the orchestrator of the scheme was a Black student activist named Kayla McKelvey. The Twitter account went live on the day of a large rally—of which McKelvey was the principal coordinator—organized in response to allegations of racism against a Kean University professor and the school's student government. This rally was part of a nationwide attempt by students to raise awareness of racial problems on different campuses, in solidarity with Black students dealing with—or, as it would turn out, fomenting—racial hostility at the University of Missouri.

Note that both the accusation against the Kean professor that inspired McKelvey's rally and the majority of the alleged hate incidents at the University of Missouri themselves turned out to be complete hoaxes. Here we see a common trend on college campuses—hate hoaxers falsifying incidents in homage to racial incidents that were themselves hoaxes.

McKelvey left her own rally—perhaps upset by what she perceived as a lack of enthusiasm—about halfway through it, went to the campus library, and set up @keanuagainstblk. She then tweeted out the account's first two messages, expressing hate for Black students and threatening to kill Black classmates, tagged the police department, and went back to the protest. McKelvey then "spread awareness of the threats" by pulling up her own tweets in front of a crowd of hundreds to demonstrate the prevalence of racism at Kean. That night, on her personal Twitter account, @ACarribeanDream, she posted both pictures taken at the rally and snapshots of the threatening tweets. McKelvey's header message, above the photos, read: #PrayforKeanUniversity, #KeanUniversityThreats, #StudentBlackout, #ConcernedStudents1950. McKelvey then went peacefully to bed, as chaos spread.[7]

And it spread quite far. Because McKelvey had set up @keanuagainstblk on a university machine rather than her own computer, and apparently deleted all tracking cookies after doing so, it proved almost impossible to chase her down. But because the crime McKelvey threatened in her posts was mass murder, and she had linked to and taunted one of the police agencies that ended up investigating her, the authorities turned out to be deadly serious about doing exactly that. State and local police as well as university law enforcement "were dragged into the fray almost immediately," and the FBI and Department of Homeland Security became involved not long afterward. As journalists from conservative political blog Hot Air and New Jersey's Bergen *Record* have pointed out, "This wasn't some simple prank that disrupted a few classes." The total tab for the investigation into McKelvey's hoax came to roughly $100,000.[8]

As a result of the extraordinary institutional costs caused by her crime, Kayla McKelvey attained a dubious distinction: she became one of the very few American college students ever to be tried and jailed for faking a hate crime. State prosecutors in particular refused to "go light" on her, bringing false public alarm charges and pursuing a sentence of ninety days in county jail. The presiding judge in McKelvey's criminal case agreed, imposing that sentence and also ordering McKelvey to do a hundred hours of community service with the county sheriff, undergo anger management therapy, and remain on probation for a period of five years. Perhaps most painful, for a new college graduate, McKelvey was ordered to pay restitution "in the amount of $82,000" to cover the tab for the massive response of local, state, and federal law enforcement to her stunt.[9]

In the wake of the incident there was also some talk about stripping McKelvey of her 2014 homecoming crown. This small side point sheds light on what may be the most significant element of the entire McKelvey case. The perpetrator was not some maladjusted chartreuse-haired dorm-room rebel or an inner-city student majoring in "Fanon and Revolution" and struggling with middle class norms. She was literally Kean's homecoming queen, as well as the president of the Pan-African Student Association. She graduated from Kean in 2015 with a degree in personal fitness and wellness and currently works as a high-end personal trainer.[10]

The Kean case demonstrates how leftist activism and Identitarian protest is becoming the absolute norm on American campuses. The homecoming queen at a good-sized university was investigated by Homeland Security for falsifying murder threats to make her school look more racist. And this happened in suburban New Jersey, not at Berkeley!

TALKING ABOUT SHOOTING ANYTHING IS RISKY: MATTHEW SCHULTZ AND THE YIK YAK SMILE CONTROVERSY

In one of the most absurd recent campus hate crime scares, a student was expelled from a top technical university and arrested on a felony charge for threatening to smile at his classmates.

In November of 2015, Michigan Tech student Matthew Schultz uploaded a post to the Twitter-like social media app Yik Yak: "Gonna shoot all black people ... a smile tomorrow!" Schultz intended the post as a light-hearted response to the unrest caused by a series of alleged racial incidents, themselves mostly fakes, on the University of Missouri campus. The lawyer that Schultz ended up hiring, Steven Pence, says that his client had "the intent of pointing out" the ridiculous and overblown style of most "trolling" racial threats (such as "shoot all black people") and of "mocking the illiterate language" used by dueling racists and activists at Mizzou ("Gonna"). As Pence points out, the fact that what Schultz threatened to shoot out to his classmates was a big smile is pretty good evidence that the young mechanical engineer is not a murderous racist.

But unfortunately for Schultz, social justice warriors generally have a poor sense of humor. Michigan Tech student Ryan Grainger took a screenshot of the post before it was deleted from Yik Yak, tweeted it to the university, and also sent a copy of his screenshot to the MTU police department. But Grainger had altered the picture he sent to the campus police, so that the phrase "a smile tomorrow" had been removed and the post read only "Gonna shoot all black people!" Unsurprisingly, given this change, the campus police department issued a formal statement condemning "an anonymous social media threat against members of our African American community." The frenzy grew and spread from there. The next day an excited spokesperson for Michigan Tech told the local TV station that an anonymous terrorist had "said they wanted to shoot all Black people" on the MTU campus: "We called public safety immediately. They sprang into action. We sent a note out to the entire campus informing them of the nature of the threat." When Schultz was identified as the author of the Yik Yak post, he was arrested for domestic terrorism—a felony generally carrying a twenty-year prison sentence—and hauled off to jail.

Now the story, already absurd, moves into Kafkaesque territory that only college disciplinary bureaucracies seem to inhabit. We now know that Michigan Tech police arrested Schultz after Yik Yak executives identified him, despite being aware that he was in no way a threat. According to Campus Reform's Amber Athey, Yik Yak did "flag and remove" Schultz's original post from the platform—presumably because it contained a reference to shooting anything at a human being, and this is America in the twenty-first century. But the site's response team quickly determined that the "post was not a threat of any kind." In response to a search warrant and request from Michigan Tech, however, they did identify Matthew Schultz as the poster of the harmless message. In short, Schultz's arrest for making the post occurred because Yik Yak identified him as the poster when asked, despite knowing full well that his message was legal and harmless.

As it became increasingly obvious that Schultz (1) was not guilty of anything and (2) was known to be innocent by the social media company he allegedly offended against, all charges initially brought against him were dismissed by the Houghton County district attorney. In a crisp professional statement, that worthy district attorney explained that there was: "no evidence to indicate an actual ongoing public danger, nor was there evidence of motive, [n]or intent." However, even this did not stop the Michigan Tech bureaucracy.

The same day the charges were dismissed, the MTU conduct board held a closed-door hearing from which both Schultz and his lawyer were barred and placed him on full disciplinary probation for eighteen months. When Schultz, now known to be innocent, elected to appeal this decision, Michigan Tech's associate vice president and dean of students chose to *expel* him, with no right to appeal the decision. According to Schultz's attorney, the university then launched a media campaign against Schultz, despite being fully aware that the post as reported to them "had been altered" from what Schultz orig inally posted. Schultz, out of school "with no hope of resuming his studies anywhere after having been labeled a virulent racist,"[11] filed a lawsuit naming not just Michigan Tech but also fellow student Ryan Grainger—who would seem to be responsible for the (hoax) hate crime in this case—and "twelve school officials" as defendants.[12] MTU eventually settled the case for $42,000.[13]

Good for Schultz! But the absurdity of how he was treated merits a final comment. Evil, as Hannah Arendt pointed out, is usually banal. People engage in it for boring, mundane reasons: to make a buck, or to get laid, or to get high. Most people who do evil things are relatable in some way; most of us *are* those people on occasion. Michigan Tech's decision to destroy Schultz's future is a bit more difficult to understand. A reputable public university expelled a rock-solid student for "racism," after the public prosecutor declared him to be innocent. MTU was pilloried in the press for this. It is hard not to ask, *Why the hell would they do that?*

The short answer seems to be: fear. Tensions at MTU had been running high since an event at which several students wore blackface. A Confederate flag was spotted on campus during the fall 2015 semester. A "Rally for Racial Harmony" took place in November, the same month the Schultz/Yik Yak atrocity occurred. In light of all this, and of the things being said around campus about Schultz's tweet, which was taken by many Black students as an actual threat, it would have been too risky not to punish him—even though every single Michigan Tech administrator at the decision-maker level had to know he was innocent. To quote Pence, MTU executives had to portray themselves as "good guys and enlightened Administrators," fighting a dragon, but one that "did not exist."[14]

With St. Georges like these, it is hard not to cheer for the dragon.

BY JALEN—IT'S HAPPENED AGAIN!
THE HOAX HATE CRIME WAVE AT CAPITAL UNIVERSITY

Most individuals who fake a hate crime do so only once. Amateurs! One troubled young man—Jalen Mitchell, a Black student at Capital University—turned out to be responsible for an entire wave of fake hate crimes.

Mitchell's catalogue of false reports was uncovered by Capital University police in early 2017, after he allegedly found a note filled with vile racial and homophobic epithets taped to the back door of his university apartment. On January 26, 2017, Mitchell reported the note to campus and local law enforcement, and an investigation was launched by the CU police. But when the cops asked Mitchell for a standard handwriting sample to eliminate him as a suspect, events took a bizarre and dramatic turn. Not only did Mitchell admit to fabricating the note, he also confessed to submitting multiple fake hate crime reports to the university police over the years.

The phony hate crimes Mitchell claimed to have experienced were not minor inconveniences. During the fall semester of 2015, he had reported finding a note even more offensive than the one he faked in 2017. The 2015 note contained not only threats and racial slurs but also multiple hand-drawn swastikas. Police had investigated Mitchell's report of the note, but "didn't find any fingerprints or incriminating evidence" from which to identify likely suspects. More recently, and more seriously, Mitchell had reported an actual physical assault, which he claimed occurred during the fall 2016 semester. On that occasion, he told university police that he had been "attacked on campus by a man with a knife" during his walk home from a social gathering. Mitchell described his supposed assailant in great detail, as a white male "in his late 20s or early 30s," with recognizable facial features and "a full beard."[15] Mitchell claimed to have received cuts and severe scratches on his arms, legs, stomach, and neck during the attack. This incident was reported in a widely circulated campus safety bulletin.

It is worth noting that, for all Mitchell's presentation of Capital University as a hate-filled sewer where he was attacked for racial reasons not once but three times, each of his accusations was in fact greeted with the usual frenzy of collegiate virtue-signaling. The College Fix noted that the school responded "as you might expect" to the 2015 incident; a campus-wide array of major events took place including "an open conversation and an inclusivity march"—a literal parade through campus—to "raise awareness of … hate crimes on campus."[16]

Though less has been said about it in print, the reaction to the 2016 allegation seems to have been similar. At no point does anyone appear to have alleged that Mitchell was falsifying these incidents that he reported annually to the local cops.

When he was finally cornered by the police request for a hand-writing sample, Mitchell gave a simple and plausible explanation for his crimes: he was going crazy. In a conversation with the CU student newspaper, he described his false reporting of the first incident as "a way to try to get attention, to say 'Someone notice me; I'm dying on the inside.'"[17] According to Mitchell, falsifying the first hate incident and observing the positive reaction he got "helped the feelings (I) was having," but "didn't solve what was really happening on the inside," because initial positive reinforcement was never actually followed by appropriate psychiatric treatment. The problems that caused the initial hate hoax thus spiraled out of control and led to the subsequent two reports. In his final analysis of the situation, Mitchell claimed that he was almost glad that campus police "responded promptly to his claims," exposed him, and got him help, because he was "in a bad place" and just "not stable mentally" before that happened.

I find myself surprised to write these words, but Mitchell is a sympathetic character. A Black and apparently gay—and very young—man, he seems to have been dealing with serious depression while working his way through a fairly difficult college in the good-sized city of Columbus, Ohio. He was quoted by The College Fix as saying that he "didn't mean to cause alarm, didn't mean to scare anyone." Instead, "I just wanted to be noticed. Not for fame, just acknowledgement." Mitchell has apologized profusely for what he did, and he noted—perhaps in reference to the campus-wide cere-monial that followed his first accusation—that he "never thought this would go as far as it did." Campus disciplinary authorities referred Mitchell's case to the student judicial affairs office, rather than back to campus police or over to the Columbus department, and I would speculate that his punishment will primarily consist of mental health counseling and community service rather than a suspension or expulsion.[18]

But while Mitchell is probably not himself a terrible person, the Mitchell *case* provides the best possible illustration of why discerning observers should be suspicious of essentially all campus hate crime reports. Over the course of less than two years, one troubled young man at a fairly typical university reported no less than three verbal and physical attacks to campus authorities. On the first occasion, the university literally threw him a party, including a solidarity parade through campus. On the second occasion—after police found no fingerprints or other evidence that the crime was not a hoax when investigating the first incident—his allegation was reported in the campus security bulletin as a troubling example of crime at CU. Even on the third occasion, police responded quickly to the allegation, and they uncovered Mitchell's duplicity only due to his unexpected response to a *pro forma* request for a handwriting sample. The Cap-ital University police are by all accounts a good, small department, and what Mitchell did was certainly not their fault. But as long as colleges continue to respond to almost all hate crime allegations with massive outpourings of public support, they will continue to see more false accusations brought by attention-seekers like Mitchell.

Interestingly, Mitchell himself pretty much admits that his actions will make others more skeptical about reported hate incidents on college and university campuses. He acknowledged that those who have experienced real hate crimes have a right to be "angry" with him, and he expressed fear that his actions had "delegitimized the reporting of hate crimes." Mitchell noted plaintively: "Some are legitimate. I'm sorry what I've done takes away from that."[19]

A worthy sentiment, mate—but a bit late.

IT TAKES AN ELECTRONIC ARMY OF MILLIONS TO HOLD US BACK: THE UNIVERSITY OF CHICAGO HACKER HOAX

As we have already seen, the internet provides hate crime hoaxers with a brave new world to exploit. In another case that sparked my interest in the phenomenon of fake hate crime and helped to inspire this book, University of Chicago student Derek Caquelin claimed that hackers had taken over his Facebook page, adding disturbing "racist and violent" content to it in retaliation for his work as a campus activist. This allegation resulted in the launching of a major federal investigation, before being proven untrue.

According to a number of well-known Midwestern publications, including the *Chicago Tribune*, Caquelin first claimed that his personal Facebook page had been hacked on November 18, 2014. According to Caquelin, at least one post made to the hacked page included explicit language, direct threats, and a reference to raping him. An implicit threat to Caquelin also allegedly came in the form of a threat made to his friend and fellow dorm-room-radical Vincente Perez: "You're next, Vincente!"[20] Caquelin blamed not a lone enemy but a group of hackers for the attack, attributing it to the "UChicago

Electronic Army (UCEA)," a "shadowy hacker group" presumably made up of conservative or Libertarian students. The UCEA, which may or may not have ever actually existed as an organized entity, had previously been accused of "feud(ing) with" feminist activists, after those "wombyn" (a term for cisgender women) circulated a printed list of all males on the University of Chicago campus suspected of being sexual threats and subsequently experienced blowback from the phallo-American community.

Caquelin claimed that he too had drawn the baleful attention of conservative hackers because of his liberal activism at the university. Although he proved to be a liar, Caquelin truly was an involved campus activist—by all appearances one slightly to the left of Che Guevara. As The College Fix points out, his Facebook-hacking allegation was simply the culmination of "a long list of racial grievances" brought against the University of Chicago by Caquelin and Perez. Immediately before this incident, Caquelin had posted a series of online diatribes condemning Halloween costumes that depicted wearers as Mexicans, criminals, and Native Americans for being prejudiced and inappropriate. This apparently ignited a major controversy on UChicago's Hyde Park campus. He supported a university-wide petition cowritten by Perez that called for "The university to mandate a 'campus climate survey' and 'mandatory cross-cultural competency programs,' as well as 'clearly' lay out its responses to 'racially insensitive actions,' incorporate racial and ethnic studies in the core curriculum and diversify the faculty."

Caquelin's hacking allegation seems to have been designed to boost campus-wide support for this petition and similar causes. I am under the impression that, unlike many of the hoaxers we have encountered so far, Caquelin did not desire national attention and was a bit dismayed to receive it. He almost certainly intended only to provide a little bit of (fake) evidence for his pet claim that the costume incidents revealed a larger "culture of intolerance" at the University of Chicago. This is what The College Fix has argued as well, pointing out that, in conversations that took place before Caquelin admitted to the hoax, Perez steered questions about the hacking back toward a dialogue about "the entire culture" of structural bigotry at the university. Caquelin himself refused to talk to The College Fix and most other off-campus media outlets—something Perez explained by claiming that Caquelin didn't want to distract from the fight of UChicago activists against campus culture.

For a few days the University of Chicago played along with the Caquelin script almost letter for letter, saying on November 20 that the "hateful and anonymous Facebook posts" to which this brave young radical had been subjected were part of "a larger pattern" on the UC campus and pledging to fix the problem.[21] But the FBI became involved in the case at almost exactly this same time—when UChicago "partnered with federal authorities to investigate" the threats to Perez made in Caquelin's fake post—and the FBI has a notoriously bad sense of humor and low tolerance for bullshit. By November 24, 2014, the *Chicago Tribune* was able to report the conclusion of the university and law enforcement that "Nobody 'broke in' to the Facebook account in question and ... in fact the posting was not (an) anonymous threat to a student."[22]

A panicked-sounding Caquelin took to Facebook to apologize profusely. His lengthy *mea culpa* read, in part: "Do not defend my name. I am behind this, and only I. There is no excuse for hate, which includes what I did." In an apparent attempt to protect Perez and perhaps others from criminal investigation, he went on to state, "No others were involved, so I really would like to ask you ... to leave them alone."

Amazingly, given that he wasted a week of a federal agency's time by falsely accusing a hidden army of conservative hackers of attacking him, even Caquelin himself ended up not having to worry about prosecution. The UChicago case became one of the most extreme examples of a phenomenon discussed throughout this chapter: a campus community behaving exactly as though the falsely alleged incident actually happened, even after it was proven to be fake. In Hyde Park, Caquelin's hoax was followed by all parties involved coming together to condemn campus racism. To quote The College Fix: "The students behind the ruse, the hood-winked university, and the school newspaper have argued that the hoax—which provoked a federal investigation—should not detract from fixing the school's culture of racial intolerance." Apparently no campus leader, whether faculty, staff, or student, called for "any punishment against the students who cried wolf."[23] The formal position of the university's *Chicago Maroon* newspaper, given the day after the *Chicago Tribune*'s feature article on the Caquelin hoax, is absurd enough to be worth quoting at some length: "The sentiments that existed before the Facebook post still ring true, and should be treated accordingly. The conversations surrounding diversity and inclusion on campus must continue in light of recent developments. The revealing of the hoax should not de-legitimize the issues of racism that have been raised, or mitigate the seriousness with which they should be addressed."[24]

Of course, by far the most serious "issue of racism" raised on the UChicago campus in the year surrounding this incident was Caquelin's false claim that he had been hacked, insulted, and threatened with rape by white conservatives. Journalist Matt Lamb probably sums up the bizarre situation best: "The hoax appears to have worked."[25] That is a true pity. The University of Chicago, known for its world-class economics faculty, should have kept one of the golden rules of that discipline in mind during this controversy: where bad behavior is rewarded, more of it will occur.

BACK TO THE BAD OLD DAYS: "ART" AT UBUFFALO

One of the more disturbing "hate incidents" in recent years took place at the University at Buffalo, where bathroom facilities and water fountains were festooned with the "Whites Only" and "Blacks Only" signs associated with segregation in the Jim Crow-era deep South. Fortunately and predictably, the whole thing turned out to be nothing more than a hoax.

In September of 2015, an unknown individual posted the signs reading "Whites Only" or "Blacks Only" over multiple water fountains on the UBuffalo campus and at the entrances to several student bathrooms. Unsurprisingly, the signs upset students of all races. According to the college newspaper, the UB *Spectrum*, students took to social media and the campus quad almost immediately to voice their "strong opposition" to the signs. Several called themselves "disgusted," and even more said they could not believe that this sort of "old-school" racism existed at their college. All students obviously agreed that the signs were racist, and at least one publicly argued that they constituted an "act of terrorism." One student interviewed by the *Spectrum*—Deidree Golbourne, a Black Studies major—claimed that that the signs had caused her "cultural trauma" and made her feel unsafe. She summed up her reaction in one poignant sentence: "Wow—not our University."

UBuffalo Chief of Police Gerald Schoenle estimated that he received eleven calls within two to three hours of the discovery of the signs, "starting at around 1pm Wednesday." His officers went into action, rapidly removing at least four signs from UB's Clemens Hall and nearby buildings. Around the same time, major campus student organizations such as the Black Students Association (BSA) called "an open meeting for the general student body" for that night and used social media to promote it across campus. The meeting, which replaced normally scheduled organizational meetings, was intended specifically "to give students an opportunity to discuss the signs." When it officially began at 7:00 p.m., a large room in UB's student center was packed with more than seventy students.

Things took the hard turn toward the absurd that we, gentle reader, have come to expect and treasure. Shortly after the meeting began, a Black graduate student named Ashley Powell stood up and admitted to having placed all of the signs. She had done so for all of the usual reasons people cite for faking hate crimes—to call attention to actual racism, and so forth. However, one fact definitively set Powell's actions apart from most hate crime hoaxes: she described herself as an artist dealing with "Black trauma and non-white suffering," and claimed that the signs were an example of her art. In fact, she had actually submitted this unique art project to the university for a grade and course credit. She had designed the signage stunt as an end-of-semester project for her 400-level Installation in Urban Spaces art class, which required her to create at least one professional-level art installation in an urban setting. It is worth noting that Powell's supervising professor would almost certainly have had to approve a project of this magnitude. It is perhaps unsurprising that tenured Professor Warren Quigley was completely unavailable when the *Spectrum* attempted to contact him on September 15, 2015.[26]

As usual in cases of hate crime hoaxes with a political component and no federal agents involved, the University at Buffalo did essentially nothing to respond to the incident that had generated a dozen-odd calls to their busy campus police department. The university's official statement on the matter, in fact, is worth reading as a typical example of the politically correct bureaucratese with which these cases so often conclude. After opening with two long sentences praising campus diversity, the university went on to say that "this week's student art project is generating considerable dialogue. The university is encouraging our community to discuss how we negotiate the boundaries of academic freedom in a safe and inclusive environment that values freedom of expression and further builds a culture of inclusion. The University at Buffalo stands strong in our commitment to ensuring that such discourse occurs in a safe, inclusive, and intellectually open environment."[27]

Brilliant stuff! Now we know *just* what their policy on hate hoaxes is!

Almost immediately on the heels of the UBuffalo statement, "artist" Powell took this whole situation to the level of "social justice" absurdity that earned it a spot in this book by issuing her own statement, in the form of a 2,170-word letter to the *Spectrum*. The student newspaper published it in full. Rather than owning up to being the perpetrator of an annoying campus prank, Powell described herself unambiguously as a victim. "I am in pain," she began. Powell explained that she studies art primarily to "express" the "suffering" she had experienced as a minority victim and to "advance the process of healing" from the disease of racism. Years of dealing with an oppressive American system that "threatens, traumatizes, brutalizes, stunts, and literally kills non-white people every day" had allegedly caused Powell to develop a set of "symptoms"—the actual word she used—including "self-hate," "trauma," and (my favorite) "an unbearable and deafening indignation." Only through revolutionary art could she heal such wounds!

While admitting regret for any trauma she had caused her classmates, Powell closed her letter by stating flatly: "I do not apologize for what I did … suffering must be allowed its moment." According to Powell, "hurt was necessary to call us to action" against the real racism out there somewhere, no doubt ready to explode into outrages far more severe than the decoration of a giant campus building with literal segregation-era signs.[28]

In contrast to such nonsense, it is worth taking a second look at the sensible and measured responses of other students at UBuffalo, a well-integrated campus located in one of New York's biggest cities, to the signs episode. An undergraduate who preferred to remain nameless pointed out that Powell's project fell well below normally accepted ethical standards for university-level research work or artistic design: "The first thing you do when planning something like this is see whether it's ethical or not, and that was where the line was crossed." White freshman Chelsea Whitney noted that the installation was pointless at an urban university not plagued by racism: "There was no excuse to put the signs up. Even white students were offended." Most succinctly, Buffalo graduate Eric Turman summed up the actual campus reaction to the signs in a sentence: anti-racist white students "didn't care about the signs," while "we (Black students) are still hurt by them."[29]

If only students speaking plain common sense got as much respect in the modern academy as goofs ranting about nonexistent oppression. If only!

CUTTING OUT THE MIDDLEMAN: THE GUSTAVUS ADOLPHUS DIVERSITY COUNCIL

During most campus hate crime scares, a troubled individual claims an act that either never happened or that he himself committed is the work of racist fellow students, Nazis, or Klansmen (or whatever), and then he reports this nonevent to the police or to campus diversity authorities. But in the spring of 2017, the Diversity Leadership Council at Minnesota's Gustavus Adolphus College decided to cut out the middleman.

Beginning on March 20, 2017, students on the pleasant if chilly Minnesota campus of Gustavus Adolphus discovered racially provocative flyers posted all around the college. The flyers, boldly worded and written in giant font, encouraged "ALL WHITE AMER-ICANS" to report "ANY AND ALL ILLEGAL ALIENS" to U.S. immigration and customs enforcement authorities because "THEY ARE CRIMINALS!" Following a few more lines of nativist bold-face, the flyers closed with the declaration that "AMERICA IS A WHITE NATION." At least two dozen of these flyers were reported on the small campus, found everywhere from the school quad to the academic hall.

Unsurprisingly, the appearance of the flyers caused quite a furor. The virtue-signaling began immediately. According to investigative reporter Anthony Gockowski, social media reactions to the white nationalist signs ranged from "What the fuck?—disgusting" to the still more succinct "Fuck. That." One activist alumna encouraged all other GAC alumni to express their disgust with any professors thought to have contributed to the "climate of bias" on campus and encouraged professors to "take five minutes from tomorrow's lesson plan to talk about how fucked up this is with their students." Many apparently did so. For whatever reason, the business school came in for some criticism, with at least one commentator saying, "It isn't a … surprise that something like this was posted at Beck Hall." Beck Hall houses the well-regarded Departments of Economics and Man-agement. Finally, of course, the flyers were reported—many times over—to the diversity bureaucrats who spring up like mushrooms on every modern college campus, in this case the Campus Diversity Leadership Council and Campus Bias Response Team.

At this point, the story gets bizarre. After a fairly long period of initial silence and a bit of hemming and hawing, GAC Dean of Stu-dents James van Hecke explained that the offending flyers had been posted *by* the Diversity Leadership Council. They were part of a series of "educational 'invisible theater' events taking place this week," that had been organized by a coalition including the "I Am We theater troupe, the Diversity Leadership Team, and the Bystander Intervention Committee" in order to teach students the importance of opposing hatred and bias.[30] Going into a bit more detail in their own separate statement, the men and "wombyn" of the Diversity Leadership Council admitted to posting the signs but said they had done so only "in an attempt to educate peers and the campus community about issues of bias, and the importance of being an active bystander."

A recurring theme in the speeches and statements of the various GAC "diversicrats" was that the poster campaign had been a response to previous real incidents of bias crime which had taken place on campus. The Diversity Leadership Council's formal statement read, in part: "We want to help put an end to the bias-related incidents that happened in our campus" in the past, by "forcing students to have dialogues about forms of hate and bias." The statement concluded by asking members of the Gustavus Adolphus community to "reflect on today's events, and join us in ensuring that no one student, or group of students" would ever again be the victim of an actual hate crime.[31]

Strong stuff.

There is absolutely no evidence, however, that a real-world wave of hate crimes ever did happen at Gustavus Adolphus. Four of the first ten Yahoo search results for the phrase "Gustavus Adolphus hate crime" are articles discussing the flyer hoax mentioned above.[32] Across the other top six articles and the next page of search results, exactly one alleged potential hate crime at GAC appears on the record. Back in 2013, a student at the college found his name and a mild racial slur spray-painted on a campus sidewalk during homecoming weekend.

Even assuming that the spray-paint incident occurred exactly as reported—and given the usual pattern, it seems quite possible that it was a hoax—St. Peter Police Chief Matt Peters pointed out that it did not qualify as a bias incident under Minnesota law: "It would not reach that type of level in the state."[33] The paucity of hate incidents at GAC is not surprising. In addition to being absolutely suffused with Midwestern niceness, Gustavus Adolphus College is more than 85 percent white and less than 2 percent Black. There simply are not many non-Asian minorities there to be discriminated *against*. So the Diversity Leadership Council intentionally garnered negative international attention in an attempt to highlight a problem that never existed on their campus at all.

In an even more absurd twist, the Gustavus Adolphus "fake flyer" stunt may have been inspired by *another* fake hate crime, which took place on October 9, 2007 at George Washington University. The link between the two is speculation on my part, but on that date left-wing activists from the Socialist Workers Party famously sabotaged the Young Americans for Freedom (YAF) event "Islamo-Fascism Awareness Week" by posting racist flyers across the George Washington campus that claimed to be YAF ads for the event. These fake flyers were headlined "Hate Muslims? So Do We!" and they listed the characteristics of a typical Muslim male as "lasers in eyes, venom from mouth, hatred for women, hidden AK-47, and ... peg leg for smuggling children and heroin." The YAF event was effectively discredited, to such an extent that the right-wing pundit Michelle Malkin wrote critically about the incident for her national website.[34] It is hard not to notice that the GWU posters, with their boldface text and faux university seal of approval, were suspiciously similar to those at GAC. Bad ideas, like good ones, can spread instantaneously and globally in the internet era.

Whether or not the Gustavus Adolphus and George Washington poster incidents are related, the fact that two "racist flyer" scandals that drew national notice turned out to be hoaxes should provide grounds for a healthy suspicion the next time something like this is reported. My take? If you ever see a poster on the ivy-covered wall of a college dormitory, on a campus that is 96 percent liberal and 94 percent white, and it says "KILL ALL WETBACKS," be aware that it is probably a hoax rather than the opening salvo of a race war. Tear the disgusting thing down, if you wish—but don't be surprised if some kind of diversity activist runs up to complain that you're ruining his work!

IT'S NOT JUST THE STUDENTS: RAMANI PILLA AND THE CASE WESTERN RESERVE HOAXES

In American academia in the modern era, it's not only the students who are faking hate crimes. Just ask Ramani Pilla—if you can find her.

In 2006, the then-rising star of the statistics department at Case Western Reserve University invented a phony wave of hate crimes against herself as part of an internal departmental power struggle. According to several conversations between the troubled academic and various law enforcement authorities, Professor Pilla dated the first "offense" against herself to the early summer of 2006—claiming that she had returned home from an academic conference at Stanford to discover that an unknown stranger had entered her office at Case Western, "moved things around on her desk," and turned off her air conditioner during a local heat wave.

From that point forward, the bad things that were allegedly happening to Pilla steadily got worse, and more bizarre. The professor alleged that in August 2006, "someone...slipped an envelope 'filled with derogatory remarks'"—ugly personal and racial slurs—under her office door. The next week someone opened the mail sent to her via her departmental address. Then she started receiving phone calls

like something out of a horror movie, involving male strangers calling her office and breathing or muttering into the phone before
hanging up. During a typical call "all she could hear was heavy
breathing, then the dial tone." By December of the same year, Pilla's
unseen attackers apparently crossed the line to directly threatening
her. The last anonymous communiqué she received was a blatant
threat, "albeit one with curiously formal grammar." It read: "Last
warning ... fucking bitch. You don't belong in the Department. Be
gone, or else face dire circumstances!"

Pilla attributed the letters and other abuse to her colleagues in the
highly ranked (at the time remarkably dysfunctional) Case Western
Reserve statistics department. She apparently laid blame on them as
part of a broader strategy of attempting to paint the "multiple tenure
rejections" she had experienced as the result of race or gender bias.
According to the records of the later court case, she named "three
suspects," all of whom worked at Case Western in tenured or tenure-
track faculty roles, as the probable masterminds of the campaign of
harassment against her, and she argued that the profane letters were
specifically acts of retaliation for an earlier discrimination claim she
had filed against the university.

Pilla's attempt to punish her department-mates for "harassing"
her took her on a journey through the hierarchy of contemporary
American law enforcement. She tried reporting the first hate letter—
apparently with little or no success—to "campus security and the
University Circle Police." When those departments failed to identify
her harasser (perhaps because there wasn't one), Pilla "went with her
lawyer to the Cleveland Fifth District Police Station" and asked the
city force to pursue the case. By January 2007 she had moved past
even the CPD and was "discussing the threats with FBI agents," passionately asking the *federales* to track down the authors of the four
threatening letters she said she had received. Around the same time,

the Pilla case took on a civil legal dimension. By December 2006, the professor had doubled down on the claim that her three colleagues mentioned above were indeed the attackers and actually sued Case Western, "alleging the university had failed to protect [her] from the threats."

Not long after that, the whole charade came to an end. Contacting the FBI was probably Pilla's fatal mistake. As we have seen, actual federal agents are like the Wu-Tang Clan of hoax hate crime investigations: they ain't nothing to fuck with. Pilla's complex cover stories and alibis unraveled after several weeks of federal investigation, and she eventually admitted she had "written the letters ... herself."[35]

Ironically, given that Pilla was a professor of statistics, statistical illiteracy played a major role in her capture. The feds quickly began to see it as mighty weird—and statistically significant—that she kept getting letter after letter from *different* members of her small circle of colleagues. The statistical insight that led to Pilla's comeuppance is quite easy to explain in layman's terms. If the chance of any single person being an insane breathe-heavily-on-the-phone-to-a-colleague-level bigot is one in a hundred, the chance of four such bigots occupying one small human space is roughly one in a hundred million. This was exactly what Pilla claimed was happening, and the claim immediately attracted skepticism when made to sophisticated professional investigators. As the blog University Diaries on Inside Higher Ed's website has pointed out, had Pilla been "smart enough to still her pen after one or two letters," she almost certainly would have gotten away with the whole hoax.[36] Alas, such is the price of hubris!

Interestingly, perhaps because of her status as a professor rather than a student, Ramani Pilla was one of a minority of hate crime hoaxers to be shown little or no mercy by the authorities. When the full extent of her duplicity was discovered, federal criminal charges were filed against her, with prosecutors alleging that she had "perpetrated a hoax" on both Case Western Reserve and the FBI. Case Western itself also found Pilla's antics less than humorous. The university banned the former employee from campus, contemplated a lawsuit, and even harshly criticized several of Pilla's academic publications. Pilla's lawyer, sounding surprised, described his client's former employers as "doing everything they can to destroy her." At the end of Pilla's criminal trial in November 2007, she was sentenced to six months in federal prison and ordered to pay back $66,000 that the university and the FBI had spent investigating her false claims.[37]

No problem there; it is my personal opinion that all hate crime hoaxers should be punished this way. Although she was treated more harshly by the lawmen than most, however, Pilla appears to share with virtually all other hoaxers the conviction that she did nothing particularly wrong. When contacted about her case by the *Cleveland Scene*, she expressed her position concisely and simply: "Everything you have heard is wrong. I've done great work. I will continue to do great work."[38]

But maybe not on campus now, eh?

HERE COME THE YOUNG TURKS (WAIT, IS THAT RACIST?): A MAJOR HATE CRIME HOAX IN HIGH SCHOOL

Unfortunately, collegians are not unique among young scholars when it comes to faking hate crimes. High school students, especially prep school students, are beginning to do it too.

Probably the most notable recent case of a pre-college hate crime hoax occurred in 2013 at St. Peter's Preparatory School in New Jersey, where a Black underclassman—whom I will leave nameless here because of his age at the time—claimed to have received multiple racist text messages during his campaign to become the majority-white school's first Black student body president. The texts were ugly ones. The first read, in part, "We have never had and will never have a nigger to lead our school!" This message went on to refer to then-president Barack Obama as "Hussein" (admittedly his middle name) and call him a nigger as well. It concluded: "We will never make that mistake again. Drop out right now."

The texts kept coming! (Because their "victim" was sending them.) A second message opened, "[From] whites! You're a waste on this earth, a waste at this school, and most importantly a waste for this campaign." According to the *Jersey Journal*, the next line of this text used a number of racial slurs and called the Black student government candidate "a slave." The third message received by the student warned him to drop out of the race and included several implicit threats. Finally the young man received a fourth and last text simply reading: "COMEONE [sic] your [sic] Black!!! Lol your [sic] a joke for even trying to run."[39]

The usual flurry of virtue-signaling followed. Someone, probably the student candidate himself, brought the texts "to the attention of school officials," who called in the kid's father and the local police. Because the messages had been sent using a phone number generator called TEXTME, it took some time for police to figure out that the sender and receiver of the messages were the same person. During this period the *Jersey Journal* took an interest in the case and published the first of what would be several articles about it.[40]

In an impassioned interview with the *Journal*, the lad's father explained how prevalent contemporary racism had hampered his son's political career. After all, St. Peter's was "a predominantly white school." (And you know how they are.) Many students at the school were no doubt "fearful of a new face trying to get in office." In contrast to these bigots, the boy who had received the threats was a good kid, "the type of boy who does not want any kind of trouble." After getting the hate texts, the poor kid was "extremely nervous," and felt "threatened." In fact, his main focus was on preventing any harm to the public's perception of St. Peter's: "He did not want the image of the school to be tainted."

And so on. In the end, of course, it was revealed that the recipient of the texts had sent them all to himself. By August 26, 2013, the law enforcement probe into the case had successfully concluded. St. Peter's spokesman James Horan read out a public statement admitting that the hate texts had been a hoax, praising local law enforcement, and concluding: "The entire St. Peter's Prep community is relieved that this extremely distressing incident has found closure." The *Jersey Journal* ran a final article on the case headlined: "Jersey City High School Candidate … Sent Racist Texts to Himself." When contacted by a *Journal* reporter around this time, a source at St. Peter's discretely confirmed that the student hoaxer "no longer attends the school."[41] How politely put.

The true tragedy of the Jersey City hoax scandal is that the hoaxer appears to have been a genuinely nice kid who caught a terminal case of "social justice." He had solid grades, was popular enough to run for student body president, and does seem to have had genuinely warm feelings for St. Peter's. He narrowly lost the presidential race (before his hoax was uncovered), but he was elected vice president of the student body. It is truly unfortunate that the Continuing Oppression Narrative managed to snare this well-adjusted upper middle-class kid, possibly convince him that his beloved prep school really was a hotbed of virulent racism, and certainly convey the message that faking a hate crime is a wholly legitimate way for a Black political candidate to win a tightly contested election. Without this poisonous logic, St. Peter's would have had a fine Black vice president in 2013. Instead, the school now bears the burden of having been accused of racism on the national stage.

Even more unfortunate, the St. Peter's Prep case was not one solitary incident. My research has turned up quite a few recent examples of fake hate crimes in high school, many involving social media. In one notable situation, which made the nightly news on the Baltimore CBS affiliate WJZ, a fourteen-year-old Black female student at Maryland's Anne Arundel High School created a fake racist organization called the Kool Kids Klan, tweeted out "We're planning to attack tomorrow" on the Twitter account she set up (@KoolKidsKlanKKK), and posted phony racist petitions around her school. This enterprising young rapscallion received only a "juvenile citation for disruption of school activities" before being released to her parents. She plans to attend college.[42]

With understudies like this in the high schools, the wave of hate crime hoaxes on the big campus will not be ending anytime soon.

THE MOTHER OF THEM ALL: UNPACKING THE UMIZZOU HATE HOAX EPIDEMIC

Probably the greatest string of hate crime hoaxes and exaggerations in recent history—and the most appropriate case to cap off this review of the fake hoax epidemic on university campuses—took place at the University of Missouri over a span of more than three months in 2015. By the time the "Mizzou Scandal" had come to an end, the Ku Klux Klan had been reported on a university campus, a Division I football team had threatened to cancel its season, and the president of the entire University of Missouri system had resigned in disgrace. As we shall see, almost all of the original incidents that led to this chaos have since been exposed as lies, probable lies, or wild exaggerations.

The Mizzou Scandal began on September 12, 2015, when Missouri-Columbia student government president Payton Head, a gay

Black man, claimed on Facebook that several white males riding in the back of a pickup truck had passed him on the street and yelled racial slurs at him. In what became a fairly famous social media post, he linked this incident to a broader pattern of "bigotry, anti-homosexual, and anti-transgender attitudes at the school," and encouraged students to resist this institutional oppression. The university heeded his call, almost immediately holding a major on-campus rally against racism. But this response did not satisfy many radical students, who organized a second major rally on September 24, 2015, to protest the fact that university officials had thus far "done nothing to address Head's concerns." An abashed Mizzou immediately promoted yet a third rally. During this "Racism Lives Here" event on the picturesque Columbia campus, hundreds of protesters filled the campus quad and chanted, "White silence is violence—no justice; no peace!"

Sadly, but perhaps unsurprisingly, these back-to-back-to-back rallies did not succeed in eradicating racism from our fallen world. Only three days later, on October 4, a single drunken white student disrupted the meeting of an African American student group, the Legion of Black Collegians, as the men were preparing for homecoming. Allegedly the white student used a racial slur when asked to leave the event, and a short scuffle ensued before he was removed. The university community, already on edge after the "attack" on Head, went from moderately woke to peak virtue signalling. The Legion of Black Collegians' members seemed to view themselves as victims of a serious hate crime, with one describing the group as having been "made victims of blatant racism in a space where we should be made to feel safe." Similar sentiments were voiced across the Missouri campus.

The university heeded the plaints of its students. The noisy sheep bleated and were fed. By October 8, the university chancellor, R. Bowen Loftin, had ordered every single student and faculty member on the Missouri-Columbia campus to undergo "diversity and inclusion training" during the upcoming 2016 school year. This training, he declared, would make all Missouri Tigers "conscious of how to be inclusive" in every one of "our words and deeds." Still unsatisfied, campus activists condemned Loftin for not doing more. In an open letter to the chancellor published in the campus newspaper, student radical Jonathan Butler—we will get back to him later—admitted that the mandatory diversity training was "a step in the right direction," but criticized Loftin for failing to acknowledge the work of Black students in developing past diversity programs and the sweeping "breadth of racial issues on the campus."

The saga continued. On October 10, protesters tried to block the car of another top university official, President Tim Wolfe, during the Mizzou homecoming parade. Wolfe unforgivably refused to leave his car to engage with protesters and listen to them scream complaints. After he kept driving down the road, one protester claimed to have been struck by Wolfe's car, "inflaming tensions." After this incident protesters also accused the local police of brutality—specifically of "using excessive force to clear the street" down which the parade was proceeding. Payton Head, the student government president whose "targeting" by "racists" less than a month before had sparked the crisis, re-entered the campus fray, posting on Facebook that President Wolfe had rudely "smiled and laughed" during the parade protests. "He laughed. In our faces. This is your President. This is America. 2015."

The University of Missouri, already in what the alt-right might refer to as "full-on cuck mode," did not do much (and what more *could* they have done to appease the activists?) to respond specifically to this latest wave of accusations of racism. A student group calling itself Concerned Students 1950 followed up on the car incident with a list of "demands" of "racist Mizzou." These included a formal public apology from Wolfe, his immediate removal from his position and the campus, and a "comprehensive racial awareness and inclusion curriculum overseen by minority students and faculty."[43] This curriculum would presumably have been taught concurrently with the campus-wide diversity training mandated by Loftin, to which the student radicals did not object. The University of Missouri ignored these demands for the nonce.

But then the braying horns of the apocalypse blew; the Four Horsemen rode onto the Mizzou campus, with locusts in their scabbards and deserts in their eyes. The Poop-Swastika was found! On October 24, 2015, someone apparently used human feces to draw a swastika—the Nazi symbol—on the wall of a residence hall bathroom. This was alleged by campus activists, including Concerned Students 1950, to be obviously aimed at Missouri's Black students.

The crap swastika garnered global attention. Jonathan Butler, calling the campus "an unlivable space," launched a hunger strike and declared himself willing to die. "I'm hardly treated like a human," he told the *Washington Post*.[44]

By November 8, University of Missouri football players had announced that they would not play another game until President Wolfe was removed from office. The SEC being what it is, Wolfe resigned the next day. By the end of 2015, scarcely more than a month later, the University of Missouri had become an international symbol of both awful contemporary racism and heroic resistance to it.[45] To this day an internet search for "Mizzou Scandal" turns up hundreds of thousands of results.

But what really happened in Columbia? Let's unpack it. First, there exists no evidence, besides his uncorroborated word, that anyone ever actually yelled anything at Head. The alleged "verbal assault" occurred in a modern college town with a professional police force and red-light cameras installed, and yet no video or pictorial evidence of this incident has ever surfaced. Even more telling is the fact that Head's credibility is deeply compromised by the fact that he told major lies throughout the Mizzou Scandal. Most notably, on November 11, 2015, Head claimed that Ku Klux Klan members had been spotted on Missouri's campus, and that he was in direct communication with the military about the incident.

This was a truly astonishing lie. Head's full tweet read, "Students please take precaution [sic]. Stay away from the windows in residence halls. The KKK has been spotted on campus. I'm working with the MUPD, the state trooper [sic], and the National Guard." As sports journalist Clay Travis rapidly pointed out, this was blatantly untrue. No Ku Klux Klan members had been "spotted" on the University of Missouri campus, and the National Guard does not typically liaise with the student government president when conducting operations. Head had obviously told an out-and-out falsehood.

Given this lie, it is difficult to believe his earlier hate crime accusations. And, notably, even if some fool did yell racial insults at Head, Travis and others have confirmed that the location where Head reported hearing the slurs is some distance away from the campus. What responsibility can Mizzou possibly have for a student's hearing crude words from a non-student, off campus? For that matter, would not a more reasonable measure of the level of tolerance at the University of Missouri be the student body's willingness to elect a gay Black man to school president in the first place?

Other widely reported incidents in the Mizzou Scandal narrative collapse just as readily as Head's claims. Multiple easily accessible YouTube videos show clearly that the homecoming protester "struck" by President Wolfe's car was barely nudged and suffered no visible injury of any kind. Police cleared the overall site of the march in a respectful, professional fashion. And hunger striker Jonathan Butler was revealed to be the son of a railroad executive worth between $20 and $25 million, not an individual with reason to worry about whether he could expect to be "treated like a human" on a preppy collegiate campus.

Butler's father made roughly $7 million during the single year before his son's campus antics began. Butler himself grew up in a $1.3 million house in Omaha, Nebraska. That is a big home anywhere, but the Omaha area is known for its real estate bargains, and Warren Buffet's nearby house is valued at only $500,000 to $600,000. As Travis sardonically points out, Butler probably could have paid for health care—a secondary issue behind his strike—not only for himself but for every other graduate student on the Mizzou campus. It is also notable that Butler, a master's candidate, had been studying at Missouri for *eight years* before his hunger strike. He must have loved the place. For whatever reason, the pervasive, institutional, genocidal, systematic, and so on racism pervasive in Columbia seemed perfectly survivable until the day when claiming it was not could guarantee him a place in the national spotlight. They say good business sense runs in families!

As I discovered during the research for this book, Butler also made multiple wildly questionable statements during the Mizzou Scandal, which have for some reason gone almost unreported. On November 10, 2015, Butler tweeted, "Death threats are being made to Black students and NO ADMINISTRATORS are responding effectively."[46] This is yet another inflammatory claim from a witness whose other statements call his credibility into question. The post garnered 410 shares and 233 likes on social media. Making the conservative estimate that each re-share of Butler's tweet was seen by only 30 people, almost half of the campus probably saw it. The university felt compelled to respond to it in detail, pointing out in a tweet that no "credible threats" to Mizzou's campus or students had been reported, and further that the campus was flooded with security, "MUPD," and "campus officials" who were all following up on the previous fake hate crime allegations. Unfortunately, this probably did little to undo all the harm caused by Butler's earlier message. In the screenshot of UMissouri's tweet that my saintly research assistant Jane Lingle obtained for me, it had only 40-odd retweets or shares and 50 likes—about one-tenth the reach of Butler's earlier dubious message.

Continuing the "everything said during the Missouri Protests was a lie" theme, there also appears to be at best inconclusive evidence for the Poop-Swastika. Of everything I have discovered in the course of my research on fake hate crimes, this surprised me the most. It seems utterly counterintuitive that a supposed hate crime could have garnered sympathetic international attention in the absence of any evidence that it ever actually occurred. But that is exactly what seems to have happened in Columbia.

Andrew McCarthy of *National Review*, one of the very few writers to even raise this point, has noted that in an era where nothing noteworthy happens "without its being captured by the camera capabilities of ubiquitous cell phones," there seem to be no confirmed pictures of the Poop-Swastika. A picture widely circulated by activists on Twitter purports to depict it, but McCarthy notes that Google and Reddit searches for the same image show it to date back to at least 2014. It seems virtually certain that this earlier image was used knowingly and unethically by activists, in the absence of any real pictures.[47]

The University of Missouri police report on the Poop-Swastika incident does note, albeit with no photographic evidence, that the first officer on the scene observed a symbol scrawled on the bathroom wall and "feces beneath it." But no actual image of the thing—accurately depicting, for example, how big it was—appears ever to have been released.[48] This police report, which differs so markedly from viral "news" about the Poop-Swastika, seems to be the closest evidence that anything even close to it ever existed. Every single

University of Missouri official contacted by McCarthy or the team from The Federalist—including Residence Hall Association President Billy Donley, Residence Life Director Frankie Miner, UMissouri News Bureau Director Christian Basi, and other campus officers—either said emphatically that they had not seen the Poop-Swastika or refused to comment for the record.[49] At "best," an earthy swastika was rapidly erased by policemen or janitors, and activists then plagiarized an unrelated photo and made it the centerpiece of a nationwide publicity campaign.

And there is one further point which no one seems to have made: even if a swastika was scrawled in a Mizzou bathroom, there is no reason in the world to assume that the group being targeted was Blacks. Swastikas represent bigotry against Jews—and to a lesser extent against Romani (gypsies), the disabled, and homosexuals. There is literally no reason to assume that this Nazi graffiti targeted Black Americans rather than some other oppressed group on the Missouri campus. Hitler is not, after all, famous for killing six million brothers. So far as I can tell, this obvious fact was never considered by activists, administrators, or mainstream media reporters covering the situation.

All in all, the only major component of the Mizzou Scandal that seems to have been based in fact was the Legion of Black Collegians' claim that a white drunk disrupted their homecoming parade preparations. And in that case, the guy lost the dumb fight he started with a bunch of solid young men. Given the international frenzy around these incidents, it is hard not to conclude that the University of Missouri was the victim of the greatest hoax hate crime wave in recent history. But the university only made the scandal worse by being a textbook example of how not to deal with hate crime fakers—from treating every dubious accusation as legitimate to firing innocent and even anti-racist campus officials to appease unappeasable activists.

Annual freshman enrollment at Missouri-Columbia is down roughly 25 percent since the scandal, with a resulting "$32 million funding deficit for the campus." Publications ranging from *National Review* to the *New York Times* have attributed this drop-off not to fear of "racism" but rather to disgust with political correctness and the antics of highly visible campus protesters.[50] When confronted with absolutely bizarre claims such as Butler's and Head's, it is usually a better idea for institutions to stand and fight than to acquiesce and pretend that such jabberwocky has a basis in fact. This, $32 million later, is the primary lesson that sane people of all races and creeds should learn from the Mizzou Scandal. And that's no hoax.

Chapter Four

THE KLAN SPRINGS ETERNAL! HOAX HATE GROUP ATTACKS AND THE REAL CRIMES THEY COVER UP

Another noteworthy category of hate crime hoaxes is made up of what I term "Klan Springs Eternal" (KSE) hoaxes, which involve POC falsely claiming to have been attacked by one or more Caucasian racists in order to conceal their own criminal behavior or mental health issues. Although no other single arena of modern American life is as rife with false charges of "hate" as the collegiate campus, all KSE incidents combined seem to be at least as common. According to the same Fake Hate Crimes website that I used to calculate the number and frequency of fake collegiate hate crime reports, there have been ninety recent nationally reported hate crime hoaxes involving African Americans and an additional eight involving Hispanics—essentially all of which fell into the KSE category.

While 80 of 269 prominent recent hoaxes detailed on the site involved college students as a primary distinguishing characteristic (29.7 percent), 98 (36.4 percent) were examples of KSE hoaxes. There is some overlap between these two categories, in that some

KSE cases also involved college students. American college and university stunts make up a ridiculously disproportionate percentage of high-profile hate crime hoaxes. My own slightly larger data set reveals an almost identical percentage of KSE hoaxes, although I employ FHC data across this and the previous chapter for the sake of consistency. Not only are KSE hoaxes common, several cases within this category—such as the "Albany Bus Beating" and the burning of Black churches and Black ministers' homes—have been among the most widely reported recent hate crime fakes.

As with the proliferation of college-campus hate hoaxes, which is enabled, if not largely fueled by, the activist Left on campus, it is my opinion that partisan political bias is largely responsible for the national attention to ugly but often faked incidents of white-on-Black crime. The mainstream media in the United States is one of the very few American social institutions that lean as far Left as the university professoriate, and it is reasonable to assume that the worldview shared by the large majority of journalists influences their coverage of racial issues.

The existence of media bias is not in serious dispute. As we have already seen, only 7 percent of those working in media identify as conservatives. That figure is from a representative nation-wide survey of local and national reporters undertaken in 2004 by the globally respected Pew Research Center, which surveyed 547 journalists working for U.S. print and television outlets. While only 7 percent of media personnel identified as conservatives, the other 93 percent identified as liberals or moderates, most of whom were left-leaning.[1] Roughly twenty years before that, a well conducted *L.A. Times* survey reached essentially the same conclusion. Of 2,700 journalists polled at 621 newspapers and other outlets across the country, "self-identified liberals outnumbered conservatives in the newsroom by more than three to one, 55% to 17%." To put this figure in context, the *Times* noted that most Americans are conservatives or moderates, and only 23 percent of American adults identify as liberals.[2]

"Liberal" and "conservative" can be vague terms, but the ideological preferences of media members are reflected in actual partisan behavior. Veteran media researcher Bob Lichter found that 81 to 94 percent of "elite" media journalists voted for Democratic candidates in every election between 1964 and 1980.[3] More recently, the Center for Public Integrity examined journalists' contributions to the campaigns of Hillary Clinton and Donald Trump. The number crunchers found that of almost $400,000 given by journalists to candidates in 2016, 96 percent went to Clinton and only 3.9 percent to Trump.[4] With regard to the actual topical issues reporters often cover, the *L.A. Times* found that "82 percent of reporters and editors favored…abortion, 81 percent backed affirmative action, and 78 percent want stricter gun control."[5] The media's 81 percent support for affirmative action is a truly remarkable finding; it contrasts with national figures of roughly 20 percent support for affirmative action among whites and only 50 percent support even among Blacks.

Several reviewers of the data have noted that biases this strong are likely to sway coverage, and this does appear to be the case. For example, while 80 to 85 percent of interracial crime is Black-on-white—according to the full range of social critics, from Tim Wise to Jared Taylor, cited in the last chapter—approximately 90 percent of national media coverage of the topic deals with atypical incidents of white-on-Black violence, such as the Trayvon Martin shooting. To give another example, 76 percent of all individuals shot by police are indisputably not Black, but coverage of these cases almost certainly makes up less than 10 percent of the total amount of coverage of police violence by national print and TV outlets.[6]

In addition to being largely on the political Left, reporters tend to be incurably sensationalist, something that naturally leads to saturation-level coverage of flashy stories such as hate crime allegations. The data on media sensationalism are at least as clear as that on artisan bias among media members. In 2016 the *Journal of Scientific Research and Studies* published my own research on the correlation between increasing media exposure and irrational fear of non-threats such as kidnapping, under the headline "Hearts All A-Twitter?"[7] There is very likely a similar relationship between media-generated awareness of unpleasant events and the belief that the United States is a racist country. Turn off the damn TV!

For example, the one thousand or so people who died in fiery airplane crashes in 2014 received 48 percent more mass media coverage than the world's 1.24 million automobile crash victims put together.[8] Almost 50 percent of all evening news coverage dealing with children and young adults concerns dramatic incidents of crime or violence, such as the JonBenet Ramsey case, while only 4 percent deals with all youth health and economic issues combined.[9] Not only do media outlets like bizarre and dramatic stories about racist "oppression," they like *all* bizarre and dramatic stories. So hate crime allegations, being fascinating, graphic, and evidence that nothing has changed, are candy for reporters.

And so we see them every week or so, whether they are true or not.

WELL, SOMEONE GOT HIT: THE ALBANY BUS BEATING

One of the most absurd examples of POC activists using fake allegations of racism to cover up boorish or even illegal behavior of their own took place in the New York state capital of Albany in early 2016.

On January 30, a highly sympathetic group of young Black women, all successful students at the University at Albany, claimed that they had been the victims of a brutal incident of racism. Asha

Burwell, Alexis Briggs, and Ariel Agudio said they had been quietly riding on an Albany city bus when they were attacked by a group of white men. The men allegedly beat the women and used racial slurs against them. During this unprovoked attack on the three coeds, bystanders behaved in a disgracefully ungentlemanly and cad-like manner: "other passengers and the driver sat silently by," and no one interfered with the racial abuse.

By now, dear reader, you know the next scene in the script. The Albany Bus Beating case made national headlines, and the virtue-signaling blazed at a thousand lumens from Berkeley to Scarsdale. The case was reported to the Albany Police Department as a potential felony, and the mandatory "rally against racism" was held on the University at Albany campus. It drew hundreds of people, who spent more than two hours listening to "young Black women speak of the subtle racism that stamped their daily lives."

The bus beating victims pledged to remain strong. "We are shocked, upset, but we will remain unbroken," Burwell told the press and the rally crowd on February 1. "We stand here with strength because we value our worth as Black women and as human beings in general!" How noble of them.

Hillary Clinton, running for president at the time, took a minute off from rearranging the hot sauce bottles in her purse and clapping authentically at Black church services to tweet about the Albany situation.[10] "There's no excuse for racism and violence on a college campus," she reminded us all on February 4, 2016. Clinton's tweet included a link to and description of Albany's anti-racism rally; it garnered 590 likes and 1,018 re-tweets.

The wheels soon came off the (in this case metaphorical) bus, and the allegations by the three women were exposed as not merely hoaxes but a cover for a serious crime that they themselves had committed. Perhaps unsurprisingly, no mob of white men had beaten three young Black students on a public bus while an integrated crowd of big-city residents just sat and watched. After several weeks of investigating the matter, the Albany Police Department said decisively that "surveillance videos did not support the accounts of the young women." Nor did the statements of "multiple fellow passengers," more than a dozen of which were quickly collected by the APD. Not only were the three young women not victims of a hate crime, but they were exposed as having actually been the aggressors in a very different crime: viciously striking a nineteen-year-old old white woman several times after an apparent exchange of insults.

Soon after the Albany police reported their findings, prosecutors filed assault charges against all three women. Burwell and Agudio, who had played primary roles in publicizing the false hate crime narrative via social media, were also charged with making a false police report. The judge who presided over the arraignment of these imaginative young ladies called the charges "if proved, 'shameful.'" Some Albany students also seemed to recognize the seriousness of what Burwell, Briggs, and Agudio had done. Olivia Bishop, an African American junior at the school, said bluntly, "I feel like they ... messed it up for the rest of us. It's like, I stood up for you, and you ... wanted this whole thing to be a hoax. It's disappointing. It's honestly the saddest thing in the world."[11]

How true. Unfortunately, however, a more common reaction to the exposure of the Albany bus beating hoax was to deny that it was a hoax at all and assert that these innocent female POC were being railroaded by The Man. The *New York Times*, in a painfully measured article, pointed out, "Activists have noted that the footage the authorities have relied on so far is incomplete." This left open the possibility that something must have "happened to provoke the young women into a physical confrontation before the videos began." Alice Green, a self-described social justice activist who directs the

Albany-based Center for Law and Justice, was one of several prominent local residents to criticize available surveillance videos of the bus
scuffle and at least implicitly advocate the conspiracy theory angle.
Quoth she, "I walked away [from a police screening of the videos]
saying 'I can't tell you what happened in that video; you haven't
shown me anything to confirm what these young women are saying,
and I can't deny it either, because it's just not clear to me." Despite
the fact that the entire incident was literally on tape and the actual
assault victim's account was supported by multiple witness statements, Green apparently did not believe that the authorities should
proceed with criminal charges.[12]

Others admitted that the three Albany students faked the attack
and even beat someone else up, but insisted that they must have been
driven to do so by racism. Indeed, they were owed a debt of gratitude
for exposing the pernicious extent of racial bias in the region. Sami
Schalk, a tenure-track professor of English at the university who was
quoted at length by the *Times*, told the paper that she was concerned
about how "the women's detractors had failed to consider the prejudice and 'racialized language'" that they had quite likely encountered
on campus before the bus ride. This alleged abuse probably "played
a role in provoking the fight."

Further, whatever the actual facts of the situation or the result of
the subsequent criminal cases, the entire incident served one critical
purpose, according to Schalk: it made "white students aware of the
subtle slights that students of color regularly encounter." As she
explained, "My white students have said this has opened up conversations." Amberly Crutcher, a coordinator at the school's Multicultural
Resource Center, went even further, telling the *Times*, "People were
forced to think about things they didn't think about before." According
to Crutcher, the real question to arise following this innovative thought
experiment was, "So, do we now stop defending Black women?"[13]

When the first question a community leader asks following the beating of a young white women by three Black women is how we can best defend Black women, we may have finally reached "peak wokeness," at least for one transcendent second. Please pause and appreciate it before we move on to the next case.

THE NEXT CASE: THE DAMN KLAN BURNT MY CAR!

One of the most insanely imaginative hate crime hoaxes in recent years took place in southern Florida in 2016, when over a three-day stretch one Volusia County man "set his ex-girlfriend's car on fire, wrote two racist notes as part of a staged hate crime, faked his own abduction, and was arrested twice."

The saga began when police and firefighters in the small Florida city of Ormond Beach responded to a "vehicle on fire" call from the Biltmore Drive area on December 10, 2016. Arriving on the scene, the first responders found a late-model Chevrolet Sonic ablaze in a residential driveway. The backseat of the vehicle had been splashed with gasoline and the back window knocked out with a brick—which was still resting on the charred remains of the backseat—and the fire had apparently been started with a flaming twist of paper. The vehicle was effectively totaled. Around this point, things started to get weirder. Searching the crime scene, police officers found a note taped to the female vehicle owner's mailbox reading, "I HAVE WATHED [sic] YOU FOR A LONG TIME AND YOU AND YOUR NIGGER KIDS DON'T Belong." On the other side of this note was one word: "TRUMP!"

Police and the owner of the car called several of her intimates, including her off-and-on boyfriend Vincent Palmer, with whom she had had the four children to whom the arsonist's note presumably referred. When Palmer arrived, things got even weirder. The twenty-seven-year-old forklift driver showed up on his scooter with "a cup of coffee and a cigarette for his ex," but began acting uncomfortable as soon as he realized that police were still on the scene. According to the initial police report on this incident, one of the first officers to interact with Palmer "said he appeared to be nervous." When, shortly after that encounter, police said that they planned to retrieve fingerprints from the half-burnt twist of paper found in the car's backseat, Palmer "got antsy" and asked others present, "They can do that?" (Pro tip: twitchily staring at the police and expressing your concern when you hear that they will be able to take fingerprints from the scene of the crime is not the best way to avoid arrest. No need to thank me.) Eventually officers ran a check on Palmer, discovered an outstanding warrant for failure to pay child support to the victim, and took him into custody. At this point Palmer had not been charged with the automobile fire or any other serious crimes.

Palmer was booked into the Volusia County jail on the misdemeanor child support charge. He posted bail and was released almost immediately. At that point things got still weirder. The very next day Palmer's sister frantically called 911. According to a transcript of the call obtained by the *Washington Post*, she had woken up that morning to find "bloody fingerprints on her car" and one of her brother's favorite jackets just "lying in the street" with a threatening note nearby. In part, it read, "This is the KKK. I hate Black men who fuck with white women. You will never see your [relative] alive again." The note appeared to link Palmer's disappearance to the earlier apparent hate attack on his ex-girlfriend's car—for which no one had yet been charged. Several law enforcement officers suggested that Palmer's disappearance might be a case of kidnapping.

At that point—and for the final time, you can relax, gentle reader—things got weirder. As the *Post*'s Cleve Wootson noted, officers quickly began to notice that "things didn't add up." Palmer didn't live with his sister, and she had seen him only occasionally during the past month or so. Why would a racist kidnapper leave the note at her place? Becoming suspicious, police from Volusia County's Ormond Beach and Daytona Beach not only mounted a search for Palmer but also asked surrounding jurisdictions to be on the lookout for the man—kidnap victim or no. After initiating tracking of Palmer's cellular phone, this impromptu task force found him calmly eating lunch at an Ormond Beach Burger King not far from the original crime scene. Not only was he obviously not the victim of any crime, he had not even bothered to leave the area where he had faked his own kidnapping.

After some initial ridiculous lies, including claiming at one point that his name was "Raquel Johnson," Palmer eventually 'fessed up, "shar[ing] his real identity and admitting to two days of deceit." Not only was the kidnapping set-up bogus, but Palmer also quickly confessed to the initial burning of his girlfriend's car. According to a police source, "The defendant told us that he wrote the note found at the arson fire" at work before leaving for the day. He then filled a soda bottle with gasoline at a local gas station and used it to light the blaze. Even the bloody fingerprints and blood droplets found at his sister's home were part of Palmer's complex hoax. He simply "pricked his own finger and spread the blood around," to add to the illusion of a violent kidnapping. After admitting to all of this—not, apparently, without some pride—Palmer was booked again and charged with second-degree felony arson.

His motives, aside from "this dude was nuts," seem to have been complex. According to both law enforcement officers and the victim's mother, his antics were part of an elaborate Byzantine scheme designed to help Palmer get back at his ex and dodge child support. His initial fake hate crime was probably designed to intimidate the woman and encourage her to move out of Volusia County, where

Palmer had already been cited by the courts for failure to pay back child support. Later Palmer faked his own kidnapping to "avoid legal trouble from the [first] staged hate crime" and establish himself even more definitively as simply not available to support his children. Dead men buy no Nikes.

But as it happens, Palmer got caught—and should have a very steady job making license plates for the next few years.[14] Hopefully, his kids will see at least some small amount of money as a result. And please allow me to recommend couples' counseling rather than his approach to any of you who may find yourselves facing a minor custody battle!

THE COUNCILMAN WHO CALLED HIMSELF:
A POLITICAL HATE HOAX

All hate crime hoaxes are to some extent political, but few are committed by sitting government officials. In February of 2016, City Attorney Brian Telfair of Petersburg, Virginia, made himself an exception to this rule.

Telfair told the Petersburg police that "between 4:00 and 5:00 p.m. on February 16," he had received a profane and threatening phone call on his office phone from an unknown male. Telfair, who is Black, said he assumed this man was white "because he spoke redneck." According to police reports, the city attorney stated that the unknown Caucasian stranger had unloaded a racist diatribe about Petersburg city politics on him, threatening to "kick the ass" of Mayor Howard Meyers, City Manager Bill Johnson, and City Finance Manager Irvin Carter—most of whom are also African American. Telfair claimed that the caller told him, "We're going to come and get your fucking nigger asses, and throw your nigger asses in the street during the meeting." In initial conversations with police and the press, Telfair theorized that this man's rage might be due to a recent hike in water billing rates. He also attempted to link the call to a broader pattern of racism in the region, telling police that Petersburg's online outreach page had received "another racist message" that "used a racial slur in describing the city's population" just three days before the call.

As the *Richmond Times-Dispatch* reported, Telfair's story caused the abrupt cancellation of an important Petersburg City Council meeting after the "frightened" city attorney spread the word that residents upset about "high water bills and other money issues the city is having" might be on their way to attack local politicians. Initially the city released a cryptic note announcing the cancellation and simply cited "safety concerns" as the reason. The next day, however, Telfair himself stated publicly that racial slurs and threats of violence against several members of the council—notably himself—had prompted the cancellation.

Police records describe Telfair as having outlined an apocalyptic scenario as the reason for canceling the meeting, pointing to the explosive combination of the racist threats, "the anger ... demonstrated by citizens" revealed by the threats, and the fact that a projected 175 people would attend the event. But Telfair apparently had reasons of his own for not wanting the session to take place. When the city council did next manage to get together, one of their first orders of business was negotiating a final separation with Telfair as city attorney. Avoiding this outcome may well have been the reason he faked a hate crime in the first place.

At any rate, the Petersburg Bureau of Police and the Virginia State Police immediately began investigating the threats to Telfair: specific threats of felony violence against public officials tend to be taken pretty seriously by the boys in blue. But what the police uncovered was a sleazy scenario straight out of HBO's *The Wire*. Petersburg City

Council Clerk Nykesha Johnson told them that shortly before the call incident Telfair had asked her if she knew of a store that sold disposable cellular telephones. When she mentioned the discount chain Family Dollar, Telfair gave her some cash and told her to purchase a "burner phone" and to activate it using a fake name. Investigators obtained a surveillance video from the Petersburg Family Dollar that showed Jackson purchasing a nineteen-dollar TracFone at 10:32 a.m., on the day the call to Telfair took place. This was almost certainly the phone Telfair used to call and threaten himself. When detectives outlined this evidence to Telfair, he confessed that "he made the telephone call to himself that was reported to Petersburg Bureau of Police as a threatening phone call."

This case has an interesting and bizarre final twist. A politician to the end, Telfair has insisted since his arrest—on a single misdemeanor count of lying to police—that he did what he did for yet-to-be-revealed heroic reasons. The *final* line of the Virginia State Police interview previously cited is, "Mr. Telfair also stated that he made the telephone call to preserve the institution of the city." And throughout his case Telfair maintained the position that the information contained in court documents relevant to his case, while technically true, did not include any of his so-far-unseen exculpatory evidence.

His lawyer, Thomas Johnson, played along with this strategy to some extent, arguing that Telfair had somehow been set up or forced into calling himself: "Mr. Telfair has been targeted because of the knowledge he possesses surrounding ... the malfeasance in the city of Petersburg government ... There is an effort to discredit and dismiss him." The disgraced politician asserted through counsel that he "looks forward to his day in court, both for this allegation and for the [upcoming] action ... against those officials who have misrepresented the facts and circumstances in an effort to defame."[15]

And so on. As it turns out, the courts have been, at least so far, rude enough to disagree with Telfair's claim that he has hidden heroic motivations. He was convicted on the single charge he faced midway through 2017. Finding Telfair guilty after a trial that took less than two hours, the district court judge, Ray Lupold, said that there was "no doubt whatsoever" that Telfair had committed the crime and expressed his disgust, saying: "This is a betrayal of trust. This is a betrayal of duty. We are held to a higher standard as lawyers." The defendant was sentenced to twelve months in jail (with eleven months suspended) and ordered to pay the Virginia State Police $7,411 in restitution.[16]

Telfair, of course, plans to appeal. Heroes do not give up! But at least he has already learned a valuable lesson: judges are harder to burn than phones.

AND THE LORD TAKETH AWAY:
THE PREACHER AND THE FELONY ARSON HOAX

One major recent hate crime hoax could very broadly be defined as an act of God.

On March 15, 2013, an arson report was made to the police of Chesterfield, Virginia, from the home of one Olander D. Cuthrell, a Black Baptist preacher and the music minister at Virginia's Gospel Shepherd Baptist Church. Like most of the crimes detailed in this book, the incident behind that report initially appeared to be an ugly and serious one. Someone had poured a flammable mixture of gasoline and oil across Cuthrell's front porch and set it on fire. The word "NIGGER" had been spray-painted on both sides of his home, obviously indicating a racially motivated attack. In addition to the damage to the property itself, a "16-ounce bottle filled with oil and gas"—in other words, a Molotov cocktail—had been ignited inside the minister's old BMW, which was parked close to the house. The entire building could quite easily have burned down.

That this did not happen is largely due to the heroism of Cuthrell's eldest son, who was woken up by the family dog, Lassie-style, and put out the gasoline fires apparently using only water from the tap. The son then promptly contacted the police. Both the Chesterfield cops and the FBI responded rapidly to the incident and began investigating it as a hate crime. The Richmond news noted that Cuthrell himself poured—if you will—considerable fuel on the fire, booking interviews and "telling several news outlets" that he had been "the victim of a racially motivated attack."[17] A popular Black preacher's house set ablaze! What could this be but a racist attack, à la Selma and Birmingham?

Well, as it turns out, the whole thing could be a complete hoax. And it was! I have noted before that FBI investigators seem to be the wolfsbane-and-garlic of amateur hate hoaxers, and this rule certainly held true here. Investigators "quickly became suspicious" of Cuthrell's inconsistent narrative pertaining to the crime, and the preacher himself became the principal target of the investigation within ten to twelve days. He was arrested April 2, 2013, and shortly thereafter he admitted to setting both of the fires and writing the racial graffiti. Although for some reason the mainstream media has not discussed this much, Cuthrell also admitted blithely to intending to kill himself and his family. According to his own statements, he went back inside his home "after setting the two fires," undressed, and went to bed "waiting for the house to burn down." Had Cuthrell's son not saved the day, five people would have died and the KKK would have taken the blame for it. The case would probably live on in history books today.

Cuthrell's motivation for setting his own home on fire was apparently money, or more specifically a lack thereof. Although gainfully employed and living in a nice house, Cuthrell had substantial financial troubles he had apparently never shared with his family. During their investigation, police learned that the minister was three months behind on the rent for the house the Cuthrells lived in and owed his landlord roughly $4,500. The most recent check he had written to the landlord, intended to pay off the majority of his debt, had bounced. Cuthrell's money woes were further enhanced by a legal case involving one of his sons, which had recently piled more bills and substantially more stress on his plate. Only days before he set the fires, Cuthrell had been told that he and his family faced eviction if he did not immediately pay his full back balance.

Assuming one can overlook the fact that his actions could have killed quite a few other people in addition to himself, it is possible to sympathize with Cuthrell. Many of us have felt depression or anger in the face of serious debt and considered frankly crazy solutions to the problem. Banks get robbed for a reason. It makes Cuthrell less sympathetic, however, that his actions in 2013 were not a one-time desperate reaction. Sadly, faking a criminal incident seems to have been his default response to serious money problems. As prosecutors noted during his eventual trial, the minister had falsely reported a felony robbery to North Carolina police twelve years earlier to cover up a substantial theft from his then-employer. He faced criminal charges in that case as well and was convicted of filing a false police report. Presumably this previous incident was one of the factors that led federal investigators to suspect that Cuthrell was the perpetrator of his 2013 house fire.

Partly because of his past antics, prosecutors pursued the case against the disgraced preacher quite vigorously. Chesterfield prosecutor Laura Khawaja presented him to the jury as a career criminal, noting that "there was a pattern to his deceit." Cuthrell was also subject to enhanced sentencing guidelines because his act of arson had involved "an occupied dwelling place," and thus "his offense was elevated in terms of the law." Despite this, however, the actual sentence Cuthrell received was quite light, as is the case for most hate hoaxers. He was sentenced to ten years in prison, but with eight of those years suspended and full eligibility for "good time"—in practice, about one year inside.

In another pattern common among hate-crime hoax cases, most of his friends and family continued to stand by Cuthrell. Some apparently denied that a hoax, and not an actual attack, had taken place. His lawyer, Richard Gates, described Cuthrell as "a good man who did something bad in a moment of weakness." Perhaps most remarkably, the senior pastor of Gospel Shepherd Baptist Church attended Cuthrell's trial and sentencing hearing to support him and announced that Cuthrell would continue on as music minister at Gospel Shepherd after being released from prison.[18]

Now, that is being Christ-like, perhaps to a fault. At the very least, I would encourage the pastor not to give Cuthrell a night-time key to the church!

FAKE HATE CRIMES GO VIRAL: THE RED LOBSTER RECEIPT AND FACEBOOK'S MEME TEAM

One 2014 hate crime received not merely some conventional mainstream media notice but also international social media attention, producing one of the best-known viral memes in recent years.

On September 19, 2013, twenty-year-old Red Lobster waitress Toni Christina Jenkins posted a picture to her personal Facebook page and YouTube channel of a customer receipt she claimed to have received while at work. The line set aside for the tip amount on the receipt read: "None." As an explanation for this churlishness, the line designated for the total bill read: "Nigger." The signature of Red

Lobster customer Devin Barnes, to whom Jenkins attributed the insulting language, was clearly visible in the screen-shot of the ticket, appearing directly under the racial slur. An understandably—or so folks thought—aggrieved Jenkins captioned the photo, "This is what I got as a tip last night ... so happy to live in the proud Southern states. God Bless America, land of the free and home of the low-class racists of Tennessee."

Jenkins's post of the receipt pictures went viral almost literally overnight. The picture was shared by hundreds of users on Facebook, and a video containing the photo racked up views on YouTube. After seeing a re-posted image of the receipt, staffers on the left-wing website Addicting Info devoted a section of their website to a fundraising campaign called "Tips for Toni," which raised $10,719 from more than a thousand contributors across the globe. Toni Jenkins stated on the record that she planned to use this money to buy a new car, and she apparently did so. Devin Barnes was less lucky. As the resident of a relatively small state, with a somewhat unusual name and a Facebook page of his own, he was rapidly doxxed and began receiving death threats and hate mail from literally around the world.

Then, as usual, the narrative collapsed. From the very beginning of the case, Barnes had claimed to his own social media followers and essentially anyone else who would listen that he is not a racist and never addressed any racial slurs to Jenkins. He freely admitted to not tipping her, but he pointed out that this was because the order in question was a take-out order, and Jenkins thus had done nothing to serve him. He remained adamant that "he never wrote the slurs on that receipt." At first these claims were generally disdained; how else would a canny Caucasian bigot, caught at his evil tricks, respond?

However, the thousands of people by then interested in the case had little choice but to pay attention when Barnes hired an expert forensic analyst to analyze images of the receipt and compare the handwriting on it to his own. The analyst examined print and cursive writing samples not only from Barnes but also from his wife and concluded that there were no "significant handwriting similarities" between either sample and the words "Nigger" and "None" written on the receipt. Either Jenkins had written the offensive language herself (ding, ding!) or someone else had somehow inserted himself into the situation and written on the receipt for unknown reasons.

Around this same time, Barnes actually wrote a personal note to Jenkins, explaining that he "never uses the n-word" and stating that he had "no idea how it ended up written on the receipt." Jenkins, who had almost certainly never intended a little harmless play-acting at being oppressed to go so far, responded to Barnes by taking a sort of self-promoting high road. Speaking to the *Daily Mail* (the British press' interest in the case says a good deal about how big this situation had gotten by then), Jenkins said that she probably "believes Barnes when he says he didn't write the slur." She had only posted the receipt pictures to "make a comment" about how prevalent racism remains today, and of course never to "draw attention to herself." Jenkins concluded the interview by saying, "I know I didn't write it. If he's claiming he didn't write it, I believe him … I'm just that kind of person!"

How big of her. In the end, however, her graceful acceptance of Barnes's claims of not being a racist ended up striking Barnes, who continued to receive constant abusive harassment online, as insufficient compensation. By May 2014, when this matter last received significant mass media coverage, Barnes had "turned to his pastor [and lawyer] Richard Duggar," and filed a $1,000,000 libel suit against both Jenkins and Red Lobster. In sometimes moving language, Barnes argued that Jenkins had libeled him by improperly using his personal information to entertain an audience of tens or hundreds of thousands, doing so "to gain publicity and money," and causing him to be "tagged a 'racist' worldwide." As for Red Lobster, the restaurant's "willful and malicious" refusal to prevent Jenkins from publicizing his name and information globally was the proximate cause of significant damage to Barnes' reputation. These are serious accusations that, if proven, would take more than even a few bowls of those delicious Red Lobster Cheddar Bay Biscuits to repair.[19]

Godspeed to Mr. Barnes in his lawsuit. What actually happened here seems stunningly obvious, and the damage caused to Barnes's reputation is real. The guy might want to consider picking Texas Roadhouse for his next family night out.

A (FAKE) GUN IN THE CAMPUS CHAPEL: ALICIA HARDIN AND THE TRINITY UNIVERSITY INCIDENT

The most ingenious motive award for a major hate crime hoaxer has to go to Trinity University's Alicia Hardin, who posed as a potential serial killer in an attempt to leave one small college for another.

Hardin's hoax was simple. In April 2005 she sent three anonymous letters to minority students enrolled at Trinity University, a small and well-regarded Christian college located about fifteen miles north of Chicago. The letters were intentionally made difficult to trace: they were all unsigned, handwritten on notebook paper, and written in a stylized hand. All of the notes were profane and offensive, containing racial slurs and threats, according to Lake County prosecutor Matthew Chancey. But the third and last missive stepped things up to a different and more disturbing level than the first two. In it the anonymous author threatened one murder, if not more, telling a female Hispanic student that the letter-writer had seen her in the campus chapel recently and stating: "I had my gun in my pocket…but I wouldn't shoot."[20] The obvious implication was that next time the writer might.

In response to Hardin's third note, Trinity University completely flipped out. Almost immediately after the short letter was discovered, campus administrators bused *every* undergraduate minority student at Trinity to an off-campus hotel, where they would presumably be safe. After several hours of consideration, the college decided that this did not represent a sufficient precaution against a potential murderer and sent the buses back to pick up all the minority grad students as well. Several edgy-but-serious websites have pointed out one obvious problem with this strategy: all of the "apparently worthless" white students at Trinity were simply left unprotected on campus, despite the fact that Hardin's notes had included race-neutral as well as racist comments about Trinity students. Midwestern Christians tend to be pretty well armed, and the website Bogus Hate Crimes half-jokingly described Trinity's white students as having spent the first few days after the note "skulking from bush to bush...looking for snipers and men named Jason wearing ski masks."[21]

Of course, they did not find any; no *actual* crazy killer had ever existed at Trinity. Early on in the police investigation that followed the third note, detectives deduced that their perp "had to be a Trinity student," and after several classmates pointed fingers in Hardin's direction she was interviewed and eventually confessed. The panic came to an end.

Hardin's motive itself was unusual. She hoaxed Trinity because she disliked the primarily white Christian campus and wanted to transfer to the larger and historically Black Jackson State University. According to Mississippi leasing agent Angela Toon, Hardin lived in an apartment near the Jackson State campus, located in the downtown of Mississippi's largest city, for at least part of the 2014 fall semester. While there, she apparently fell in love with the university and spent so much time on campus that many Jackson State students thought she was a fellow Tiger. Toon recalled Hardin saying that she "knew a lot of students at Jackson" and "had to be a student." In contrast, Hardin apparently hated the predominantly white Trinity University. One of the minority students evacuated to an area hotel after Hardin's hoax said how Hardin was constantly complaining about Trinity University, "talking about how she hates this school, she doesn't like it here."

More noteworthy than Hardin's motivation for her hoax was the "thought universe" of beliefs, shared by her and many other minority Americans, which underlay the stunt and made it effective. This disturbed student's actions and the results she expected them to have illustrate the incredible paranoia about racism that exists on the activist Left. The ultimate goal of Hardin, who is from inner-city Chicago, was to convince her parents that a religious school in suburban Bannockburn was *too dangerous* for her to attend. According to Chancey, Hardin "wanted to attend a different college" and faked racism on campus to convince her parents that Trinity was such an unsafe environment that they would allow her to transfer.

In reality the Trinity University campus, while perhaps a bit pious and stifling, is a well-integrated and conventionally anti-racist place. The *Chicago Tribune* describes the Trinity student body as "13 percent African American, 3 percent ... Asian or Pacific Islander, 4 percent Hispanic," and 6–7 percent "other" or foreign-born.[22] The place is less than 75 percent white, and many of the white students are city kids from the Chicago metro area. Besides Hardin's hoax, no serious hate crimes have been reported at Trinity University in the past decade. Once again, the activist Left narrative is simply wrong: middle-class Black Americans are not in terrible danger when they attend pleasant little suburban colleges. But many of our countrymen believe that they are, to the extent that Hardin could assume that her claims about murderous racism at Trinity would be taken so seriously that she would be freed to attend another college. How terrible the belief in the evil of our own society must be for far too many minority kids.

Although her motives may have been a bit more complex than those of most hate hoaxers, Hardin received fairly typical treatment after her exposure and arrest. She was charged with one criminal count of moderate severity—disorderly conduct—and went to trial in 2006. She was apparently convicted, but it is difficult to uncover what happened to her after that. Records of this case seem to have been subjected to the same net-scrubbing treatment that appears to have been applied to so many non-PC hate hoax stories. Several stories referred to in secondary sources as covering the situation have been removed from the internet, and the hyperlinks to them are all dead.[23] Ah well—in ignorance of the facts, at least we can hope that Hardin did a few months and got some counseling. That might not be the change of scenery she wanted, but it might well do her more good.

THE FIRE THIS TIME: A PHONY KLAN ATTACK IN LOUISIANA

One of the more sympathetic recent hate crime hoaxers appears to have committed her crime because of genuine issues with mental illness, rather than simply to garner attention. And she paid for it. In addition to the punishment handed down by the American legal system, Louisiana's Sharmeka Moffitt will bear the literal scars of one poor decision for the rest of her life.

On October 21, 2012, a 911 operator received a frantic telephone call from Moffitt, then a twenty-year-old student. The young lady claimed that three men wearing hooded garments had attacked her, "doused her with flammable liquid," and set her on fire in a popular local park near the jogging trail.[24] Although Moffitt described these men as racially indeterminate, there seemed to be little doubt about their affiliation and motive. Before leaving Moffitt for dead, the trio allegedly wrote "KKK" and a racial slur on their victim's car. Moffitt somehow survived and managed to summon up the strength to call police before collapsing. She was evacuated to the Louisiana State University Health Sciences Center, where doctors diagnosed her as having suffered second and third degree burns over fifty percent of her body and scheduled her for emergency surgery. Moffitt was declared to be in critical condition at the time of her hospital admission and remained in that state for some time.

The response to what was universally assumed to be a horrific hate crime was everything that could have been hoped. Police mobilized immediately and aggressively. Less than a minute after Moffitt's call hit the 911 switchboard, the first officers from the Louisiana State Police, Winnsboro Police Department, and Franklin Parish Sheriff's Department were arriving at the crime scene in the park. With dozens of officers screaming toward the location, the big toys came out. State police arrived by helicopter with a full mobile crime lab to gather outdoor evidence shortly after Moffitt was taken to the hospital for medical treatment. Law enforcement agencies gathered potential clues and pieces of evidence from the apparent crime scene throughout the night, finishing their in-situ analysis of the location within a day. Kevin Cobb, the Franklin Parish sheriff, gave an impassioned speech promising to root out any racist activity in his parish and "seek justice" for the injured Moffitt.[25]

Perhaps less useful, but even louder, the NAACP also got involved in the case. Social media accounts across Louisiana spread the story of the apparent attack, and civil rights activists got wind of the incident quickly. According to BET, the NAACP "stepped in to urge police to investigate the possibility of this being a hate crime," well before local authorities or the FBI had finished looking into the role that race played in the apparent attack.[26] Otis Chisley, president of the NAACP branch closest to the crime scene, promised to wait for all facts to come in before arriving at any conclusions about the case. He argued, however, that Klan activity, "although hidden," was still a problem in Louisiana, and reasonably enough, seemed to point the finger at the KKK as the guilty party.[27] The less restrained Louisiana NAACP Conference president Dr. Ernest L. Johnson Sr. pronounced himself "shocked" by the malicious actions of the perpetrators in the Moffitt case and demanded immediate investigation of the situation as a hate matter.[28] As jaws worked and phone lines buzzed around the state, some less moderate activists threatened retaliatory riots.

Then, once again, it happened. The meticulous police work of the literally dozens of detectives and investigators focused on cracking this case proved to be Moffitt's undoing. According to the *Franklin Sun*, Moffitt's fingerprints were quickly determined to be the only ones on the cigarette lighter discovered hidden in the park and presumably used to set her on fire. A can of lighter fluid also bearing her prints was recovered from the dense "wooded area near the crime scene." In addition, several indicators pointed to Moffitt as the individual who had used toothpaste to write the slurs on her car. Only a few days after her original call, a visibly disturbed Sheriff Cobb announced at a press conference, "All forensic evidence pointed toward Moffitt concocting the story and setting herself on fire." Winnsboro police agreed, with Chief Lester Thomas noting, "There is more physical evidence … that backs this up." The investigation into Moffitt's attackers was closed, and charges were eventually prepared and filed against her. The record indicates that she was convicted, although I have been unable to find a report of her exact sentence. As this case came to an end, both of the lawmen just quoted referred to it as a very disturbing one.[29]

And it was. Unlike the exposure of some college punk out to make himself famous, the uncovering of Moffitt's deception is nothing to gloat about. She was clearly battling demons, depression or some other mental illness, and scarred herself for life after losing a round against them. Her family responded to both the initial claim and its unraveling in a classy way, saying, "While this was not the resolution we had expected, it is a resolution, and we appreciate the thorough investigation by the local and state police as well as federal agencies. We are sincerely sorry for any problems this may have caused and wish to express our appreciation for the outpouring of love, prayers, and support we have received."[30]

I thought about not mentioning this case, given the sympathetic nature of the perpetrator and her family. But the Moffitt case, for all its complications, is an important one to analyze because it demonstrates an absolutely critical point: there is no race war going on in the United States. There simply are not groups of Klansmen roaming urban Louisiana wearing hoods and writing "Nigger" on cars with Optic White toothpaste. If someone says that there are, that claim is almost certainly a lie.

BEWARE OF "RACIST GRINGOS": THE FAMOUS TAGGER AND THE FAKE STABBING HOAX

In contrast to Sharmeka Moffit, Jesus Francisco Cabrera may be one of the least sympathetic hate crime hoaxers of all time. Cabrera is a Palo Alto graffiti vandal who claimed that a mob of whites attacked him. His motive? To explain away injuries he had received in a gang fight.

On July 15, 2015, Cabrera was admitted to a California hospital with a serious leg wound and opted to file a police report. Speaking to investigators, he claimed that he had been peacefully walking to his vehicle, located in a downtown parking garage, when he was set upon by a group of white males. First, "the three white men approached him" and began making "derogatory comments about his [Mexican-American] ethnicity." When he shot a few sharp comments back, the racist gringos told him that he didn't belong in the United States.[31] The men argued, and the situation escalated.

This is the point in the narrative where major inconsistencies appear. Just before the scuffle in which he claimed to have been injured, the pack of three white guys in Cabrera's narrative appear to lose a man. While "three white men" originally approached him, the alleged victim described a fight with "two white guys." Thus an attacker Cabrera had described in detail simply vanished from the story without explanation. Several commenters have observed that this inconsistency in Cabrera's story should have "sent up red flags for the police." But it didn't.[32] Cabrera claimed that the two white males viciously attacked him: one grabbed him from the back and forced him into a hold, while the other stabbed him in the leg with a screwdriver. Mission accomplished, the white men ran off.

California being what it is, and urban northern California being perhaps the most California part of California, the sensitive racial nature of Cabrera's story caused the "ultra-sympathetic" police to immediately label the attack a hate crime. Considerable resources were immediately rerouted toward solving the case. Palo Alto Police Lieutenant Brian Philip listed some of them: "overtime patrols, canvassing, follow-up interviews ... many different things [went] into this."[33] Massive expenditures of government resources—read: our tax money—aside, the Cabrera situation also ended up being used by authorities in the region as an exemplar of the horrific problem of ongoing contemporary racism. Palo Alto's human relations commission asked the police department to draw up a professional Power-Point presentation about the frequency of hate crimes and best practices for responding to them in response to this "racially motivated attack," and the coppers duly did so.[34]

By now all of you know what happened next. According to SFGate, "after months of investigating," police were forced to conclude that Cabrera had simply made up the whole story.[35] As in the case of Payton Head's allegations that same year in Missouri, no video-camera images of the suspects in the screwdriver attack ever surfaced, and police were never able to confirm that the men Cabrera accused of attacking him even existed. Perhaps unsurprisingly, given his confusion in the initial police report about how many attackers there had been in the first place, "Cabrera kept changing his story." Finally, after a tense interview with investigators, the 'hate crime victim' admitted that he had been lying all along.

So far, all of this is pretty much par for the course. It is Cabrera's motivation for his lie that stands out as uniquely unsympathetic, even for a hate crime hoax. As it turns out, he was a graffiti artist—one of greater Palo Alto's more well-known graffiti vandals—and had actually been stabbed by a rival crew during a gang fight in East Palo Alto while he was tagging one of the city's major bridges. According to at least one contemporary source, Cabrera considered the man who stabbed him "a friend or acquaintance," and concocted his story because he "didn't want to snitch on his homeboy." In contrast, random white citizens could apparently be insulted at will. As a result, of course, all of the police resources named by Lieutenant Philip were simply wasted chasing wild geese.

Cabrera did receive some punishment. He was charged with the single count of a misdemeanor false report that seems to be *de rigeur* when hate hoaxers face any criminal charges at all. But he seems to have escaped jail time. There is no word on whether he continues to paint. Whether or not Cabrera or the city of Palo Alto learned any lessons from the results of this charade, there are certainly some conclusions the rest of us can draw from the case. As one local commenter pointed out, the police should be "more interested in fighting crime than in propping up political correctness."[36] If they were, it would not be especially hard for them to figure out that—for example—a graffiti artist claiming that a mob of random citizens attacked him with building tools, who forgets how many of these attackers there even were, is probably lying. Such allegations could be tossed out *before* millions are spent investigating them!

At least outside of California, that is a lesson for all of us to take to heart.

A HARBINGER OF THINGS TO COME: RACHEL DOLEZAL AND THE TWO NOOSES

The case that will close this chapter illustrates the link between the reporting of dubious and false hate crimes and the Continuing Oppression Narrative promoted by the activist Left. Over the course of roughly six months in 2009, one woman reported no fewer than six hate crimes and other hate incidents to the FBI and local police in Washington and Idaho. That woman's name was Rachel Dolezal.

According to accounts published by Washington's *Spokane Spokesman-Review*, Idaho's *Boise Weekly*, and the Associated Press, Dolezal first claimed that in April 2009 "three skinheads" walked unopposed into her office in Coeur d'Alene's Human Rights Education Institute and asked her a series of "personal questions," including where she lived and what school her young son attended. Shortly after this, her Idaho home was burglarized, and Aryan Nation fliers were distributed in her neighborhood. By August 2009, to escape the abuse and allow her little boy to attend school in a "racially diverse classroom," Dolezal had temporarily moved from Idaho to Spokane, Washington. But this proved no escape! Almost as soon as she got there, Dolezal claimed that "someone wrote a misspelled racial epithet" on the concrete sidewalk outside her new home "with an arrow pointing to the house." Just a few weeks later, in early September, Dolezal's Idaho house was allegedly burglarized a second time. According to media accounts, she stated that "$13,000 worth of personal belongings," including a television, a laptop computer, "every penny from her son's piggy bank, DVDS, and video games" were taken.[37]

Then came the nooses! On September 23, 2009, the website for Idaho regional TV station KHQ "The 6" ran a feature piece noting that Dolezal had contacted police to report that someone had left a hangman's noose on the porch of her Washington home in an apparent threat against her "Black family."[38] Dolezal drew on her experience as a civil rights activist and community organizer to expound on the meaning of the noose as metaphor. "I spent a lot of time in Mississippi, so...when I saw that rope, I knew what it was," she told the *Coeur d'Alene Press*. "You have to learn and practice how to tie a noose. It's a very intentional thing."[39] But not, apparently, a one-time thing. According to a separate story, which opened with the words "Racism is alive and well in Northern Idaho," Dolezal claimed to have found a second perfectly tied noose—this one at her Idaho home—on or before June 21, 2010. Amy Heizfeld, Dolezal's boss at the Human Rights Education Institute, used this incident as a fundraising opportunity, saying that the discovery of the noose really "underscores the importance of our work." The *Boise Weekly* soberly opined that "the Treasure Valley isn't immune."[40]

Coverage of this Normandy-style wave assault of hate crimes against Dolezal was immediate, sympathetic, and national in scope. The Associated Press, the *Boise Weekly*, the *Coeur d'Alene Press*, The Street, and the largest newspaper in Spokane all ran features based on Dolezal's claims. Much of this coverage focused on Dolezal as a proud Black woman under attack. The AP called the first noose found on Dolezal's porch "an apparent threat against a Black family," while the *Spokesman-Review*'s three-page story was headlined "Latest In a String of Incidents Targeting Black Woman."[41] Partly as a result of the apparently racial nature of the case, the FBI got involved.

The reveal in this case is a bit different than usual. None of Dolezal's accusations has ever been proven to be a hoax. But so far as I have been able to tell, no suspects were ever identified in most of the incidents reported by Dolezal. You, dear reader, will have to judge for yourself just how likely it is that one woman was the victim of seven different serious hate attacks in two different states inside roughly one year. And as you judge, it seems fair that you should take into account her—subsequently demonstrated—level of honesty and credibility. That brings us smoothly to the *un*usual reveal just promised.

Rachel Dolezal is white. For those of you who have not already figured this out, she is the "Black" civil rights activist who was very famously exposed as Caucasian in 2015 after pretending to be Black for years, attaining a high position in the Washington State NAACP, and teaching Black Studies at an accredited college. After being exposed, Dolezal—rather than admitting her mistakes and entering therapy—wrote a best-selling book called *In Full Color* in which she discussed living as a "white Black." In explanation of how she was able to pull off such a bizarre masquerade for such a long time, Dolezal has noted, "I certainly don't stay out of the sun."[42]

The Dolezal case is an almost perfect metaphor for the relationship between the activist Left and the Black community. For almost half a century now, activists on the Left have ginned up charges of racism. They use faked or at best atypical incidents to create a false impression about the level of racism in America. And many of the activists playing this game are not Black. A surprising number—not just Dolezal, but probably at least 60 percent of BLM and antifa stalwarts—are not African American.[43] And those who are biologically

Black—the Nation of Islam, "the Moors," the "Back to Africa" brothers—are completely out of touch with mainstream Black America, which is culturally conservative, respects Christianity, and is imbued with a nuanced but real patriotism. (Anyone who doubts the patriotism of Black Americans should take a quick look at rates of military service by race. African Americans make up 13 percent of the U.S. population, but 30.27 percent of active-duty enlisted men.)[44] Tragically, fake hate crimes and the activists who exploit them are succeeding in convincing African Americans that our country is much more racist than it actually is. Removing this parasitic contingent of outsiders from positions of influence would do the Black community more good than almost anything else.

Chapter Five

THE TRUMP HATE CRIMES: DONALD TRUMP'S ELECTION AND THE RESULTING WAVE OF HOAXES

An entirely new category of hate hoaxes has sprung up since the 2016 election of the tough-talking forty-fifth president. This is not really surprising. Probably the primary mainstream media talking point regarding President Trump is that he is a "racist" or a "white supremacist," and a close second is that his campaign unleashed a "wave of hate."

According to Professor Brian Levin at Cal-State's Center for the Study of Hate and Extremism, there was a five percent increase in hate crimes between 2015 and the end of 2016. However, many of the cases included in that 2016 number were probably fakes, which can take some time to be exposed. As we shall see in the next chapter, the much-touted rise in anti-Semitic hate incidents, in particular in the year after Trump's election, is almost certainly explained by an increase in hate hoaxes rather than an increase in actual hate crimes.

The constant presentation of Trump as a bigot has indisputably triggered a wave of hate crime *hoaxes* of many kinds, beginning several months before the Trump election. Many of the most famous hate incidents associated with Trump, such as the hijab-ripping attack on Yasmin Seweid, were fakes.

There is little ambiguity in the media's coverage of Trump. On January 11, 2018, CNN host Don Lemon opened a nightly news broadcast with the following: "This is CNN Tonight. I'm Don Lemon. The president of the United States is racist."[1] We have already seen a plethora of stories that come up on a quick search for "Donald Trump white supremacist," such as "How White Nationalists Learned to Love Donald Trump" and countless others.

Of course, truth is an absolute defense to libel. The prevalence of headlines calling Trump the second coming of George Wallace raises the question: Is Trump a racist? The answer seems to be "probably not," in any real sense of that word.

The man is not exactly the king of tact. In fact, he's the archetypal obnoxious native New Yorker ("Oudda my way, jackass!"). He has made many bold statements unusual for a politician, including summing up a riot between neo-Nazi thugs and antifa street fighters as "really bad people…both sides," and calling the struggling island nation of Haiti a "shithole."

But honestly, 95 percent of Americans might agree with those sentiments in private. Neither KKK nor antifa members would make very welcome neighbors in most subdivisions—those guys just never keep up the lawn!—and Haiti is a poor and fabulously dangerous disaster zone, however many brave and striving people may live there. There seems to be little if any evidence that Trump is an actual racist—that is, a person who believes that some races are genetically inferior. Prior to his election, Trump appeared on G-Unit Radio with 50 Cent, maintained friendships with Oprah and Russell Simmons, and regularly hosted famously diverse business and modeling talent shows. While his administration is a bit less diverse than Obama's, one of his most respected cabinet secretaries is the African-American Ben Carson, his UN ambassador is the Indian-American Nikki Haley, his FCC czar is

Ajit Pai, and so on down the line. I can find almost literally no evidence of Trump being called a bigot in mainstream print before he chose to run for president against the hot-sauce toting Hillary Clinton.[2]

If anything, Trump seems to be guilty of saying that which must never be said, rather than of *evil racism*. Unfortunately, honest discussions of race and class are absolutely taboo in today's America. The media chatters on endlessly about "white privilege," but serious conversations about race—on any issue from crime rates to affirmative action—are verboten.

Regardless of whether he and his supporters are actual bigots, it cannot be denied that Trump's name has been associated with brutal hate crimes since before his November 2016 election date. It is hard to forget Yasmin Seweid, the young Muslim woman who claimed that a group of boorish white males tore at her hijab on a New York public train. Or the torching of Mississippi's historic Hopewell Missionary Baptist Church, which was burned nearly to the ground and left with the words "Vote Trump" defacing one ruined wall. Or the preppy Black Bowling Green State coed who was attacked by white fraternity types—who threw stones at her like she was a damn dog. Or the multiple Philly storekeepers who had phrases such as "Sieg Heil" spray-painted on the windows of their lovely little shops the very night Trump was elected. How could anyone not sympathize with the victims of these heinous crimes, and question the character of the new president and his supporters?

The easy answer: they were all complete fakes.

THE CASE YOU'VE ALREADY HEARD OF: YASMIN SEWEID AND THE (UN)RIPPED HIJAB

Probably the most famous Trump-related "hate crime" took place on December 1, 2016, when a young Muslim student claimed that she was attacked on a New York City subway train by "drunken,

hate-spewing white men shouting 'Donald Trump!'" As we have
already seen, she made the whole thing up.

According to the *Daily News* and the *Washington Times*, Baruch
College coed Yasmin Seweid initially reported that she was taking the
train home on a late afternoon in December when she was surrounded
by three Caucasian males who "taunted her" and "tried to snatch her
hijab off her head."[3] Seweid described a blood-chilling scene to the
police, and apparently later directly to the papers. Quoth she, "They
were surrounding me from behind and they were like 'Oh look, it's a
fucking terrorist.' I didn't answer. They pulled my strap of the bag
and it ripped, and that's when I turned around." A frightening physical scuffle then allegedly followed. Invoking the shade of Kitty Geno-
vese, Seweid castigated her fellow New Yorkers for callousness,
alleging that multiple observers did nothing to aid a damsel in distress.
"Everyone was looking, no one said a thing, everyone just looked
away." She also specifically blamed Donald Trump for her victimization, saying, "The president-elect just promotes this stuff and is very
anti-Muslim, very Islamophobic."[4]

Seweid's story attracted frenzied national attention, to the point
that I will not bother listing all of the major papers and networks
which reported on it. As a result, most of you had probably heard of
Seweid before reading this book. The Long Island teenager became
something of a social media star, posting an emotional and widely
shared account of her train experience on Facebook. It opened, "I was
harassed on the subway last night. And, it was just so dehumanizing.
I can't speak about it without getting emotional." New York City
police got involved almost immediately, treating the case as a hate
crime. The NYPD's finest have been justifiably a bit coy about this,
but it would appear that the coppers placed Seweid under some kind
of surveillance, to such an extent that police detectives were soon able
to say that they had spotted one of the suspects following her "when

she got off the subway at Grand Central Terminal" on a later date. Pretty specific.

Of course, given that Seweid's claim was a hoax, it can safely be assumed that this "suspect" was simply a random white man. Nonetheless, top-notch police work! Still, this level of police attention rapidly turned up multiple holes in Seweid's story. Perhaps most notably, none of the probably tens of thousands of New Yorkers riding the rails at the time of her alleged attack reported having noticed a violent scuffle between a *hijabi* Muslim woman and three white guys. For some time, however, police believed that all of the inconsistencies in Seweid's narrative were due to the severe extent to which she had been "traumatized." According to at least one police spokesman, Seweid had "numerous opportunities to admit nothing happened"—without much punishment, early on—but "she kept sticking to her story."

Seweid's narrative finally collapsed after she apparently panicked and simply disappeared for a while. She vanished from her home on Wednesday, December 7, and she was officially reported missing the next day. Media coverage of her disappearance was national in scale and frenzied in tone. But when Seweid turned up on December 9 with not a mark on her, police were able to confirm their suspicions. A breaking point had finally been reached. Previously treated with kid gloves, Seweid was now subjected to tough questions from NYPD detectives. By Wednesday, December 14, she confessed: "She said she had made it all up."[5]

The reaction to Seweid's confession was predictably significantly more muted than the response to her original claims. While the *Daily News* did run several multi-page articles on the new revelations, a more typical example of the mainstream response, at least on the left, was the lengthy statement made by Albert Khan, attorney for the New York State Council for American-Islamic

Relations.[6] Cahn argued that Seweid's embarrassing admissions should not "diminish concern about anti-Islam incidents" that had followed the election of Trump. Cahn spoke sympathetically of Seweid, saying that he was disturbed by "these distressing developments," but insisted that there were "numerous" real reports of hate crime coming from the Muslim community in New York. The governor of the state, Andrew Cuomo, seemed to share this view, creating a "special task force" focused entirely on hate crimes less than a week after the 2016 election.[7]

Interestingly, the mainstream media—even the doughty *Daily News*—seems to have almost totally ignored the real story of oppression threaded throughout the Seweid case. That true story is that violence against women is epidemic in most traditional cultures and among immigrants from many of those cultures to the United States. Seweid's motive for her lies has been lightly reported, but it will receive proper notice here: she made up her wild story because she was genuinely terrified of getting in trouble for breaking a family curfew after staying out a bit late drinking with friends. Her strict parents, both practicing Egyptian Muslims, objected to any use of alcohol and were apparently also upset that she was dating a Christian man. She may have feared serious physical violence, and there is strong evidence that such a fear would not have been unjustified.

After her dishonesty was revealed, her parents apparently forcibly shaved Seweid's head, and she appeared bald at her few post-hoax court appearances (on the usual misdemeanor false report charge) with adult relatives who did things like "cover [her] face with a black down jacket." The right-wingers at the Red State website may be on to something when they say, "This is Domestic Violence. Violence against Women. Whatever you want to call it."[8] There was probably a real story here under the fake one, but the mainstream media almost universally chose to ignore it.

"LIKE THE SIXTIES," WITH A TWIST: THE BLACK-BURNED MISSISSIPPI BLACK CHURCH

Although the alleged hijab-tearing attack on Yasmin Seweid was probably the most widely publicized "hate crime" linked to the election of Donald Trump, the most morally disturbing—at least to any student of American history—has to be the burning of a beautiful old Black church in Greenville, Mississippi.

The national narrative around what became known as the "Trump church burning" began on November 1, 2016, when Mississippi's historic Hopewell Missionary Baptist Church was burned and vandalized, roughly one week before the presidential election in which Donald Trump defeated Hillary Clinton. The church was more than 110 years old at the time of its destruction, having been founded in the heart of Greenville's African American community in 1905. During that period of more than a century, Hopewell had grown into a stable congregation of more than two hundred members—mostly working middle class Black folks—and, as area records indicate, had produced multiple distinguished veterans of World War II, Korea, and Vietnam.

The attack on Hopewell was an act of evil. The arsonist used a combination of incendiaries to set virtually the entire church building ablaze. Reporters affiliated with Memphis's Channel 3 News quoted the local fire chief's comments that the church "sustained heavy damage" in the fire, while even an attached kitchen and the pastor's office "received water and smoke damage."[9] The conclusion of pretty much every stakeholder interested in rebuilding the church was that doing so would take months, and might not be possible at all. *Business Insider* noted that, while a few of the church's stout "beige brick walls" survived the fire, the entire interior of the building was destroyed, and church leaders frankly said the structure would "have to be razed." Further, to add insult to injury, the church-burner used spray paint to write conservative political slogans on the outside of the ruined building. The graffiti urging "Vote TRUMP!" naturally caught the attention of the national media.

You can figure out the story from there. Major media outlets including CBS, NBC, Red State (which admittedly had bit of a different take), CNN, *Business Insider*, and dozens of other national television and print sources sprinted to cover the Greenville case. The mainstream media narrative was that a racist was abroad and loose in the land: the campaign of Donald Trump had emboldened one or more hard-right bigots, who were running around setting Southern Black churches ablaze.

In a refreshing side note, the actual residents of Greenville did not take this narrative of racial tension to heart. In that city, an integrated "New South" community where citizens of different races regularly "work and eat lunch together," the predominantly white First Baptist Church immediately offered displaced Hopewell parishioners First Baptist's own facilities to worship in. During a good chunk of a year, Hopewell congregants conducted services in one of the sizable chapels inside First Baptist. Hopewell's bishop, Clarence Green, said that the kindness of the neighboring church demonstrates that God's "unlimited love transcends social barriers." For his part, James Nichols, the senior pastor at First, said that his fellow Christians from Hopewell were "welcome to stay as long as they need a home." Members of both congregations noted that Hopewell, by no means a tiny or poverty-stricken church, would have offered the same accommodations if the positions of the two congregations were reversed.

A beautiful story. But the narrative of continuing oppression held sway nationally. Imagine the shock, then, when the police investigation into the case turned up a Black suspect—who was a member of the church! By December 21, 2016—just before Hopewell would normally have been holding Christmas services, to blatantly tear-jerk for a minute—Mississippi Department of Public Safety spokesman Warren Strain was able to announce that Andrew McClinton, an African American male, was in custody for first-degree arson against a place of worship. Perhaps unsurprisingly for a Black dude in Mississippi, McClinton does not appear to have been a Trump supporter. (Greenville's home county voted 11,380 to 5,244 for Hillary Clinton over Trump.) Police and fire department sources noted quickly that "the fire wasn't (actually) politically motivated," although it certainly seemed to be "meant to look that way." Still, one possibility is that a Black liberal may have framed white conservatives for a horrendous crime in order to get more Clinton voters to the polls.[10]

That said, speculation is not science, and McClinton's actual motives remain a bit of a mystery. Mississippi Department of Corrections records show that McClinton has a felony record as long as LeBron James's arms, including convictions for grand larceny (1991), receiving stolen property (1992), attempted robbery (1997), and armed robbery (2004). McClinton almost certainly would have racked up more free trips to various county and state hotels if he had not received a serious sentence—eight years—in the most recent robbery case. He was released in 2012, four years before the 2016 felony arson.[11]

Several observers of the case have noted that an individual as damaged as McClinton could have burned the church for any reason or none at all: perhaps he had a problem with the minister. A critical task of all churches, especially those in economically deprived areas, is to minister to at-risk individuals in their home communities. That cross is a heavy one; in this case Hopewell's outreach to McClinton failed dramatically, despite all that many good women and men could do. Jesus, as they say, wept.

Moving from spiritual to practical facts, it is worth noting that "hate crimes" committed against churches seem just as likely to be hoaxes as any other highly publicized hate crimes. Doing deep background research on the McClinton case, I almost immediately turned up two other recent hoax hate attacks on heartland places of worship, one of which also involved Trump's name. In 2015, a Black man in Colorado Springs was arrested after being exposed as the sole source of multiple profane signs posted outside a large Black church saying things such as "KKK" and "Black Men Beware."[12] More recently, the organist at St. David's Episcopal Church in Bean Blossom, Indiana, was discovered to be the person responsible for writing "Heil Trump!" and anti-gay slurs across the outside walls of the main church building. He admitted to having done so to "mobilize a movement" against then-candidate Trump, describing himself as "fearful of the election results."[13]

Perhaps he should have tried prayer.

NABRA HASSANEN: THE ILLEGAL IMMIGRANT MURDER THAT BECAME A "HATE CRIME"

I hesitated, thought long and hard, and actually asked friends for ethical advice before including Nabra Hassanen's story in this book. In this case a human being—by all accounts a fine, truly top-notch young woman—was attacked and died. But in every other way the case fits the typical profile of a fake hate offense: (1) a real or apparent crime occurs, (2) conservatives or whites or taxpayers or society at large are initially blamed, but then (3) the actual perpetrator turns out to be a POC criminal or radical with unsympathetic motives.

The Hassanen case, which quickly vaulted a stricken family and community into the national spotlight, began on the warm Virginia evening of June 18, 2017. Hassanen, a rising junior at South Lakes High School in Reston, Virginia, was spending a summer night during the Muslim holy month of Ramadan with roughly fifteen teenage friends. The teens met at the All Dulles Area Muslim Society's mosque, and—not having eaten all day—decided to set out for a McDonald's after dark fell and the day's fast had ended. After they ate, while making their way back to the *masjid* on foot and bicycles, the teens became involved in a dispute with an older man who attempted to drive past them in a red car.

Unexpectedly, after a few words were exchanged, the man in the car began acting frighteningly irrational. He first drove up onto the curb, trying to pursue the teens onto and down the sidewalk. When that failed, he followed them down the road to a parking lot, "chased the youngsters down and got out [of his car] swinging a bat." The man apparently reached Hassanen first and "beat [her] as her friends scattered." He then left the scene briefly before he returned, tossed Hassanen into his own vehicle, "assaulting her again," and drove away.[14] Hassanen's lifeless body was found floating in a Reston pond. Police, who discovered the corpse around 4:00 p.m. the next day, confirmed that she had been murdered—killed by foul play after a struggle. The cause of death was ruled as blunt force trauma.

Hassanen's death prompted immediate nationwide outrage, centered on the assumption that this brave young woman's death was a hate crime committed by an Islamophobe. Tara Isabella Burton of the center-left website Vox claimed almost immediately that "Hassanen has become another example of an innocent victim of Islamophobia."[15] Ibrahim Hooper, spokesman for the Council on American-Islamic Relations (CAIR), argued provocatively that there is "a strong possibility" the attack on Hassanen would never have happened "if the teenagers weren't Muslim." Lawyer and Muslim activist Rabia Chaudry agreed, tweeting: "if you think for a minute that her appearance had nothing to do with this crime, you're lying to yourself."[16] Perhaps most movingly, Hassanen's distraught father stated that he believed "100 percent" that his daughter was killed because of her identity as a Muslim, noting her hijab and her traditional dress at the time she was attacked.[17] It seems fair to say that the activist Left was bracing for a major campaign against Islamophobia, with President Trump as a primary target.

And then it happened. Virginia's Fairfax County police conducted a quick, competent investigation and had a suspect in custody the day after Hassanen was murdered. This man, Darwin Martinez Torres, was not in fact a Trump-voting conservative white guy. Instead, he was not only Hispanic but also an illegal immigrant to the United States, having snuck into the country from El Salvador years before. Further, while undoubtedly a sociopath, Torres was not a racist and appeared to have no problem whatsoever with Muslims. During a news conference shortly after the arrest, a county police spokeswoman noted that his attack on Hassanen was a pure "traffic dispute" and that "no evidence has been uncovered that shows this murder was motivated by race or religion."[18]

Chief Edwin Roessler of Fairfax County police confirmed that law enforcement authorities had "absolutely no evidence" that Torres had disliked Muslims in general, or Hassanen in particular, before his roadside clash with her.[19] It is no exaggeration to say that Torres's arrest was the ultimate nightmare for many lefty pundits: the expected white male who could become the center of a national social-justice campaign instead turned out to be a non-racist, illegal alien named after Charles Darwin, and his arrest launched conversations about immigration policy and race and crime in America.

Of course, it is difficult to persuade fanatics of any variety that they are wrong. The actual reaction of the activist Left to the fact that Hassanen's killer was not white and her death was not a hate crime was ... educational. As is surprisingly often the case, many activists simply refused to accept that the left-wing narrative had collapsed. In a nationally circulated column published in the *Washington Post*'s features section, Petula Dvorak opined that, while Torres' attack on Hassanen might not have technically been a hate crime, it "feels" like and "has the effect of one."

Totally ignoring the fact that the sole perpetrator in the case was an unprejudiced Hispanic guy who had already been captured, Dvorak questioned whether worshippers at the Dulles Area mosque should organize "deeper security" and armed "patrols" for the remainder of Ramadan to avoid becoming "targets of hate." Women came in for some unsolicited care and concern as well; perhaps they might now recognize that their pleasant "bedroom community" was not a safe place to "walk around in." Blacks, always sacred objects to liberals of a certain stripe, were invoked—could Hassanen have been attacked because her parents were born in Egypt and thus she was "African American"? And so on.[20]

The Continuing Oppression Narrative never changes. But, of course, we are free not to believe it. Those who do not believe the narrative and want to pursue actual solutions to America's greatly improved but still real racial problems can do two things to commemorate the tragic death of Nabra Hassanen. First, they can take a moment to genuinely mourn a brave young woman. More importantly, they can recall that while all the ecumenicalism and kumbaya singing in the world would not have saved Hassanen from Torres, actual enforcement of the immigration laws would have.

THE BROTHER WHO TAGGED SOUTH PHILLY

On a much lighter note, one of the funnier recent fake hate crimes—no one was killed or even hurt, and journalists got off some genuinely good lines about the whole thing—involved a Black guy terrorizing Philadelphia's tough interracial South Philly district with pro-Trump graffiti. Perhaps the reason it seemed like a joke is that the residents of South Philly are a bit more tough-minded than the precious snowflakes on college campuses. And they have a better sense of humor. Like many a good joke and sad story, this one began on election night.

According to Michael Tanenbaum of PhillyVoice, this case, which does not yet have an ominous-sounding nickname assigned to it, started when police received reports of an energetic spray-can campaign in South Philly during the wee hours of the morning on November 9, 2016. In one single incident, "three vehicles and one house" were tagged in huge black letters with political slogans. One message read, "Trump Rules"; another said, "Trump Rules, Black Bitch!"; a third consisted simply of a giant-sized letter T.

These acts of vandalism occurred on the 900 block of Philadelphia's South Sixth Street, on the border between the sub-neighborhoods of Bella Vista and Queen Village. In another incident, on Broad Street, a spray-can vandal scrawled the words "Trump" and the phrase "Sieg Heil 2016" on a small storefront's glass window. Overall damages were estimated at well over $10,000. A sixty-two-year-old grandmother, the owner of an expensive white SUV that had been defaced with the words "Black Bitch," noticed the graffiti shortly after it had been placed there and immediately called the cops. Using street camera footage, the police were able to put together a description of the suspect as a hoodie- or jacket-wearing male "of unknown race."

Given this vague description, local activists could come to only one logical conclusion: the vandal was a white conservative male inspired by Donald Trump! Several large-scale protests took place, and Philadelphia Mayor Jim Kenney issued a strongly worded (in fact, rather eloquent) statement condemning the incidents. Quoth he, "In the wake of the election, Philadelphians must work tirelessly to bridge the divides that have plagued this nation for decades. I know that many residents are planning to take part in rallies and vigils tonight and in the days ahead, and I urge you to gather respectfully and peacefully." The Philadelphia Anti-Defamation League quickly condemned the graffiti, although they noted that the pro-Trump messages might be "an isolated matter." Senior detectives from Philly's South Detective Division began investigating these "hate incidents" as a priority.[21]

And then it happened. Philadelphia's South Division turns out to maintain an impressively comprehensive criminal tip line, through which aspiring snitches can report a crime by texting tips to the number "773847," submitting one of several online forms, or by calling either the police station or the detective division directly. (At 215-658-3013 and 215-686-8477, respectively—should you ever need to snitch on someone in Philly. No need to thank me. I live to serve others.) Informants get paid. Within one day of the division's announcement that they were seeking information about the pro-Trump tagger, "an anonymous ... tipster" had called in to provide the vandal's identity. By November 22, after a bit of additional investigation, police arrested William Tucker, an African American man from Camden, New Jersey, who had been visiting Philadelphia the day of the 2016 election.

Tucker's motives frankly remain a bit of a mystery. Unsurprisingly, he does not appear to actually be a partisan Trump supporter. So far as I have been able to tell, he is not registered to vote at all, for any party. He certainly does not fit the "business self-starter" stereotype of a northeastern Republican; the fifty-eight-year-old Tucker still lives with his mother, a no-nonsense woman who answers the phone at the one contact number provided for him with a crisp "No comment." On the advice of their counsel, both Tucker and his mum appear to have said nothing whatsoever on the record about the graffiti case. The police do not seem to have taken him very seriously as a hate criminal, charging him with "criminal mischief" and releasing him on his own recognizance before the first preliminary hearing.[22] Perhaps Tucker simply found a couple of spray cans, and decided to have fun tagging some big shiny trucks with names he had recently heard on TV. Inquiring minds remain unsatisfied.

The Tucker case, almost amusing to everyone other than the owners of the ruined Escalades and Suburbans in question, is not especially important in the great scheme of things. Tucker may end up doing a few weeks in the can—or not. He seems unlikely to offend again, at least in this way. However, there is one *very* critical general lesson to take from his case. Any time someone does something like write "KKK" or "It's Trump, Bitch!" across multiple homes and vehicles in a tough Black and Italian neighborhood in the northern U.S., it is a fairly safe bet that a hoax or prank has taken place ... and not an actual Klan raid, worthy of global coverage and speeches by the mayor. As the old Army maxim goes: if you hear hoof-beats, think horses, not zebras.

THROWING SHADE AT TRUMP: THE HOAX ROCK ATTACK AT BOWLING GREEN

While the story of the apolitical Black guy who pretended to be a pro-Trump tagger borders on the humorous, many other alleged pro-Trump hate crimes would have been truly despicable—if they had actually happened. On the Bowling Green University campus in central Kentucky, for example, a young Black woman claimed she had been chased for several blocks by Trump supporters shouting racial insults and throwing rocks at her. Unsurprisingly, she was lying.

On November 9, the day after a 2016 election that seems to have been a sort of national April Fool's day for hate hoaxers, Bowling Green student Eleesha Long filed a police complaint alleging a pro-Trump hate attack on her person. It read, in part, "While I was walking down Crim Street to ask for [presumably pro-Clinton] yard signs, three boys began to throw rocks at me." Long went on to say that the men who attacked her were all white males "wearing Trump shirts," and that they had followed her for some time, shouting profanity and tossing fist-sized stones. Long's complaint was remarkably detailed, describing not only the appearance of each of the three male attackers but also exactly what each of them was wearing.[23]

The usual reaction followed. Bowling Green police officers took the complaint very seriously, asking Long to return to the police station and give a lengthy formal statement, which she did. A post to her Facebook page about what had happened went viral, garnering probably thousands of likes, shares, and other emoji-based online reactions. Perhaps more importantly from Long's perspective, her claims gained her a great deal of sympathetic local attention, including multiple displays of support on the Bowling Green campus, such as a sympathetic social media post from the university's vice president for student affairs and a full-scale town hall meeting on "Respect within Our Community."[24] This last reaction was exacerbated by Long's legitimately upset father, who told attentive area media and police that he "couldn't locate" his twenty-four-year-old daughter "for some time" after the reported attack on her. Imagine, for a moment, this poor man's genuine fear.[25]

That fear turned out to be unmerited and unnecessary, however, as is common in these cases. The Bowling Green University campus police, a typical small force, quickly discovered that Long had simply made up the entire attack. Several police sources have noted that Long changed her story at will "multiple times" throughout the investigation. Lieutenant Dan Marcuso told Action News, on the record, "Several times the complainant changed her story about what happened, where it happened, and when it happened." After becoming aware of these inconsistencies, police obtained a digital search warrant for Long's Facebook and Verizon history—and discovered that she had apparently never been where she claimed she was at the time of the alleged attack. Lieutenant Mancuso was blunt: "[this] proved she was not in the location when she said it occurred."

Entertainingly, the search of Long's phone and internet histories revealed that she herself seems to be quite the racist, and an extreme political partisan. Local news stories and police reports describe her phone records as "laced with racist remarks against Trump supporters," which were sent not only to peers like her boyfriend but also to her mother. Among these were: "[Trump] is why you should take an IQ test to vote"; "I haven't met a decent Trump supporter yet"; and "I hope they all get AIDS." From this evidence, it would appear that what we have here is the case of a left-wing political activist attributing a fake hate crime to right-wing operatives in order to delegitimize the results of a valid election—an ugly way to play the game. The authorities apparently thought so. Whether or not the charges against her were boosted by the discovery of her prejudices, they were unusually serious: criminal falsification and the obstruction of the police's "official business."[26]

But in the end Long, who pled guilty, was given only a $200 fine and two years of probation.[27]

There is one positive postscript to the Long case. We in the United States are one country, no matter how hard the activist Left and the alt-right—both movements for losers—attempt to deny it. The response of actual Bowling Green students to Long's attempt to divide the campus was exactly what one would hope. Hispanic Bowling Green coed Monica Florez dismissed Long in a sentence, telling ABC 13: "I think it's terrible someone would want to start lying about something like that." Karl Hinshaw, president of the large and long-integrated Kappa Alpha Psi men's fraternity, had thoughts along the same lines: "I feel like as a country, we need to get away from the whole race issue." A third Bowling Green student stated the obvious: no matter which candidate students had supported in the presidential election, "We all have to move forward and make peace."[28]

How true, and what inspiring young folk. *E pluribus unum* and all that. Now let's move on to the next cynical attempt to divide the country!

GO BACK TO ACTING SCHOOL: THE FAKE CAMPAIGN OF THREATS AT NORTH PARK

Another would-have-been-absolutely-despicable-if-it-actually-happened-but-it-did-not hate crime occurred within a week of the 2016 election (again), took place on a Midwestern college campus (again), and actually drew the attention of Donald Trump (okay, admittedly not typical). This hoax, like my birth and many other epic events, took place in the flyover states' undisputed capital, Chicago.

On November 14, 2016, Taylor Volk, a student at North Park University in the city's Albany Park neighborhood, took to social media to protest an apparent wave of unprovoked hate incidents targeting her. The sophomore, who describes herself as openly bisexual, claimed first that she had found a "hateful note" taped to her dorm room door the previous Friday. The anonymous note, written in black marker, read "Back to Hell" and "Trump." It also allegedly contained a series of homosexual slurs. In addition, Volk claimed to have previously received two similarly threatening anonymous e-mails and experienced some more generalized harassment on campus. So she went public about her situation, not merely posting some of the alleged content to her Facebook page but also apparently contacting North Park University officials. "This is a country-wide epidemic," Volk informed the campus and the local media.[29]

The reaction to Volk's case was even more frenzied than the norm in these cases, perhaps because of its setting in a big town. The school president, David Parkyn, released a statement, vowing, "When student safety is compromised...when institutional values are not maintained, we will respond with resolve." NPU's marketing director also spoke out, striking a similar note: "Any incident that is reported to North Park is taken extremely seriously."[30]

Most students on campus quickly heard about the hate notes, probably as a result of Volk's social media campaign, and responded with alarm. "The fact that somebody reached out to do this to her specifically is shocking," said Kelsey Stevens, a North Park senior. Stevens blamed Trump: "I think those who have these feelings have been emboldened by this election." Even the president himself responded to this incident—and others similar to it—telling supporters "spouting hatred in his name" to "stop it" during a prime-time broadcast of *60 Minutes*.[31] The Volk case was covered by NBC Chicago, *Forbes*, the *Washington Times*, and at least a dozen other sources.[32]

And then it happened. Although details of the Volk investigation are difficult to come by, we know for sure that by November 24, 2016, Volk's complaint had been fully checked out by NPU authorities and found to be a hoax. President Parkyn spoke again—a bit more drily this time—in a public letter to North Park students about the situation, saying: "We are confident there is no further threat of repeated intolerance to any member of our campus community stemming from this recent incident," because "the incident and related messages were fabricated." The discovery of Volk's lies apparently had at least some real-world consequences. With the exquisite politeness that perhaps only a Christian private school can summon up, NPU has responded to inquiries about Volk's status on the campus from myself and others by simply saying she is "no longer enrolled at this school."[33]

This is my own speculation, but Volk's rapid fall from grace may have had something to do with the fact that she apparently never contacted the actual Chicago police about the "threats" against her. Her neglect to notify authorities was in obvious contrast with her public presentation of herself as being in a panic. The Chicago police have stated on the record that none of its law enforcement officers has ever been able to find "any report" from her.[34] This, to me, is a red flag: the person claiming a hate crime makes a big noise on social media, and perhaps contacts a friendly campus police department. But other people and institutions a crime victim might reach out to in a time of genuine stress—city cops, relatives, federal agents, gun stores, travel agents, and coaches—are not contacted. When the person reporting a threat knows it to be false, his goal is to publicize the alleged event rather than to survive it. It is very possible that law enforcement noticed that pattern in this case.

One amusing final note about the Volk hoax: in covering her case, the folks at Campus Reform almost incidentally mentioned some 2016 incidents that were considered to be *real, non*-hoax offenses by academia. One alleged "racial incident" under serious investigation at Edgewood College involved an election-related Post-It stuck to a door that read "Suck It Up!" and included a mild slur.[35] Instead of balling it up and throwing it in the garbage, Vice President of Student Development Tony Chambers responded to the note by saying, "A great deal of fear, sadness, and anger … resulted, for those that gather in (that office). The message was hateful and harmful … it violated every value that this institution considers to be at its core." The Post-It note incident was officially investigated as a hate crime. In another major national case, professors at the University of New Hampshire called for the expulsion of Trump-supporting students who dressed as Richard Nixon and Harambe the gorilla for a campus prank.[36] While I estimate that between 15 and 50 percent of widely reported hate crimes are frauds, these incidents fall among the "real" ones, the ones that are *not* hoaxes.[37]

At least those incidents actually happened. Since Volk's did not, let us leave her in justifiable obscurity and move onto the next hate hoax.

A HATE HOAX FROM ACROSS THE POND:
THE PRO-BREXIT ATTACK THAT NEVER HAPPENED

Mixed in among the many faked pro-Trump hate crimes in fall 2016 was a fake pro-Brexit hate crime. For those of you that pay attention mostly to U.S. domestic affairs, the "British Exit" or "Brexit" was a referendum in Great Britain on the question of whether the United Kingdom should leave the European Union in response to pressures such as mandatory mass immigration from the Middle East. In general, conservatives were pro-Brexit, liberals anti-Brexit. Obnoxious social justice activism knows no boundaries, boys!

This Euro-hoax began on the afternoon of November 15, 2016, when Ann Arbor "wombyn" Halley Bass claimed that a man jumped out and attacked her, "slashing her face with a safety pin" or some similar small sharp object as she walked past that city's Graffiti Alley to see a show at the Michigan Theater. Bass very specifically claimed that her attack was part of the (largely fictional) "surge in hate crimes following the election … a week earlier," and told police that she had probably been attacked because she was wearing a "solidarity pin" associated with the left-wing position on Great Britain's contemporaneous Brexit vote. "The person must have seen the pin and picked on me," said Bass. There was "no other reason why he would target me."

Bass's police report, like many reports in hoax hate crime cases, was remarkably specific and detailed. According to the report itself and to detailed coverage of the incident by the MLive news website, Bass described her attacker as a roughly forty-five-year-old male with a day's worth of stubble on his face, "wearing a black hat pulled low over his face, a grey hoodie with the hood down, and sweat pants." The credibility of Bass' story was further bolstered by the fact that she actually had multiple cuts—superficial but ugly—on her face. The police repeatedly noted "several scratches" when discussing her condition.

Bass did contact the local police, but she also made extensive use of social media to promote her narrative of what had happened outside that theater. According to MLive, she posted about the alleged slashing incident on Facebook "the same day" that she reported the attack to the police and possibly did so before contacting the authorities. Bleeding or not, a girl has to have priorities! Bass's Facebook post went viral regionally, garnering dozens of shares and more than 100 likes. Sounding rather proud, Bass told detectives that her message "blew up a little more than I meant it to," and described the post as an important one, meant to convey that "all people are equal and deserve to have their voice heard and not feel endangered."

And then it happened. On November 17, Bass was called in to the Ann Arbor police department for an interview with not only Detective Robin Lee but also FBI Special Agent Sean Nichol. As I have noted, FBI investigators are to amateur hate crime hoaxers what holy water and elephant garlic are to vampires. This case proved no exception to that rule. During a sometimes rambling interview, both law enforcement professionals noticed some inconsistencies in Bass' story. The very next day, they and other Ann Arbor detectives obtained and "scoured" surveillance camera footage from the East Liberty Street area near the Michigan Theater. Shockingly, none of the law enforcement officers saw Bass anywhere near the alleged crime scene in any of the videos. Later that same day Nichol and Lee questioned Bass again, challenging the veracity of her story and telling her frankly that it seemed to be "over the top."

By the end of a long, tough interview, Bass had confessed. Her story reads like an intentional caricature of campus snowflakes. She eventually told police that she had slashed her own face after being 'triggered' during an undergraduate seminar in women's literature. Quoth she, "I had been in a discussion in my women's lit...and there were a few people in my class that sort of said things that scared me." She claimed, "It was...like I wanted a concrete reason to be scared," and self-harm provided that. Later, in court, she told a similar but slightly different story, explaining that she had been "suffering from depression at the time" of the faux attack and became embarrassed and ashamed after making some superficial cuts on her face. "It was visible, and I was embarrassed...so I made up a story."

Clinical depression is a bear—a serious mental condition that affects a large percentage of Americans at one point or another—and I feel considerable sympathy for Bass. The judge, however, apparently did not. On March 6, 2017, Bass was convicted after pleading guilty as charged to making a false report. According to the last written account of this case I was able to find, her final gambit was to request via her attorney, Douglas Mulkoff, that she be sentenced through the Michigan 15th District's "mental health court" rather than the banal "and now you go to jail" judicial process. Assuming that Bass's mental state legitimately does qualify her for such differential treatment, I wish her luck and hope she receives the care she needs.

One final note on the case: Bass seems to have been inspired to make a false report at least partly by a sense of solidarity with other Ann Arbor residents who had reported serious hate crimes following the election of Donald Trump. MLive points out that she had heard of "other incidents on campus," including the case of a hijabi woman who claimed a white man threatened to set her on fire if she did not take her head-covering off.[38] But—surprise!—most of those cases turned out to be hoaxes too. In the hijab-attack case, Ann Arbor police formally "determined that the incident was a hoax" shortly after Bass's own deceit was uncovered, and they considered prosecuting the hoaxer but for unknown reasons decided not to.[39]

In short, a woman who falsely reported a serious felony was inspired to do so by an almost-honorable sense of solidarity with victims of previous well-known atrocities—who also turned out not to be telling the truth. Such is the American university campus today.

THE MAYBES: FELONY TRUMP HATE CRIMES THAT VICTIMS "CHOSE NOT TO PURSUE"

I have chosen the last cases for this "Trump hate crimes" chapter because they almost perfectly illustrate a point that I touched on above. While a significant percentage of high-profile hate crime allegations are eventually categorically proven to be hoaxes, the fact that a specific allegation is never proven false does not mean that it is true. Many, many cases fall into an intermediate area. This seems to be especially true for hate crimes related to Trump. One of the highest-profile cases from my first data set provides a good example of the genre.[40]

That incident, like many of those in this chapter, occurred on November 9, 2016, just after the presidential election. A Muslim female student at San Diego State University reported that she had been the victim of a strong-arm robbery. According to the student, who shall remain nameless, she was walking down the stairwell in a campus parking garage when two males confronted her and grabbed her school-bag, purse, and car keys.[41] The young woman stated that her car "was … missing when responding officers arrived." So this crime, if true, would be a felony case of grand theft auto. According to this Muslim student, both of the men who accosted her bragged "about President Donald Trump" throughout the encounter, telling her, "Trump is president. Get ready to start packing up and flee!"

She described her attackers as a white male adult and a light-skinned Hispanic adult male.

By now, we know what the university's response was. After President Trump's election, but before the alleged robbery, SDSU's administration had already issued a heartfelt missive bemoaning the Trump election and calling for "campus unity" at this challenging "moment of transition." After the robbery allegations, they issued a *second* statement condemning the specific "hateful act" and reminding all students, "Hate crimes are destructive to the spirit of our campus. We urge all members of our community to stand together in rejecting hate!" (Yes, yes. Despite that college's frenzied panic about the purported hate crime, the mascot of SDSU is not only a Native American, but literally an Aztec in full historical warrior gear.)

The robbery story also ran in the *Daily Aztec* student newspaper, in a page-long article by senior Will Fritz, and attracted at least a few TV news crews to the campus. College Republicans even issued an apologetic statement—in full-on cringe mode—the day after the supposed attack. This one read, in part: "We understand that the GOP does not have the best reputation in this country, and we understand the perceptions about us. But, our club does not condone these events. Nor will we stand idly by as our Muslim peers are harassed or molested. This needs to stop." The overall mood on campus was perhaps best summed up by Aisha Sharif, a senior sociology major and good friend of the alleged victim. Sharif said,"I think this absolutely relates with [Trump's victory]. It's sad that it hasn't even been 24 hours since he's been elected and we're already getting this type of hate."[42]

The horror! The humanity! A highly focused police investigation into the student's charges began almost immediately. And then it happened...well, in this case, only maybe. The police were quickly able to verify that major aspects of the alleged victim's story were simply not true. For example, her report of a felony car theft was false. According to SDSU Police Lt. Greg Neil, "The student's report of a stolen vehicle was unfounded, since the student forgot where she had parked." In other words, cops soon found the missing car unscathed, parked several spots away from where the student remembered leaving it. Using common sense, we can only assume that no keys or access fobs had ever actually been taken from her. Perhaps by now a bit suspicious, police announced plans to move forward with a comprehensive investigation of all questions remaining in the case by "looking at all surveillance video" from the garage, contacting the victim as often as might prove necessary, and attempting to verify multiple statements "relevant to the entire case."

In perhaps a completely unrelated coincidence, the student picked this moment to decide that she no longer wanted to pursue justice for herself. In early January 2017, SDSU police stated publicly and NBC News reported that the young woman had decided not to pursue any charges in the case. Police sources described the student as not "willing to testify" and said she "no longer wanted to pursue the matter criminally." She actually appears to have stopped working with police several weeks earlier, with officers noting that they had already suspended the case because "the victim no longer wants to cooperate" and was not doing basic things like answering phone calls.[43] It seems fair to say that shortly after officers discovered that her car was not stolen, the student dropped off the map and stopped assisting with the investigation into the purported crimes against her.

Another case often reported in panicked early reports about the post-election "wave" of pro-Trump hate crimes concluded in a basically identical manner. On November 10, 2016, Philadelphia's Villanova University launched a probe into the allegations of a Black female student who claimed she was knocked down and assaulted by a mob of white men yelling "Trump! Trump! Trump!" By December 3, however, the University had closed the probe—after police got involved and the student unequivocally said "she no longer wanted to pursue" the matter.

In a bravura performance, Villanova spokesman Jon Gust managed to answer almost literally no questions when speaking to the *Inquirer* and other Philadelphia news sources. Among other things, Gust declined to say whether he thought the incident actually happened, why the student no longer wanted to cooperate, and whether the university knew the identities of any of the males allegedly involved. He also had nothing to say about "what the university's probe into the matter uncovered." Gust closed simply: "We're not going to comment on what occurred." He broke from opaque bureau-speak on only one occasion, taking a long moment to laud diversity and note that academics must be ever on the alert for racism, whether the alleged evidence for it is real or not, saying that the closure of the investigation "[did] not diminish the concerns and discussions that have taken place on campus, as they have in many places, and that have led to some important dialogues on campus."[44]

Sure, Jon. That said, it must be noted that neither of the questionable hate crimes just discussed has been proven to be a hoax. Neither would fall into the category of "demonstrably false" hate allegations that the University of Wisconsin recently concluded make up roughly 15 percent of all campus hate crime reports, or the block of hate crimes I coded as "proven fakes" when working on my data sets 1 and 2. One or both could theoretically have actually occurred.[45]

Readers will simply have to make up their own minds about how likely this is. Do people very often truthfully report that someone violently stole their car, only to have it turn up unscathed twenty feet from their usual parking space?

If cases like these were added to the statistics, the University of Wisconsin's 15 percent estimate would have to be revised upward—dramatically.

Chapter Six

FAKE RELIGIOUS, ANTI-LGBT, AND GENDER BIAS INCIDENTS

Most hate crime hoaxes are perpetrated by college students and POC radicals. But false reporting appears to be very common across all categories of hate crime allegations. Both my data sets and the Fake Hate Crimes set contain literally dozens of hate hoaxes perpetrated by individuals who initially claimed they were targeted because of their status as Muslims, Jews, lesbians, or gay men. On the one hand, some of these incidents, such as the burning of Velvet Ultra Lounge or the murder of Iraqi Resistance figure Shaima Alawadi, are among the best-known cases in this book. On the other hand, I may be the first writer to comprehensively document the astonishing case in which virtually the entire "epidemic" of threatening calls to Jewish Community Centers reported after the 2016 election turned out to be a hoax orchestrated by two men—Black American Juan Thompson and a nameless Israeli hacker now in custody. The reality of actual violence against gays or Muslims, as opposed to spoiled college kids, means that hate crime allegations against members of these groups should be treated with even more than normal seriousness by law enforcement. But fraud is near normal here as well.

It is a *fact* that, unlike 6'3" Black guys or campus PETA marchers, social minorities such as gay men frequently do experience real incidents of hate-based violence. Social scientists Caitlin Ryan and Ian Rivers note that, of gay people nationwide, 44 percent report experiencing serious sexual orientation-related threats, 30 percent report being followed or chased, and fully 80 percent report verbal abuse in environments such as schools and locker rooms.[1] Homophobic violence was the most frequent sort of hate crime legitimately reported in the United States through the early 1990s, despite the small size of the gay community.[2] Until quite recently, such behavior was not effectively punished by society at large. I recall reading as a high school student in 1995 that a Midwestern judge had made headlines for asking whether gay-bashing was "actually a crime."

But two things can be true at once. The huge majority of serial killers are white, but very few Caucasian men are serial killers. And while there are many hate crimes against gays and Muslims, many hate crimes reported by gays and Muslims are hoaxes. American Muslims, in particular, seem very likely to falsely report hate incidents. According to the Fake Hate Crimes data set, 31 hate crime hoaxers out of 269, or 11.5 percent of all hoaxers, were American Muslims of Middle Eastern or South Asian descent. In my own Data Set 2, 34 hoax perpetrators out of 409, or 8.3 percent of all hoaxers, were Muslims.

These are remarkable figures. While around ten percent of all serious hate crime hoaxers over the past decade or so have been Muslim Americans, less than one percent of Americans are of Muslim faith. Statistically speaking, members of this small population are 4.24 times (424 percent) more likely than Black Americans and 24.14 times (2,414 percent) more likely than white Americans to fake hate crimes. These fakes are no morally better or worse than hoaxes perpetrated by whites or Blacks, but they are more common.

A CAIR PACKAGE: THE NATIONALLY PUBLICIZED GROCERY STORE "TORCHING"

One of the most initially horrifying anti-Middle Eastern "hate crimes" took place not far from where Rachel Dolezal reported her seven allegations of vile graffiti and nooses in the garage, in the mid-size but diverse Washington city of Everett.

During the early morning of July 9, 2004, that city's popular Continental Spices Cash and Carry, a grocery store specializing in Indian, Pakistani, Arabic, and other Middle Eastern food staples, was almost entirely destroyed by a fire. The three-alarm inferno caused an estimated $50,000 in damages. After putting out the roaring blaze in proper heroic fashion, firefighters found significant evidence that a hate-based arson had taken place, including an empty and half-burned can of gasoline, "a spray-painted obscenity" targeting Arabs, and a white Christian cross drawn on one wall. The manager and part-owner of Continental Spices, Mirza Akram, was discovered near his ruined business in a deeply traumatized state. Rupinder Bedi, the manager of the 7-11 next door, found him in tears. Akram told Bedi that he had recently been harassed by a group of Caucasian customers, who didn't stop their abuse until the grocer threatened to call police. Akram suspected these same men of being behind the burning of his store.

Like most flamboyant hate crime reports, this case immediately generated considerable regional media attention. The *Seattle Times* ran a story, as did the *Everett Herald*. The latter paper included a fair-sized block of doomful quotes from Akram, including his comments that some local men were angry because "he had been born in

Pakistan," and his theory that the fire had been set "in retaliation for attacks on Americans in the Middle East." However, the Continental Spices fire became a truly national story when it attracted the attention of the Council on American-Islamic Relations (CAIR), a NAACP-style advocacy group that claims to represent the interests of American Muslims. The day after the fire, July 10, CAIR issued a national press release decrying the "arson attack" on Continental Spices. Titled "Arsonist Torches Muslim Store," the presser demanded that all "national leaders address the issue of growing Islamophobic prejudice." Cameras swarmed to Everett, and headlines and a police investigation followed.

And then—well, you know the story by now. On August 19, following a comprehensive investigation including multiple suspect interviews, police got their man, arresting Akram in his store on federal arson charges. His story was a complex and bizarre one. A genuinely hard-working immigrant businessman—although perhaps not the ideal instructor for a business ethics class—Akram had been in the process of buying Continental Spices from Seattle's Z.A. Trading Corporation. He was doing so on a long-term installment basis and, having already paid $52,800, owed less than $35,000. But several factors, including a regional economic downturn and a possible *actual* backlash to the Iraq War, had caused sales at the store to drop from $11,000 per month in 2003 to $3,000 per month in 2004. No longer able to make both the $640 monthly purchase payment and the $1,200 monthly rent, Akram chose to "stage an arson and make it look like a hate crime."[3]

Although driven to crime by financial hardship, Akram frankly does not seem to have been any good at it. The arsonist he employed, Naveed Khan, was a U.S. Navy sailor and family friend who required at least two separate visits to the store to set the joint on fire. (Pro tip: sailors specialize in *water*.) On the second occasion, Khan almost killed himself Richard Pryor–style, dropping burning incense into a pool of gasoline and narrowly escaping the resulting explosion. Akram and Khan left a trail as wide as a cattle drive, with phone records obtained by police showing eleven calls between the two men "between midnight and 4 a.m. … the day of the fire." Most laughably, Akram made the rookie mistake of not checking the fine print of his insurance policy. Perhaps because of the ongoing transfer of ownership, the insurance policy did not cover the store building, and Akram essentially torched his own business for *nada*. Akram was duly convicted of arson after a one-day trial and sentenced to four years in prison.[4]

While the bumbling arsonist Akram is a somewhat sympathetic character, CAIR strikes me as less so.[5] The organization appears to have a substantial history of publicizing dubious or false hate crimes. On July 14, 2006, for example, CAIR headlined its national website with the banner "Blast at Arab American Restaurant Suspicious," and described in detail the plight of Musa Shteiwi, a Muslim American restaurateur whose business had been destroyed in an apparent act of arson. When police demonstrated that Shteiwi had burned his own eatery, the story vanished: "CAIR went silent."[6] In May 2010, CAIR brought eight complaints alleging various forms of bias and shoddy treatment against the St. Cloud, Minnesota, school district. Seven were rapidly dismissed. And so on.[7]

It is deeply depressing to see some recent immigrants adopting the Continuing Oppression Narrative and attempting to find success in the United States via a strategy of protest and half-baked claims of oppression, rather than by means of the hard work that has made so many immigrants of all races successful. Let us hope that the contagion does not spread—that viewing life in the world's richest nation as "genocidal oppression" does not infect more striving immigrants of color.

Only time will tell. Akram's prison sentence recently concluded. Let us hope that jailhouse ramen kept his taste for foreign food alive, he has started another successful business, and he chooses not to burn this one down.

"CONCERNED CONSERVATIVE CANADIAN" CRACK-POTTERY: THE CONCORDIA COLLEGE CAPER

Another apparent hate attack on a peaceful Muslim resident in the West, arguably even more offensive than the Continental Spices torching, took place in Canada during early 2017. Fortunately, this one did not actually happen, either.

On March 1, an unknown entity calling itself the Council of Conservative Citizens of Canada sent a letter to a number of major Canadian media outlets, threatening to "DETONATE once per day a small artisanal … explosive device where Muslims hang out." (That has to be the most casual terrorist threat ever made.) The missive specifically referenced President Trump: "Now that Trump is in office south of the border, things have changed." (Note that to Canadians, the diverse and crime-ridden state "south of the border" is the United States.) The letter described Muslims as legitimate targets for violence, noting that "[our] only aim is to injure some Moslem students," and actually apologizing in advance for the fact that "unfortunately some non-Moslems might be collateral damage." A widespread perception among members of the Canadian media was that the Council of Conservative Citizens was an offshoot of the American racialist group known as the White Citizens Council, which was referred to repeatedly by church shooter Dylann Roof in his rambling "manifesto." The online magazine Vice described this connection as possible.

Coverage of these bizarre threats was widespread throughout the frozen north, where the only competing major story at the tail end of a Canadian February was a series of polar bear attacks in suburban Montreal. (Okay, that—unlike February in Canada—is a joke.)

Multiple media outlets ran feature stories. On the campus of Concordia University, one of Canada's largest four-year colleges and a location mentioned by name in the threatening letter, panic reigned. Three of the largest buildings on campus were evacuated on March 1, and all classes scheduled during the business day were canceled. Dozens of police officers were "on-site, investigating" within hours of the media outlets receiving the letters. The consensus was that an anti-Islamic hate crime had occurred, with a larger one in the works. The Concordia University Muslim Students Association released a statement demanding that law enforcement investigate the letter as a hate crime. "A threat against one of us is a threat against all," the group declaimed.[8]

Then it happened. Following an investigation that apparently included suspect interviews and fingerprint analysis, Canadian police got their man, literally the day after the threatening letters were received. He was, of course, not an alt-lite, right-wing, white Canadian. Instead, the Canadian Broadcasting Corporation (CBC) announced the arrest of one Hisham Saadi, a forty-seven-year-old immigrant student of Lebanese origins. Saadi was taken down by a massive-force operation, including double-digit numbers of elite Montreal SWAT and canine officers, who descended on his modest apartment in the Darlington Avenue area in the early afternoon. Probably wisely, Saadi, a candidate for a Ph.D. in economics, went along without resistance. He was charged with a laundry list of serious crimes, including criminal mischief, making terrorist threats, and "carrying out a terror related hoax." Saadi was sent directly to jail pending a bail hearing and, unsurprisingly, ordered to undergo a full psychological assessment before any further legal proceedings.

The reaction on Concordia's campus to the arrest was entertaining. Quite a few students simply refused to believe that the culprit was a POC. Aouatif Zebiri, a Concordia University student and member of the Muslim Students Association, clung hard to the fact that the original threatening letter had come from a group calling itself the Council of Conservative Citizens of Canada, which claimed to be white nationalist in its political leanings. "Since it's still unclear if the [Middle Eastern] man who was arrested ... is linked to that group," Zebiri argued, it did not yet make sense to start "feeling reassured." Perhaps unclear on the concept of a hoax, she declared that she for one would not "be going to the buildings that were targeted anytime soon."

Along with many of her peers, Zebiri also complained about the 'insensitivity' of Concordia's resuming classes only one day after the hoax terror threats. "Students had been through a traumatic experience. How do you expect them to go back to school[?]," she asked. Some undergraduates, while continuing to insist that the real mastermind behind the letter incident was a white male still on the loose, also bemoaned the presence of additional security officers on campus following Saadi's hoax. "Students from minority groups may feel uncomfortable with having more...guards around," one of them opined.[9]

While the usual nonsense went on amidst the leafy groves of academe, grown-ups in the justice system continued apace with the prosecution of Saadi, who was the only suspect in the case. Saadi was released on bail but banned from coming within a hundred meters of a college or university campus.[10] Ultimately, Saadi "admitted he sent the threats in an effort to avoid having to write a mid-term exam," was convicted, and received a jail sentence of eighteen months.[11]

In an ironic twist, in the time between his arrest and his trial, Saadi became afraid of being attacked by right-wing terrorists or activists in revenge for his hoax. According to the CBC, after receiving threats following widespread reporting on the case, he was so afraid for his safety that the court and media outlets were asked to reveal no information about his whereabouts.

As it happens, I have Saadi's probable current address. However, I will not publish it here; it would not do to have someone send him a nasty letter!

INSULT TO INJURY: A DOMESTIC MURDER PLUS A HOAX

Unlike the last two cases, one recent anti-Muslim hate hoax contains no elements of humor or whimsy. The brutal murder of Shaima Alawadi deservedly attracted global attention and ratcheted up tensions between POC and whites, before being revealed as the work of an estranged husband rather than a bigot.

On March 21, 2012, Fatima Alawadi stumbled across her mother's unconscious body in the family dining room. Shaima Alawadi had been beaten literally to a pulp, struck so hard that the bones in her skull had shattered in multiple places. Next to her bleeding body was a note that read: "Go back to your own country." She survived a trip to the intensive care ward at the local hospital, but her condition continued to worsen, and family agreed to take her off life support on March 24, 2012. The cause of her death was listed in medical records as severe head trauma.[12] Because of the discovery of the anti-Middle Eastern note, and because Alawadi wore a hijab, police began to investigate the attack as a hate crime.[13]

Like the Black church burning discussed two chapters previously, this was a difficult case to write about. The violent abuse of a woman is always horrible, and the victim in this situation appears to have been something of a hero. Shaima Alawadi arrived in the United States from Iraq in 1993, after her family fought in the uprisings of moderate Shiite Muslims who were brutally suppressed by Saddam Hussein. The Alawadis continued their resistance to the dictator stateside. According to multiple sources, several members of the Alawadi family "worked for the U.S. Army training soldiers who were to be deployed to the Middle East." Shaima Alawadi herself apparently sometimes assisted with this effort, but she preferred to think of herself as a housewife—volunteering at local charities and religious centers and raising five children.[14] Her death was a great tragedy.

Because of Alawadi's status in her community and the brutal nature of her killing, her murder made international news. The U.S. State Department offered formal condolences, and Iraqi government officials attended her funeral. On the activist left, many commentators attempted to link Alawadi's death to the "murder" of Trayvon Martin, which had taken place less than a month earlier. Just as Martin's trademark hoodie was said to have contributed to "racial paranoia" on the part of the Hispanic man who shot him, Alawadi's hijab, clearly tagging her as Muslim, was argued to have served as a red flag to the person who beat her to death. In the *Washington Post,* Elizabeth Flock noted approvingly that the temporally proximate deaths of Martin and Alawadi had inspired at least one large-scale "Hoodies and Hijabs" rally. Preparations for the law enforcement investigation into the Alawadi matter were massive in scale and unsurprisingly centered on the working assumption that it had been a hate crime motivated by Islamophobia.[15]

And then it happened. Local police, assisted by the FBI, discovered records indicating that Alawadi was considering filing for divorce from her traditional-minded Muslim husband and moving from San Diego to Texas. When officers began investigating Kassim Alhimidi as a suspect, evidence against him rapidly began to pile up. Alhimidi had apparently been angry for months about his daughter Fatima's relationship with a Christian man and was attempting to arrange a marriage between her and a cousin in Iraq, which the women of the house vigorously opposed. Actual divorce papers were found among Shaima Alawadi's possessions, and multiple screaming fights between her and Alhimidi were reported by witnesses.[16] Most damningly, a brave relative of Shaima's came forward to say that she had actually heard Kassim apologize to his wife for what he had done "when she was in the hospital dying." After the focus of professional investigators finally and fully shifted away from fantasies about hoodies and white vigilantes to an abusive husband under the same roof, Alhimidi had little time left as a free man. He was arrested on November 8 and charged with his wife's murder.[17]

From that point, the case turned from tragedy to something of a farce. Claiming that they needed to "look through [the] evidence," defense lawyers delayed the trial for nearly two years, into late spring 2014. When it finally did get underway, Alhimidi pled not guilty and insisted on taking the stand in his own defense. As a result, as Listverse noted, "The...proceedings turned into a circus," as "Kassim's outbursts and antics halted the trial." Much of the early testimony at trial focused on "the actions of...Fatima," and retrograde concepts such as honor killing, rather than the actual murder. Much later, when a sentence was finally announced, Alhimidi's sons reacted so violently and angrily that police deputies had to drag one of them out of the courtroom. By the end of the hotly contested trial, Fatima Alawadi had refused to participate further, sending the court a short statement "showing her disgust" with both her father's actions and the complicated legal process.

After all that, however, the system worked fairly well, with Kassim Alhimidi being sentenced to twenty-six years to life with limited options for parole.[18] A middle-aged man, he will most likely die in jail. That seems fair enough: a life for a life.

ONE OF THE ONES THAT STARTED IT ALL: CHICAGO'S VELVET ULTRA HOAX

Moving from fake hate crimes against Muslims to fake hate crimes against gay people (sorry: members of the LGBP2TTQQIIAA community),[19] we come upon one of the cases that inspired me to write this book—the 2012 burning of Chicago's popular Velvet Rope Ultra Lounge in 2012.

Velvet Rope entered the national consciousness on June 3, 2012, when the "bar, lounge, and dance-floor experience" in Oak Park, Illinois, an inner suburb of Chicago, was destroyed by a suspicious fire. Firefighters responded quickly to the first reports of the blaze, arriving on the scene at 6:30 a.m. and extinguishing the flames in "minutes," according to Oak Park spokesman David Powers. But the blaze, which had clearly been set by someone and boosted with an accelerant like gasoline or ethyl alcohol, had already done considerable damage. The Velvet Rope was so badly damaged that it never reopened under that name, and neighboring businesses Flat Top Grill and Geppetto's Toy Box also sustained enough fire and secondary water damage that they had to close for months.

The narrative that the burning of the Ultra Lounge had been a hate crime took root almost immediately and ensnared hundreds of thousands of Chicagoans, including myself. While not exclusively a gay bar, Velvet Rope catered extensively to a young and upscale gay clientele, and owner Frank Elliott quickly began arguing that "the bar was targeted because it catered to [the LGBT community]." Shortly after the fire, according to OakPark.com, Elliott stated that he had discovered multiple anti-gay messages "scrawled on the walls" inside the burned nightclub and informed reporters that he believed the fire to have been a homophobic act of arson.

The people of Chicago, unlike those of New York, are not as rude as outsiders like to think. The gay and hipster communities of the city, which *are* as large as outsiders probably think, responded to Elliott's plight with an outpouring of support, and they were joined by legions of allies. A benefit charging at least $20 per head was held at the Hideaway Bar in nearby Forest Park and raised thousands of dollars to support Elliott in his future business ventures. Several of my friends attended, and a substantial chunk of Chicagoland's population, again including me, monitored the case closely to make certain the arsonists were brought to justice. Using insurance monies and profits from the Hideaway Bar fund-raiser, Elliott was soon able to buy *another* bar as principal owner, opening a location called Bonsai in Chicago's Boys' Town neighborhood.

And then it happened. Parties familiar with Chicago's court system, once again including *moi*, became aware that Frank Elliott had been in financial trouble for some time before his club mysteriously burned. By early 2013, multiple parties were suing him for nonpayment of bills. The list included Ellen Betterhausen—a former part-owner of Velvet Rope and Elliott's lender on a large promissory note in 2008—and wholesale food vendor U.S. Foodservice Inc. Lack of money and desperate need for it is probably the major motivation for arson among businesspeople, and state and local investigators began examining whether there existed probable cause to pursue Elliott for that crime. The answer was an emphatic yes.[20]

As Elliot's associates began to flip—including at least one individual facing a DUI charge, who agreed to cooperate with police in a sort of undercover capacity—the real story of Velvet Rope's burning began to emerge. It was a disturbing one. According to the Coalition Against Insurance Fraud's "Insurance Fraud News" (which is apparently a thing), the consensus among cops and prosecutors by November 2013 was that "Elliott and a friend went to a liquor store and bought several bottles of Everclear alcohol. The two doused the bar with the alcohol and spray-painted gay slurs on the walls before igniting the bar ... Elliott then filed a $150,000 insurance claim." (For anyone not lucky enough to have partied at a Big Ten university, Everclear is 198 proof—99 percent—grain alcohol. Essentially, gasoline you can drink.) Largely on the strength of this account, the former club owner was arrested, taken to the Cook County Jail, and charged with two counts of arson and one of insurance fraud.[21]

Given the nature of the criminal counts he was facing, Elliott got off very lightly. By 2015 he had pleaded guilty to one charge of arson and one charge of insurance fraud, and he was sentenced to two years of probation and payment of $107,000 in reparations to two insurance companies. Elliott did not have to serve a single day in jail. So far as I have been able to tell, he is once again a successful businessman.[22]

Elliott's case did have one additional consequence. It got thousands of Chicagoans interested in the phenomenon of fake hate crimes and inspired me to write this book. Let us hope that, long term, that last side effect makes antics like Elliott's far less rewarding and frequent.

PARIS IS (NOT, ACTUALLY) BURNING: ANOTHER ARSON FIRE HATE HOAX

Another hate crime hoax masquerading as an act of anti-gay arson took place just a year after the burning of Velvet Ultra Lounge, in the ambitiously named town of Paris, Tennessee.

This case seemed at first like an absolute tragedy. Joe Williams, a thirty-two-year-old gay man, was by all accounts inordinately proud of his business, Healthy Thyme, a well-reviewed little health-food store with a campily cute name and surprisingly large inventory. On November 20, 2013, he came close to tears while reporting to police (and later insurers) that he had been "beaten unconscious by three men" during a probable "anti-gay hate crime" at the store. According to the *Huffington Post*, Williams claimed that multiple men had entered his store, beaten him nearly to death, robbed his till of $1,200, and written "a three-letter homophobic slur across his forehead in permanent marker." (The reluctance of the mainstream media to publish racial and gender insults often approaches the absurd. We all know what "a three-letter homophobic slur" and "the n-word" are.) The suspects also allegedly set the front rooms of Healthy Thyme on fire, causing at least $5,500 in damages.

Williams blamed the attack on a hostile customer he said he had encountered earlier that same day. This unknown man had entered his shop about mid-afternoon and "asked him about his sexuality" before becoming aggressive and telling Williams that he could no longer patronize Healthy Thyme if the owner was gay. Williams's take was that this unpleasant fellow had returned with reinforcements near closing thyme (see what I did there?) and beaten him badly while calling him "similar derogatory names." Williams seemed terrified by his ordeal, telling reporters, "I just fear for my life. I'm to the point now where I'm worried to even go outside. I live my life as a gay man and wasn't ashamed of it and I just feel that I was targeted for that reason."[23]

Coverage was, as usual, massive in scale. The *Huffington Post* ran a feature piece on the case, and the apparent brutal attack on Williams received prime-time coverage on several news channels, in the pages of *The Advocate*, and (from a critical perspective) on the website The Other McCain. Prominent local citizen Robert Spicer's view of the matter was probably typical of local and national attitudes. "I'm extremely surprised and dumbfounded [about] why someone would do that," he said. "I figured we've come farther as Americans than to disgrace somebody about their beliefs, especially in 2013."[24]

Then a comprehensive police investigation began, and—guess what? It happened. By December 28, 2013, investigative journalist Bob McCain was able to definitively state that Williams had been arrested on a false report charge: "A man who told police he had been robbed and beaten at a Paris health food store a few days before Thanksgiving was arrested after he allegedly withheld information about the incident, and has now been charged."

The proximate cause of Williams' arrest was multiple dishonest "inconsistencies" in his original report. According to Sergeant Ricky Watson, Williams had been given three separate opportunities to explain away contradictions in his story and had consistently failed to do so. When informed that he faced arrest for impeding an active police investigation, he turned himself in at Tennessee's Henry County Jail on December 20. Police were very careful to note—as I do here—that they had not been able to "verify" that absolutely every element of Williams' fire-and-beating narrative was a hoax.[25]

In comparison to false allegations made on college campuses or by racially identified Blacks or whites, fake hate crime allegations brought by religious minorities or LGBT taxpayers seem much more often to be aimed at material gain—such as insurance money or avoiding prosecution for a crime—than at illustrating some obscure moral point. The case studies in this chapter provide several excellent examples of this phenomenon. Frank Elliott pursued a $150,000 insurance payday after burning down his own bar and received more than $100,000. Williams himself went after almost $6,000 in damages, and Kassim Alhimidi faked a hate crime to cover up the murder of his wife. In contrast, many campus or racial hate hoaxers seem to have been motivated by the desire to point out prejudice (which may or may not actually exist).

One counterintuitive explanation for this discrepancy suggests itself. More research is needed to test this theory, but it may well be the case that anti-LGBT and anti-religious hate hoaxes are likely to be more mercenary than ideological because so many *real* hate crimes are committed against gays and Muslims. Recall the Ryan and Rivers data which opened this chapter. The media leans left and almost always covers hate attacks on gays or religious minorities. Faking such a crime is certainly a workable way for a cynical citizen to escape a financial bind. But there is no need for activists to falsify hate crimes against these groups simply to make the point that they sometimes occur. We all know they sometimes occur. In contrast, it is probably accurate to say that real, violent hate attacks against minority students at far-left leaning universities almost never actually happen. In order to justify that new $15,000,000 Chicano student center or fully funded campus visit from Ta-Nehisi Coates, it may sometimes be necessary to fake a little hate.

Moving on, the level of media coverage of the Williams case made possible an empirical comparison between the amount of media coverage given to an initial report of a hate crime and the later amount of coverage of its exposure as a fake. The original report of Williams' beating in Healthy Thyme was covered by at least six major media outlets, including Fox and local ABC. Fewer than half of these outlets ever ran a follow-up story mentioning his subsequent arrest, and those pieces were on average much shorter than the stories in the first wave of coverage.

The *Huffington Post*, for example, ran a page-long feature story on the original accusation, but only a twenty-five-word "update" mentioning that the entire situation had turned out to be a hoax and noting that readers could access another less liberal news site to read about new developments in the case. Reporters at The Other McCain drew attention to this pattern, pointing out that the discovery that the Williams case was a hoax had not been "reprinted in bold headlines" by most of the outlets that "reported the story originally."[26]

Obviously, no single case study is proof that the media generally devote more column inches to "sensational" liberal stories than to responsible follow-up pieces, but this one does provide a very instructive example.

The prevalent social justice narrative may almost always be wrong, but you wouldn't know that from the mainstream media. Let's change that.

THE CAMERA FOR THE WIN: THE WHOLE FOODS HOMOPHOBIC CAKE SCANDAL

One of the most absurd, and frankly funny, recent hate crimes hoaxes involved an openly gay preacher struggling with $27,000 worth of debt suing Whole Foods for allegedly selling him a cake that called him a "faggot."

In April of 2016, Jordan Brown—chief pastor of the Open Door Church in Austin, Texas, a "love and acceptance" focused church with a "particular focus on outreach to lesbian, gay, bisexual, and transgender Christians"—went to his local Whole Foods and asked the grocery store to provide him a cake decorated with the "Love Wins" slogan of the pro-gay marriage movement. According to Brown, the cake was baked and given to him, but an anti-gay slur had been added to the original slogan: the top of the cake read "Love Wins, Fag" in pretty blue icing. Brown did not take this lying down. He recorded and released a tearful video about the incident, showing the offensive cake he had supposedly been given inside a sealed pastry box. The clip went viral, garnering tens of thousands of views.

Brown also filed a lawsuit. In a case brief claiming intentional infliction of emotional distress and seeking substantial money damages, the pastor made some unique legal arguments. Claiming that he had spent a day or more in tears as a result of the cake incident, he argued that the risk involved with a store employing in-house cake decorators is extreme. According to Brown, "The potential for racial, sexual, religious, and anti-LGBT slurs to be written on personalized cakes is high, and Whole Foods knew or should have known that slurs or harassing messages could be written on cakes and then presented to a customer without any oversight or prior warning." Free range cakes being frosted in stores: there oughta be a law!

Whole Foods opted not to simply pay out money to end the bullshit. Put in the difficult position of having to prove a negative, the company managed to do so inside a month. Stores, especially high-end stores where king prawns and elephant garlic are sold by the quarter pound, have surveillance cameras in them. As a result, Whole Foods' corporate office was quickly able to obtain video footage from the store location in question. And it showed that Brown had made up his entire story; the surveillance video had captured a content-looking Brown checking out of the store with a normally decorated cake in a sealed box. In online discussions of this case, multiple employees and supporters of Whole Foods have pointed out the obvious: customers get to *see* cakes before they accept and pay for them, and very few professional bakers are going to risk losing a union job by turning out a profane cake that insults the guy standing right in front of them.

Equipped with actual, you know, evidence, Whole Foods immediately threatened a countersuit, claiming that Brown had "intentionally, knowingly, and falsely accused Whole Foods and its employees of writing (a) homophobic slur ... on a custom made cake." Facing unexpectedly stiff opposition, Brown panicked and gave up his case. Business Insider's Hayley Peterson quoted him as saying unequivocally, "The company did nothing wrong." Instead: "I was wrong to pursue this matter and use the media to perpetuate this story."[27] Brown went on to apologize to Whole Foods as a corporate entity,

to the store's employees and team members, and to the totally innocent bakery associate who had apparently been fired because of
Brown's original lie.

Clearly, as demonstrated by Brown's rapid retreat from his original set of charges, the best defense against phony hate crime accusations is a thousand-pound offense. Whole Foods, more merciful than
I would have been, abandoned their legal action against the abashed
hoaxer. In a company statement quoted at length by Julie Zauzmer
in the *Washington Post*, the company said, "We're very pleased that
the truth has come to light. Given Mr. Brown's apology and public
admission that his story was a complete fabrication, we see no reason
to move forward with our countersuit to defend the integrity of our
brand and team members."[28]

Like most anti-gay hate crime hoaxes, Brown's actions would
seem to have been motivated by the simple desire for money, rather
than any kind of higher purpose. Easily available records show that
he owes more than $25,000 in student loan debt and has been sued
for non-payment on at least one previous occasion. Lawsuits usually
lead to money damages, and a bold-faced stunt like the one he pulled
must have seemed like a rare opportunity for the pastor of a small
and left-leaning storefront church to make good "bread."

Well, let him eat cake!

RAINBOW DRAGONS AND RELENTLESSLY GAY YARDS

A similar case popped up in Baltimore in 2015, when a young
bisexual mother raised $43,000 after claiming that neighbors had
denigrated the sexual orientation of her backyard.[29]

Julie Baker, a Maryland single mother of four, claimed she had
discovered a note on her front gate criticizing her pro-LGBT yard
decorations. Referring to the multiple strings of rainbow-colored

lamps Baker used to spell out "love" and "ohana" ("family" in Hawaiian), the note referred to her yard as "relentlessly gay." It went on to say, "Myself and Others in the neighborhood ask that you Tone It Down. This is a Christian area and there are Children. Keep it up and I will be Forced to call the Police on You! Your kind need to have Respect for GOD."

In response to this hateful attack on her sexuality, Baker initiated an internet fundraising campaign. The stated purpose of her GoFundMe campaign, for which she set a minimum goal of $5,000, was to "make my home even more relentlessly gay." Her initial pitch for cash is entertaining enough to merit quoting in full. Quoth Baker, "I need more rainbows. . . . Many, many more rainbows. So, I am starting this fundraiser so I can work to make my Home even More 'Relentlessly gay.' If we go high enough, I will see if I can get a Rainbow Roof! Because my invisible relentlessly gay rainbow dragon should live up there in style! Put simply, I am a widow and the mother of four children...and I WILL NOT Relent to Hatred. Instead, I will battle it with whimsy and beauty and laughter and love, wrapped around my home, yard, and family!!! Thanks for your relentlessly gay support!"

Witty, to be fair. Initially shared only among Baker's circle of friends, her appeal for money struck many people as entertaining and rapidly went viral. Set to "public," so that essentially anyone on the internet could see or contribute to it, her GoFundMe page was being shared by major LGBT websites within two to three days of its creation on June 16, 2015. Star Trek star and geek icon George Takei posted it to his personal Facebook page, adding a sympathetic blurb to the link. Within six days, Baker's campaign had raised almost $45,000—and the donations kept flowing in. Her rainbow dragon (or her actual daughters) seemed at the very least to be well set up for college.[30]

And then it happened. Internet sleuths noticed that Baker's GoFundMe demonstrated exactly the same kind of grammatical mistakes as the original warning note she claimed to have received. The *Daily Mail* pointed out that the strange capitalization of the words "home," "relent," and "hatred," among others on the GoFundMe page, mirrored the rather unique capitalization and punctuation also noticeable in the original note.

This correlation prompted the myth-busting website Snopes to launch an investigation into the Baker case. The Baltimore police detective assigned to investigate Baker's claims told the net-based investigators that the alleged victim had done essentially nothing to help the investigation. She was "unable or unwilling" to produce the letter itself, maintaining that it was for some reason "no longer in her possession," and she had missed at least one scheduled meeting with detectives.[31] That would seem to indicate that Baker's original story was a hoax, though this has never been legally proven. You be the judge!

It is worth commenting on the involvement of both a detective-level police officer and one of the internet's leading websites with a case in which—even on the unlikely assumption that Baker's story was true—almost nothing actually happened to Baker or her gender-bending yard. Literally all that even *might* have occurred in this situation was that a Christian neighbor asked a gay neighbor, rather rudely, to turn off her lights at night.[32] After being offended by that request, the LGBT neighbor was able to raise *forty-five thousand dollars* from total strangers, and a big-city police department got involved in the case. Incidents such as this one—not to mention the recent sentencing of a Florida man to fifteen years in prison for leaving a pound of bacon in a mosque—are reason to be concerned that the U.S. is moving toward the sort of hyper-restrictive "hate speech" codes already adopted by many European nations.[33]

Let us hope not. At any rate, in the wake of the police and Snopes investigations, Baker declared that she would give back all the money raised during her GoFundMe campaign to avoid even the "appearance of impropriety." According to Bil Browning in the *Advocate*, she did pause her online fundraising on June 22 and stated that she would use GoFundMe protocols to "return the $43,000" she had raised to the original donors.[34] Actions, however, speak louder than words, and Browning wrote in late August of 2015 that Baker had by that point not returned a dollar, and "did not say when the money…will be returned." So far as I have been able to tell, it still has not been, although I welcome correction on this point.

Hopefully this substantial sum did eventually make it back to the original givers, and neither Baker nor her rainbow dragon managed to burn through it.

VASSAR: THE SEMESTER-LONG GRAFFITI HATE HOAX

In one particularly bizarre hate hoax, a biological woman who identifies as a man also chose to identify as a hate crime victim when he did not happen to be one. This case involved one of the leaders of the Vassar Bias Incident Response Team painting vile graffiti across the campus and then reporting it, essentially to himself.[35] The troubles at Vassar began during October and November of 2013 when, according to The Daily Caller, students and faculty at the prestigious liberal arts college in upstate New York began to notice "a curiously high number of bias incident reports" occurring on campus. Between the September start of classes and early November, at least six genuinely disturbing messages, including "Avoid Being Bitches," "Fuck Niggers!" and "Hey Tranny: Know Your Place," were discovered spray-painted on college buildings and reported to the authorities.

This epidemic of hate was taken so seriously that the campus Bias Incident Response Team (BIRT) sent out an urgent mass e-mail to every Vassar student on November 14, urging calm and noting that an official investigation into the graffiti had begun.[36] Edward Pittman, BIRT coordinator and dean of the College of Campus Life and Diversity, said in the message, "This is unacceptable. Members of our community should be able to work and learn in environments that are free of hurtful expressions and behaviors." A somewhat utopian goal.

So far, so typical. In this case I will skip my usual set-up paragraph describing the campus outcry and media coverage generated by BIRT's missive—by this time we know the drill—and jump straight ahead to where things got weird. BIRT's investigation apparently began swiftly and was conducted with rather surprising competence. It produced what I would consider to be the predictable result. Only five days after the original e-mail was sent, Vassar President Catharine Hill announced that "the bias incidents"—apparently all of them, although there was some confusion about this early on—"were hoaxes perpetrated by two students." She described the fraud forthrightly and honestly, without any talk about its being (say) the inevitable result of the lived experiences of brown bodies on our racist and hetero-sexist campus, stating: "It is our unfortunate duty to report that two Vassar students have admitted responsibility for creating a number of recent bias and hate-speech messages. They also falsely reported these ... Sadly, our community has been deeply hurt by these actions."[37]

The students involved were not just random members of the Vassar community trying to make a political point. One of them seems to have played a very secondary role in the entire stunt, and I will not name her here. The senior of the two, however, was campus leader Genesis Hernandez. Hernandez, a transgender activist who identifies as a young man despite being biologically female, was vice president of Vassar's powerful student government and the sole student member of the BIRT at the time of the graffiti hoax. As the holder of these positions, Hernandez was thus literally painting graffiti all over the campus he played a role in running, reporting these incidents to himself, and then playing a leading role in investigating his own crimes.

Hernandez was not arrested or charged. He was forced to step down from the vice presidency and the BIRT post and subsequently to leave Vassar.[38] My suggestion: go West, young man, and apply somewhere else.

The Hernandez case, like those previously mentioned involving a collegiate homecoming queen, a high-end personal trainer, and a prep school student body vice president, illustrate an interesting and important point. The individuals faking hate crimes on the modern campus are not moody losers or rebellious outliers. They are respected core members of the campus community in leadership positions. At the University of Missouri, the young man who falsely claimed to have seen KKK fighters on campus was the *student body president,* Payton Head. The people hunger-striking and canceling games to support him were, respectively, a multi-millionaire and the members of the men's varsity football team, which plays in the elite Southeastern Conference.

Their actions reveal the true power of the Continuing Oppression Narrative. These popular leading figures on campus are so invested in the idea that they are oppressed, by white privilege, anti-gay bigots, or whatever, that they are willing to lie and risk their hard-earned reputations to illustrate the (often quite dubious) bigotry they claim to have endured.

Exploring the motives underlying such actions is an interesting process. Some young activists seem to really believe that pleasant places like Vassar College are modern Star Chambers full of ingenious hidden oppression. But I suspect that it is more often the case that posing as oppressed appears to young people as a way to achieve cachet or stand out from the crowd. But with this path to glory often taking a turn toward exposure, disgrace, and even expulsion, the question arises: Would it really be so terrible just to admit that you are a prosperous upper-middle class citizen enjoying every opportunity for success in life?

Seriously: How do we get more collegiate radicals to "identify" as one of those?

"ANTI-TRUMP COMMUNIST ARRESTED FOR JEWISH COMMUNITY CENTER BOMB THREATS"[39]

This chapter, which has so far featured hate hoaxes against Muslim, gay, and trans people, closes with one against Jews. Unfortunately, but unsurprisingly, the chosen people have not proven exempt from either actual hate crimes or the recent wave of fake ones. In one particularly nasty case, a liberal Black man was eventually prosecuted for pretending to be a conservative white woman in order to threaten Jewish children.

The threats began in late February 2017, when an unknown individual called the national headquarters of the Anti-Defamation League using a tone-and-gender voice disguiser, and said that "a C4 explosion" would take place inside the building "within one hour." Several days after this incident, according to *Newsweek* magazine, the same person threatened Jewish Community Centers (JCCs) and Jewish youth centers in Dallas and San Diego, among other locations. On one occasion, the caller talked about "wanting to cause a 'Jewish Newtown,'" a clear reference to the bloody 2012 shooting at Sandy Hook Elementary School. During some of these anti-Semitic calls, the perpetrator gave no name, but in others used the name—well, let's say the name was Theresa Bella. I am changing it slightly to protect a woman who turned out to have nothing to do with the phone threats, but in fact to be another victim of the hoax.

Details around this early stage of the JCC threats case are a bit difficult to pin down (imagine: police don't eagerly explain their full investigative strategies to some smart-mouthed academic phoning from a college campus—disgracia!). But local and federal police got involved with the matter and apparently began to pursue the real Theresa Bella, a woman working in a junior executive role at a social services agency, as their first suspect. However, they rapidly discovered one hell of a complicated back-story. Bella, as it turned out, had an estranged boyfriend named Juan Thompson, who was a former reporter and a complete lunatic. According to *Newsweek*, authorities discovered that Thompson had in the recent past told Bella's employer that she had a serious sexually transmitted disease, falsely accused her of various highly illegal activities, and falsely reported her to the National Center for Missing and Exploited Children for watching child pornography! Bella had already secured at least one order of protection against this nut-case.

Because of incidents like the false STD and child pornography reports, police soon began to suspect that Thompson, a Black guy on the far left, was in some way involved with the anti-Semitic threats initially attributed to Bella. Upon closer examination, many of the threatening messages turned out to have either mentioned Thompson in passing or even to have been designed to look like attempts by Bella to frame Thompson. Thompson himself turned out to have referenced this phenomenon on Twitter, asking on February 24, 2017: "Know any good lawyers? Need to stop this nasty/racist #whitegirl I dated who sent a bomb threat in my name and wants me to be raped in jail."

The pretense that the criminal caller was not Thompson, but Bella trying to set Thompson up, did not hold up for very long. Several of the threatening calls and e-mails were quickly traced back to him by police. An e-mail had been sent to the organization from one of Thompson's computers saying that Bella was someone to watch for: "She is behind the bomb threats against jews. She lives in nyc and [will be] making more bomb threats tomorrow." Within twenty-four hours of sending this message, of course, Thompson called the Jewish organization posing as Bella and made one of his most vile threats. After discovering messages like this, law officers began to move toward their final position on this case: that Thompson had hoaxed the JCCS by posing as Bella-posing-as-Thompson.

Like Tolstoy's unhappy marriages, each hate crime hoax is unique, and several things about this one stand out to me. First, it is worth mentioning that Thompson himself seems to have been responsible for a large chunk of the surge in anti-Semitic hate crimes that allegedly followed the 2016 election. Between the beginning of 2017 and late April of that year, roughly a hundred serious threats, perhaps twenty more than normal, were made against Jewish Community Centers and other Jewish institutions in the United States. Thompson made eight or nine of them. This one person thus was responsible for almost 50 percent of the troubling increase.[40] This is very worth remembering: there are so few real, serious hate crimes in America that the actions of a single activist or lunatic can swell the police blotter enough to create the illusion of an epidemic.

Second and equally important, it is notable that before gaining fame as a hate hoaxer, Thompson spent years as a mainstream media journalist. *Newsweek* and The Daily Caller reported that he was employed by The Intercept as a regular contributor between 2014 and 2016.[41] Thompson apparently kept his job for years despite having been called out for reverse racism by mainstream civil rights groups in 2015. Among other antics, he is alleged to have displayed "hostility toward whites," called all white police officers "evil socio-paths," and described Barack Obama as a right-of-center racist, "a rotten [collaborator] who killed innocent people of color." To give a solid left-wing site credit where credit is due, The Intercept did eventually fire Thompson for dishonest reporting in 2016.[42] But the fact that a major high-traffic website employed an admitted bigot who later gained fame as a hate hoaxer says a lot about the point of view from which media coverage of hate allegations is coming.

Moving back to the legal details of the case, Thompson was arrested by the FBI and local law enforcement in March 2017, in St. Louis County. He was charged with making at least eight bomb and murder threats against Jewish Community Centers, and additionally with the cyberstalking of Theresa Bella.[43] In December 2017, Juan Thompson was convicted and received a five-year prison sentence.[44] Given Thompson's tweet about the conditions in American big-city prisons, we can only hope he spent the months leading up to his trial working out.

THE OTHER SHOE DROPS: THE ISRAELI HACKER AND THE REST OF THE JCC HOAX CASES

Almost unbelievably, the Juan Thompson case was only the *second* craziest recent episode involving hoax hate threats against Jewish community and youth centers. Even more bizarre is the case of the eighteen-year-old Israeli hacker who made more than 2,000 bomb and arson threats to Jewish institutions.

This case got off the ground in October 2016, after a series of disturbing warnings were phoned in to a Jewish institution in New Zealand. According to Fox News, investigators first "struggled to locate" the person behind these threats, but the investigation got a second wind when an individual with similar characteristics threatened Jewish centers in nine American states: Florida, New Jersey,

Delaware, Maryland, Tennessee, Georgia, Pennsylvania, and North
Carolina. The same person also called in a bomb threat to Delta
Airlines, causing the carrier to halt all scheduled flights for a period
of hours and forcing the grounding of an in-air flight carrying the
NBA's Boston Celtics.[45] The *Jerusalem Post* noted that the wave of
threats against the Jewish Community Centers "forced widespread
evacuations" and prompted global concerns about "a resurgence of
anti-Semitism."[46] In the wake of these incidents on American soil, the
FBI "began investigating" and took on a leadership role in the developing international case.

Investigators soon found that all roads led to the holy land. After
some dodging around internet anti-detection tools like the anonymous
web browser TOR, our *federales* found that all of the threats phoned
into our country and Canada had come from Israel. New Zealand
police and agents came to the same conclusion, identifying the address
used to threaten their Jewish center as an Israeli one and contacting
the Israeli authorities.[47] At this point, the assumption of both national
police forces seems to have been that the cyber-attacker was a genuine
anti-Semite, perhaps an Israeli Arab.

The reality turned out to be a *lot* weirder. Despite this perp's use
of "advanced disguise technologies...such as distorting software"
to cover his tracks, Israeli authorities had identified a suspect and
brought him into custody by March 23, 2017. Michael Kadar was
not an anti-Semitic terrorist, but instead a teenage hacker along the
lines of "Zero Cool." A Jew, he seemed to have no problem with
other Jews, but rather to be an internet mercenary who used the
so-called Dark Net to sell cyber-bullying services.[48] For a set fee,
clients of any race or creed could hire him to threaten their old
school, call into an airport and shut it down, distract police with
phony 911 calls on a day the clients might be planning a robbery,
and so on.

This kid seems to have been one lab accident away from becoming a super-villain. In addition to selling prank-call and phone-phreaking services, Kadar "was also accused of using undetectable web network[s] to deal in illegal drugs and sell computer kits to counterfeit official documents, manufacture poisons and explosives, and hack into social media accounts," according to the *Jerusalem Post*. He is also at least alleged to have tried to blackmail several American politicians, once apparently sending Dark Net drugs to the house of Delaware state senator Ernesto Lopez, who had spoken out strongly against the JCC bomb threats, in an attempt to get him in trouble with the law. The teen hacker's businesses were astonishingly profitable, landing him at least $225,000 worth of Bitcoin cryptocurrency and allowing him to employ two other internet operatives as sub-contractors. When the police eventually kicked in Kadar's door, he put up a fight to keep his small empire, drawing first blood before being arrested on initial charges of illegal possession of a weapon, attacking a law enforcement officer, selling drugs, and "possession of pedophile-type materials."

The full scope of Kadar's crimes was staggering. The teen had "made at least 245 threatening telephone calls" to Jewish organizations between January 4 and March 7 of 2017. These hate calls went out globally, but if only a quarter of them were made to destinations within the United States, that would be 60 threats to Jewish Community Centers and similar targets in America. In addition, according to an indictment from the state of Georgia, he was also tied to "240 hoax threats called into schools" in the U.S. and Canada from 2015 to 2016. His business was pretending to be a terrorist...and business was *good*.

Kadar eventually faced a bevy of charges, including extortion through threat, publicizing fake news (wait, why are the folks at CNN and Fox still at large?), cyber-crime, and felony money laundering. His lawyer seems to have been reduced to arguing that his client was crazy, saying on one occasion that "the defendant had a high IQ but the emotional intelligence of a five year old," and on another that he might be suffering from a brain tumor.[49] I personally think it is very unlikely that any "high-IQ" individual just happened to suffer 485 separate insane fugues leading him to phone in murder threats, with each one occurring after he was paid to make the call in question.

In the end, an Israeli court convicted Kadar of making literally hundreds of threats, and that included only the ones he made *after* his eighteenth birthday. Apart from the thousands of crimes he probably committed, another set of figures stands out.[50] Remember that this hacker called in a bare minimum of nine threats specifically to Jewish Community Centers in the United States. As we learned in the last chapter, Juan Thompson was responsible for another eight or nine of the most widely documented calls to Jewish Community Centers in 2017. Simply put, these two men were responsible for essentially all of the widely cited surge in JCC threats in late 2016 and early 2017 that is generally blamed on the election of Donald Trump and attributed to the alt-right.

This has, to say the least, not been widely discussed in the mainstream media. But more than a few sources tacitly admit it. The Wikipedia entry on the JCC threats phenomenon mentions only two individuals, Thompson and Kadar, as having ever faced serious charges in connection with the threats.[51] And the *Jerusalem Post* has briefly noted that "this bizarre case overturned an entire narrative that had formed about an increase in anti-Semitism in the U.S. by placing an American-Israeli [Jew] at the center of the mass anti-Jewish hysteria."[52] So one of the biggest hate crimes propping up the Continuing Oppression Narrative, the alleged attacks on American religious minorities around the time of Donald Trump's election, turned out to be the work of two minority hoaxers.

Chapter Seven

THROWING FUEL ON THE FIRE: MEDIA COMPLICITY WITH HATE CRIME HOAXES

One of the most remarkable things about the symbiotic relation-ship between the mainstream media and hate crime hoaxers is how long a particular pattern of reporting has been going on. When I first began my research, I half expected hate hoaxes to be a phe-nomenon unique to the social media era, the result of activists realizing that few things could get more likes than a YouTube video of a popular campus radical with a perfectly blacked eye ranting against racism. Not so. Laird Wilcox's *Crying Wolf*, published in the mid-1990s, contains nearly as many cases of note as the data set I collected over a similar length of time. In fact, it would appear that the rate of hate crime hoaxes has been fairly consistent for at least the past twenty to twenty-five years.[1] For that entire time and longer, mainstream media coverage of hoax incidents has followed the same template.

The general pattern of media coverage of fake or questionable hate crimes is (1) get wind of a sensationalist allegation of a hate attack; (2) dramatically report it, often on the front page or during prime time; (3) ignore growing evidence that the allegation is a hoax; (4) finally receive indisputable proof that the allegation is a hoax; and (5) run a retraction of the original front-page story on page twenty-six of the Leisure and Pet Cats section. This template accurately describes the coverage of Yasmin Seweid's false claim that Trump supporters attacked her for wearing a hijab—but also the reporting on the infamous rape accusations against the Duke lacrosse team in 2006 and the 1992 claims of Azalea Cooley that "Burn Nigger Burn" had been painted on her house along with a swastika. Though this has been going on for at least three decades, it has apparently never occurred to many reporters and media executives to be suspicious of wildly unlikely hate crime allegations.

To the extent that a single beginning point for this phenomenon can be pinned down, it all started with Tawana Brawley.

THE FIRST AND STILL THE BIGGEST: THE TAWANA BRAWLEY WHITE GANG RAPE HOAX

Probably the most famous hoax hate crime of all time, which made Al Sharpton into a national figure and demonstrated the shocking level of media credulity given to openly absurd hate crime claims, was the Tawana Brawley case. This sleazy case spawned the famous slogan, "Tawana Told the Truth!" But she didn't.

The Brawley case began on November 28, 1987, when a fifteen-year-old African American student—who had been missing for four days from her home in suburban Wappingers Falls, New York—was found "unconscious and unresponsive" lying in a trash bag a few feet from a New York City apartment where she had once lived. The young woman seemed to have been brutally attacked. Her body was smeared with what appeared to be stinking human feces, and her clothing had been burned and torn. After Brawley had been taken to a local emergency room, it was discovered that the words "KKK," "Nigger," and "bitch" had been written all over her body in charcoal. During a subsequent interview with the police—Brawley would only communicate with a Black officer, and only via "gestures and writing"—she claimed that she had been taken to a wooded area and raped repeatedly by three white males, one of whom she described as a police officer, apparently in uniform.

Unsurprisingly, Brawley's allegations caused an international firestorm. The Wikipedia account of the case describes it as having captured almost every "headline across the country" during portions of 1988.[2] Multiple major rallies were held to denounce the attack and demand justice for its "victim." Actor Bill Cosby, years before he himself would be accused of sexual assault by more than two dozen women, helped organize a legal fund for Brawley that raised a substantial amount of money. At least some of this cash wound up paying the legal fees of flamboyant and race-baiting lawyers Alton Maddox and C. Vernon Mason, who rapidly began handling Brawley's public relations alongside civil rights activist Al Sharpton.

It is fair to say that Sharpton, Maddox, and Mason took the Brawley matter to a level of spotlight-seeking rarely seen in American jurisprudence, before or since. On separate occasions, members of the trio claimed that the New York state government was trying to protect potential defendants in the Brawley case, none of whom would ever be found "because they were white," and accused the assistant district attorney Steven Pagones of *being* one of Brawley's rapists. Black Muslim minister Louis Farrakhan also became involved with Brawley's cause around this time, leading a march of more than a thousand activists through a working-class New York neighborhood in support of Tawana.

While all of this entertaining libel and rioting was going on, Brawley's actual legal case was falling apart. A sexual assault kit administered the night of Brawley's admission to the hospital came back negative, turning up no DNA or other evidence of sexual assault "anywhere on (Brawley's) body."[3] More broadly, the young woman had shown no sign of exposure to the elements or to inclement weather, something even the *New York Times* drily noted would be quite unusual for a victim "held for several days in the woods at a time when the temperature dropped below freezing."[4]

As a result of all this, the grand jury refused to indict any of the accused. On October 6, 1988, they went further and took the highly unusual step of issuing a 170-page legal report noting that Brawley was probably lying. According to the grand jury, there was essentially no medical possibility that Brawley had been "abducted, assaulted, raped, (or) sodomized." They explicitly condemned the "unsworn public allegations against Dutchess County ADA Steven Pagones." Among several other findings, the grand jury report pointed out that the epithets on Brawley's body had all been written upside down—a strong indication that she had written them herself—and that the feces on her body had been traced by forensic experts to a neighbor's large dog.[5] The grand jury also pointed to a probable motive for Brawley's lies. Like Yasmin Seweid almost two decades later, she apparently wanted to avoid discipline at home. Brawley seems to have spent at least the first night of her four-day disappearance with a boyfriend, and she feared violence from a strict step-father who disapproved of her spending nights with young men.[6]

The fallout from the collapse of Brawley's case was significant, though it notably did not include the mainstream media's examining its own role in promoting a transparently absurd hate crime narrative for more than a year. Consider what I just said. Brawley accused a uniformed police officer and the *assistant district attorney* of taking her to the wilderness and raping her for days ... and became a *cause célèbre*. If these claims could be believed, are there literally any allegations that could not be?

Even after her story was exposed as a fake, the activist Left essentially refused to believe that Brawley had lied. Generally speaking, even those liberal thinkers who conceded that her actual story was false argued that something similar must actually have happened. In any case, no one should doubt the Continuing Oppression Narrative that her original accusations had played into. Well-known legal scholar Patricia Williams opined that Brawley "obviously was the victim of some unspeakable crime." Issues of racial and gender violence remained to be dealt with "no matter how she got there. No matter who did it to her—and even if she did it to herself."[7] It would be hard to come up with a better short summary of the "ctrl-left" worldview.[8] If a Black woman falsely accuses a group of white men of rape, she must have done so because she was a victim of racism, and whites as a group need to figure out how best to apologize to her.

In contrast, most normal tax-paying citizens of all races were outraged and disgusted by the behavior of Brawley and her legal team. On May 21, 1990, Alton Maddox actually had his license to practice law indefinitely suspended by the state's supreme court following a disciplinary hearing "regarding his conduct in the Brawley case." District Attorney Steven Pagones, for his part, demonstrated why it is generally a bad idea to accuse a government prosecutor of being a rapist and a pedophile; he sued Sharpton, Mason, and Maddox for defamation and won a $345,000 judgment after a series of lengthy procedural delays. Cynical readers may be amused to know that Sharpton's $65,000 obligation to Pagones was not taken care of until 2001—when supporters such as Johnnie Cochran paid it, in order to retire a long-standing embarrassment to the "civil rights icon."[9]

That brings us, two decades after her allegations, back to Tawana Brawley. Pagones also successfully sued Brawley, who apparently did not bother to show up in court and contest his charges. He was awarded a judgment of $187,000 against her, but the *New York Post* noted in 2012 that she had never paid him a dollar.[10] It would appear that at least one judge read the article; roughly one month after the piece appeared, Brawley's wages were ordered garnished, forcing her to at least get started on paying Pagones—although it is unlikely she will ever be able to pay him the entire sum owed.

Some lost income aside, Brawley seems to have escaped any serious fallout from the false allegations that made her globally famous. According to a well-received documentary about her case, *The Tawana Brawley Story*, she works as a nurse in Virginia, has a relatively happy and stable life, and recently converted to Islam. A *Daily News* feature on the twentieth anniversary of her case mentions that she and her parents still contend that the attack on her actually happened. In fact, they recently "asked the New York State Attorney General...and Governor...to reopen the case," so that Brawley can finally receive the justice she deserves.[11]

What a marvelous idea. Let us hope that someday she gets exactly that.

EIGHTY-EIGHT SHADES OF FALSE: THE LACROSSE RAPE HOAX AT DUKE

Perhaps the only hoax hate crime allegation to rival the Tawana Brawley case in global notoriety occurred a bit farther down the East Coast in North Carolina, but also involved a Black woman's claim of gang rape at the hands of privileged white males, a slew of "civil rights" gadflies, and a prosecutor who ended up accused of some very serious offenses. This prosecutor, Mike Nifong of Durham County, was accused by the legal bar and the court system, not the "victim," and was apparently guilty.

The Duke lacrosse rape case began at 1:22 a.m. on March 14, 2006, when Durham police received a report of a heavily intoxicated woman refusing to leave a vehicle in the parking lot of a local Kroger supermarket. Arriving on the scene, officers discovered Crystal Mangum, a twenty-six-year-old African American college student "who worked as a stripper, dancer, and escort," behaving bizarrely. According to police, "Mangum had no identification, would not talk to [officers], was having difficulty walking, and seemed severely impaired." As police prepared to take her to Durham Center Access, a mental health and substance abuse facility, she stated that she had been forcibly raped prior to her arrival at the grocery store.[12]

Mangum claimed that the assault had occurred earlier the same night, technically on March 13, after she had been hired to dance nude at a party held in the home of two of the Duke lacrosse team's then-captains. Mangum's account of her assault was graphic and seemed complicated. Essentially, she claimed that she had been pulled into a small bathroom in the lacrosse house and sexually assaulted by at least three male college athletes. According to the most widely cited version of her account, Mangum stated that she was "suspended in mid-air and...assaulted by all three of them" for a period of at least minutes.[13]

Police began investigating Mangum's claims on March 15 and showed her photo arrays composed of potential suspects on March 21 and April 4, 2006. On the second occasion, she identified Duke lacrosse players Reade Seligmann, Collin Finnerty, and David Evans as her rapists. It is worth noting that the second photo array, during which Mangum identified three Duke lacrosse players as her attackers, included only pictures of Duke lacrosse players. This is, to say the least, not typical police procedure. Photo arrays generally

include multiple images of individuals in no way connected with a
particular case, to test for false positives. By May 15, 2006, all three
young men had been indicted on charges of forcible rape, "sexual
offense," and kidnapping.[14]

The local and national response was predictable, but extreme.
The Duke lacrosse case represents, almost certainly, the best recent
case study example of how the academic Left and the mainstream
media can operate in tandem to promote the Continuing Oppression
Narrative. Even before the indictments, when essentially no evidence
of any lacrosse player's guilt existed, nearly a hundred Duke professors
(the "Group of 88") took out a full-page ad in the local paper stating
that "something" had obviously happened to Mangum and praising
protesters—who had called for the castration of lacrosse team members and blanketed the campus with "Wanted" posters featuring their
faces—"for not waiting."

In his blog entitled "Durham in Wonderland," KC Johnson noted
that mainstream media outlets such as the *New York Times* credulously praised the Group of 88 and local prosecutor Mike Nifong,
creating a feedback loop. He states the obvious: "While not as left-
wing as the typical elite [university's] faculty, the media obviously
leans left, especially on issues of race and gender," and so the facts
presented by Nifong and by Duke's radical faculty "seemed too good
to be false." Many media outlets ended up serving as "de facto ste-
nographers" for the anti-lacrosse side of an active criminal case,
credulously passing on the biased perspective of one side as the truth.[15]
Largely as a result of this sort of coverage, long-term Duke lacrosse
coach Mike Pressler was forced to resign "under threat," and the team
canceled its 2006 season entirely.[16]

And then, despite the professors' and the media's best efforts, it
happened. Crystal Mangum's story turned out to be, forgive the crude
term, horseshit. To outline just a few of the problems with it: her

dance partner and potential prime witness Kim Roberts admitted that, while there had been a short but ugly argument with white lacrosse players at the party, Mangum's story of assault was "a total crock."[17] A police-administered DNA test "definitively" failed to connect any Duke lacrosse player to the alleged rape of Mangum, and a later privately administered test reached the same result—although prosecutor Mike Nifong apparently concealed this exculpatory evidence for at least some time.

The total absence of DNA evidence from Mangum's person was a significant finding, because Mangum was a professional escort and apparently a hard worker. Without "slut shaming," it must be noted that the same series of DNA tests confirmed that DNA from many other unidentified males was found on or inside Mangum. "According to conservative estimates," the lab work revealed that there were "at least two unidentified males' DNA in Mangum's pubic region, at least two unidentified males' DNA in her rectum, at least 4–5 unidentified males' DNA on her underpants, and at least one unidentified male's DNA in her vagina." This last sample has been described as coming from her boyfriend, who may or may not have known exactly how much of an open relationship he was involved in. In this context, it is questionable whether even the discovery of DNA from Duke lacrosse players inside Mangum would have been strong evidence of rape. The absence of any such DNA was the strongest possible legal evidence that no rape had taken place.

Further, Mangum was discovered to have previously made at least one *other* false or unproven rape claim in 1993, against a group of three young males. Further yet, Reade Seligmann, one of the lacrosse players she had accused, turned out to have a watertight alibi including ATM records from the exact time when he was supposedly raping Mangum, "photographs, cell phone records, an affidavit from a taxi driver, and a record of his Duke Card being swiped at his dorm." In the wake of these revelations, the rape charges against the three young men were dropped on December 22, and the entire case was abandoned. The prosecuting attorney even took the remarkable step of declaring all of the defendants actually "innocent" rather than "not guilty," on April 12, 2007.

The Duke lacrosse case stands out among fake hate crime cases because serious consequences actually befell some of the individuals responsible for falsely accusing the three Duke athletes of rape. On December 28, 2006, and again on January 24, 2007, the North Carolina State Bar filed serious ethics charges against Nifong. The disgraced prosecutor was accused of engaging in dishonest conduct such as downplaying the importance of significant DNA evidence and making multiple biased public statements that were "prejudicial to the administration of justice." He was taken off the Duke case totally in late January of 2007, and actually disbarred on June 16 of the same year. He also faced a criminal charge of contempt of court in August 2007 for knowingly making false statements during a criminal proceeding, and he ended up serving one day in jail.[18]

Crystal Mangum, for her part, is in prison to this day, although not for her role in the Duke lacrosse situation. In 2010 she was arrested for attempted murder after attempting to kill her live-in boyfriend Milton Walker, and—in an entirely separate case—she was then arrested for and convicted of actual murder in 2013, after stabbing a *different* boyfriend, Reginald Daye, to death.[19] Being Crystal Mangum's boyfriend seems a risky business.

It is worth noting that the comeuppance of the accuser and her supporters was an almost entirely off-campus phenomenon. The reaction to the case and its aftermath was a bit different inside the hallowed groves of Duke. Alternating between outrage and what I can only read as amusement, KC Johnson notes that many or most of the "Group of 88" signatories have "advanced at Duke," with little or no harm done to their academic careers. Prominent signer Srinivas Ara-vamudan is currently Duke's dean of the humanities. His old ally Lee Baker is a dean of academic affairs. Paula McClain, who signed her name a few lines under theirs, is dean of the graduate school and provost for graduate education, one of the most influential posts on any college campus. Other signatories have moved on from Duke to still "more prestigious posts," including professorships and chairs at Cornell, Vanderbilt, the University of Chicago, and Harvard.[20]

No surprise there, really. Modern American colleges and universities are gonna "modern American college and university," unless and until we stop them.

FIFTEEN YEARS BEFORE DUKE: SABRINA COLLINS AND THE GENESIS OF MODERN CAMPUS HOAXES

One of the contemporary era's largest hate hoaxes predated the Duke lacrosse case by seventeen years. It rocked the campus of Atlanta's Emory University in 1989, nearly thirty years ago, and the mainstream media covered the case just as they would today.

According to the *New York Times*, the Emory hate hoax scandal began in March, when freshman coed Sabrina Collins—a pre-med major from Hepzibah, Georgia—claimed that she had been the victim of a horrific campaign of racial harassment. Collins alleged that one or more unknown individuals had repeatedly entered her locked dorm room, "ransacking" the place, scrawling racial insults on the wall in lipstick and permanent marker, and slipping death threats under her door.[21] On one occasion, multiple items of Collins's clothing were soaked in bleach and apparently destroyed. Even her stuffed animals did not escape the attackers, being "mutilated" during one particularly disturbing raid. As a result of this abuse, friends in the dorm reported that Collins spent hours per day curled up in the fetal

position and had stopped speaking coherently. At one point, she had
to bc hospitalized.

As word of Collins's story leaked out, the *Times* notes that
Atlanta, at that time billed as "The City too Busy to Hate," was
"shocked by her apparent ordeal." And embarrassed by it as well, no
doubt. Hundreds of students held a massive "Rally against Racism,"
perhaps the first of its kind, to protest the abuse of their schoolmate.
Both during and after this event, student organizer Leonard Scriven
denounced the "pervasive system" of genocidal "racism" at Emory.[22]
At least four new Black student organizations took root on the Georgia university's campus during the Collins crisis, including Students
against Racial Injustice (SARI), an official chapter of the NAACP,
and the Black nationalist Brotherhood of Afrocentric Men (BAM).[23]

When Collins returned to campus from her hospital bed, she was
treated like Queen Boadicea rallying her people against the Romans.[24]
Multiple accounts record that literally dozens of student well-wishers
greeted her with kind words and small gifts, and university police
equipped her dorm room with "additional locks, a portable motion
detector, and an alarm system." At least two armed safety officers
were assigned to patrol the hallways of her dormitory. And the campus Department of Public Safety called in not only local but also
federal and state law enforcement to investigate the case.[25]

Collins was apparently less than thrilled with this last action, for
good reason. By June 1, 1990, separate investigations by the Georgia
Bureau of Investigation, individual FBI investigators, the DeKalb
County police force, and the university's security force had *all* revealed
that Collins made her story up. Ralph T. Bowden, DeKalb County's
county solicitor—basically the district attorney, for all you General
Grant lovin', non-grits-eatin' Yankees out there—who had the envi-
able task of reading every word of the police reports and deciding
whether to press charges, summed up the entire situation: "There

certainly is direct evidence, and a great deal of circumstantial evidence, that...Sabrina was the only person involved in these matters. That is certainly the conclusion of the [many] investigating agencies, and I have no quarrel with that." Fingerprint analysis, handwriting review, and several other varieties of costly forensic analysis had all fingered Collins as the sole person responsible for the letters and the damage to her dorm room. It had also become clear that the entire wave of hate incidents began just after Collins went under academic review for cheating in a tough required chemistry class.

The Emory community's reaction to these revelations established the tone for an era. In addition to being one of the first contemporary college campus hate hoaxes, the Collins case also set historical precedents in that (1) Emory decided to do basically nothing to punish Collins for her antics, and (2) many campus activists refused even to believe that she had lied. As Bowden stated, Emory was "inclined" not to push for the prosecution of Collins and he had "no quarrel with [that] inclination." In a letter to the Georgia Bureau of Investigation, Bowden said that Collins "appears to be someone who needs psychological and/or psychiatric treatment," rather than jail time or a fine.

Collins's own lawyer, James W. Howard, continued to make the dubious claim that at least some handwriting analysis had exonerated his client. Further, he argued that the "exonerated" Collins was in fact the chief victim in this entire situation, and not a perpetrator at all: "It is apparent that the person who inflicted this pain and suffering on her is not only free to do it again but has succeeded in evading the investigation." Perhaps O.J. Simpson, now out of prison again, can find that evil bigot after he catches his wife's real killers!

Otis Smith, the president of the Atlanta NAACP, said that the police findings were essentially irrelevant from a strategic perspective. To quote him verbatim: "It doesn't matter to me whether she did it or not, because of all the pressure these black students are under at these predominantly white schools. If this will highlight it, if it will bring it to the attention of the public, I have no problem with that."[26]

I read him as saying: *Hell, racism is still sometimes a problem, and a good newspaper story gets the donations flowing in—who cares if this confused college girl lied or not?* But perhaps I am a cynic and a horrible person.

Nevertheless, it seems fair to say that Sabrina Collins has earned a place in history. To a very real extent she created the template for future campus hate hoaxes: make outrageous allegations, enlist radical allies, receive massive media support, deny everything and claim insanity if caught, and avoid any real punishment. As with baseball fields and mouse traps, if you build it, they will come.

THE PERFECT VICTIM: AN EVEN WILDER STORY IN PORTLAND

After Sabrina Collins came Azalea Cooley. Almost exactly three years after Collins made her accusations in Atlanta, Cooley claimed to be a victim in Portland. The two cases were eerily similar, involving apparently stressed but high-performing middle-class Black women in integrated U.S. cities alleging entire campaigns of protracted racial harassment—which no one else seemed to be able to see. Both cases were covered breathlessly by national media outlets. And, of course, the two situations had one other thing in common: both were total hoaxes.

The Cooley matter began in May 1992, when a wheelchair-bound former correctional officer named Azalea Cooley claimed that graffiti vandals had defaced her house with a swastika and the phrase "Burn Nigger Burn." Shortly after that, she would allege that she had been the victim of another crudely painted swastika, multiple threatening letters mailed or delivered to her home, and a cross actually burned in her yard. On one occasion, to quote *Willamette Week*, she claimed to have found "a black plastic doll on the front porch, with a .38 caliber bullet lodged in its forehead." This went on for weeks, in an apparent sustained campaign of intensive abuse.

Portland, a ridiculously liberal city whose spirit animal is Bill Maher, reacted as you would expect. As the *Willamette Week* put it: "[There was] a reflexive kick of outrage. The mayor, the police bureau, the Urban League, the "No on 9" campaign, the Anti-Bigotry Coalition, the Metropolitan Human Rights Commission—everyone jumped to condemn the attacks."

Community activists rallied to defend the besieged Cooley, who was universally referred to by her first name, "Azalea." Multiple all-night vigils were held in front of her well-kept little home, and one organization set up video cameras on her porch pro bono in an attempt to catch racist raiders in the act. On November 1, 1992, allies held a massive thousand-person "Take a Stand against Hate" rally in the square of Portland's Pioneer Courthouse. It began with a "wombing," a unique ceremony during which Cooley emerged "reborn" from a symbolic representation of female genitalia before leading the crowd in chants. As one local newspaper dryly noted, none of this seemed to work: "The cameras malfunctioned, and the sinister stalkers seemed unperturbed by potlucks and prayer drums."

Police soon found out why that was. By late fall 1992, Portland Police Chief Tom Potter had gone from being baffled about his department's inability to solve the Cooley case to being suspicious that a third party was interfering with the investigation. Without telling anyone, including Cooley, he had a team of investigators set up cameras in a neighbor's apartment, focused directly on Cooley's house. In early November—ironically, within twenty-four hours of the huge Take a Stand rally—the cameras captured a grainy but recognizable image of a woman climbing the steps to Cooley's porch, sticking a foot-long wooden cross into a flower pot, and setting it alight.

Of course, the woman was Cooley. When confronted with the videotapes by detectives, she reacted in a bizarre and violent manner, half-seriously slashing her wrists and winding up hospitalized for a short period of time. A week later, in an impassioned handwritten note, she confessed not only to staging all of the hate crimes but to an impressive range of other lies. As it turns out, Cooley *didn't need to use a wheelchair.* Nor did she have cancer, the disease she had told dozens of rally organizers she was suffering from. She had been "shav[ing] her arms and dye[ing] her eyebrows to simulate the effects of chemotherapy," in order to paint herself to Portland's liberal community as an even more sympathetic victim. In fact, however, Cooley was a healthy former law enforcement officer in early middle age.

Willamette Week writer and partly recovered guilty liberal Chris Lydgate provides a remarkably lucid account of why Cooley's scam worked. The hoaxer was, in his words, "the perfect victim." Cooley was: "lesbian, Black, wheelchair-bound, suffering from brain cancer. It was hard to imagine a more vulnerable target." A fit middle-aged woman who could walk got away with pretending to be a wheelchair-bound cripple for a year because "we wanted to believe her."

In an era forty years after *Brown v. Board of Education*, when there was almost surely very little real racism visible in the anarchist capital of the West Coast, Cooley's story "seemed to confirm a dark, paranoid vision about the forces of hate running loose in America," justifying the Continuing Oppression Narrative. Lydgate even noted a phenomenon on which I have commented throughout this book: "America was so hungry for victims in the early '90s that some activists continued to champion Azalea's case even after she admitted making the whole thing up."

Once exposed, Cooley essentially vanished. She left both Portland and the public eye shortly after writing her *mea culpa*. The *Willamette Week* did manage to track her down not long ago in the blue-collar California suburb of Vallejo, where she described herself as happy: "I have a relationship. I have a dog. I am a normal person. In fact, you couldn't pick me out of the crowd if you saw me walking down the street." With unintentional irony, Cooley said that she did not want to be blamed or "harassed" because of things that had happened in the past.

The contemporary Cooley saga doesn't quite end there, however. Having been asked by Cooley to leave her alone, the newspapermen went door-to-door in the area to canvass a few neighbors. And almost all of them reported that "Azalea does not seem to be in good health. She uses a wheelchair and takes a long time to answer the door. She told them she has cancer—a tumor in her spine."[27] Some things never change.

THE CRAZIEST STORY YOU'VE NEVER HEARD OF: "YOU'LL BE WHITE TODAY!"

Today, it is almost literally impossible to find any online media record of one of the most widely publicized hate hoaxes of all time. But for more than a month's worth of media cycles in America's second city (as we Chicagoans call New York), everyone was talking about the Albanian Bad Boys.

The shock and horror began in January of 1992, when a four-teen-year-old Black boy and his twelve-year-old sister claimed that they had been attacked by a gang of white youths while on the way to school. According to the *New York Times*, the pair stated that four rough-looking white teenagers had robbed them of three dollars, "snipped off ... the girl's hair," and yelled racial slurs at the two young kids.[28] Most notably, the white toughs had splashed the Black children's faces with a pale shoe polish used to make sneakers look newer and yelled: "You're gonna be white today!" These teenage assailants were said to have described themselves as the "Albanian Bad Boys."

It is no exaggeration to say that this incident, which as described was essentially a scuffle between two groups of teens, became one of the most widely covered racial crime stories of all time. The "shoe polish hate crime" made the front page of the *New York Times* and the cover of New York City's *Newsday* magazine. Conservative writer Ann Coulter pointed out that the *Times*'s story was a remarkable 1,228 words long, roughly five pages in length at a normal font size. Accounts of the attack were picked up by the wires from New York media and received prominent coverage in the French, Canadian, and Chinese press, as well as during a prime-time spot on the *MacNeil Lehrer News Hour.*[29]

Mayor David Dinkins, presiding over what was probably America's most lawless and least governable big city at the time, was uniquely horrified by the shoe polish attack. He called it the "most despicable" crime he had ever seen—this in a city with over two thousand murders a year at the time.[30] Dinkins devoted the day after he learned about the shoe polish allegations primarily to responding to them—not only meeting with police and borough officials to plot a law enforcement response, but also calling the children's mother and offering them unlimited free counseling. Dinkins directly ordered not only the police but also New York's Commission on Human Rights to investigate the case, so that "those who committed this outrageous attack are brought to the justice they deserve." In the next few days, a $20,000 reward was offered for any verified information about the attackers, and a twenty-four-hour hotline was set up for anonymous tips.[31]

After a full month of investigation by almost two hundred police officers, New York law enforcement had unearthed exactly zero leads concerning the perpetrators of the shoe polish atrocity. Well-founded suspicion that it had never actually occurred began to mount among police and reporters. On February 7, 1992, the *New York Post*'s Peter Moses pointed out that almost none of the male victim's schoolmates believed the attack had taken place. Several noted that the boy had a habit of blaming his problems on "racism" or "white people" whenever he got in trouble. Moses also pointed out that there was a theater across the street from the alleged location of the attack and that multiple security cameras had picked up no evidence whatsoever of violence occurring during the time the scuffle allegedly took place.[32] Even the generally left-leaning *Times* paused to concede the obvious, with columnist Maria Newman stating on February 6 that one possible explanation for the continuing lack of leads in the shoe polish case was that the kids involved had "fabricated their description of the incident."[33] It is now almost universally accepted that the globally-decried New York shoe polish incident was a complete hoax.

But the fake story had real and brutal consequences. The backlash to the phony story about an attack on two Black kids involved almost one hundred *actual* hate attacks against whites and Hispanics. By January 28, 1992, the *Times*'s Linda Richardson noted regretfully that there had already been sixty-one such incidents. On one occasion, three Black males "vented their rage" at a twenty-three-year-old white guy taking a train into the Bronx, slapping him hard and saying, "This is for what happened [to those kids]." Around the same time, a homeless Brooklyn man named Thomas Peritore was knocked out by a punch—and lost his front teeth—after the two Black men responsible asked, "How about we paint you white, whitey?!" Perhaps most horrifically, a fifteen-year-old white honor student was kidnapped by several Black New Yorkers and raped repeatedly; her attackers allegedly referred to the earlier shoe polish hate crime and said that they had selected her because she was "white and perfect."

In addition to a number of genuinely awful crimes and a good deal of media yap, the "Albanian Bad Boys" incident also inspired many copycat hoaxes. Following both the shoe polish claim and the white student's rape, a twenty-five-year-old Black man from Brooklyn told authorities he had been beaten by five Caucasian males who told him "not to rape any more white women."[34] He later admitted to police that he had been going through a tough time in life and lied to get sympathetic attention from relatives and friends. More charmingly, witty twelve-year-old Hispanic lad Brian Figueroa claimed that an exact repeat of the original shoe polish mauling had happened to him—with several white teenagers attacking him as he waited for the bus to school, painting him white with polish and makeup.[35] Figueroa's case seems never to have been definitively exposed as a hoax, but multiple conservative authors were more than a little suspicious that his first post-report question was, "Do I get to meet the mayor too?"[36]

Like the Sabrina Collins matter, the shoe polish atrocity helped to develop the blueprint for future hate crime hoaxes. The two Black tweens' false allegation of an act of violence against POC caused a backlash of actual acts of violence against whites and an upsurge in other hate hoaxes by canny tricksters of all races. The combination of the original fake allegation and the real, but anti-*white,* wave of backlash crimes was then used by primarily left-leaning reporters to argue that "race relations are problematic in America."

And the more hate hoaxes there are fomenting hostility between minorities and whites, the more problematic race relations in our country will become. Shoe polish-style hate hoaxes continue to occur in contemporary America, followed by similar backlash waves of real crimes. To see perhaps the best example of this phenomenon, simply

Google "Trayvon Martin revenge crime." You'll get literally hundreds of relevant hits. But in total disregard of the risk that credulously reporting hoax hate crimes will lead to real ones, new hoaxes are inevitably covered in exactly the same way as their predecessors. Apparently a very significant chunk of the media simply doesn't mind feeding the fires of racial animosity and violence, at least among people of color.

A QUICK SWING TO THE WHITE: SUSAN SMITH AND THE "BIG BLACK" CAR THIEF

Both in the past and today, mainstream media feeding frenzies have generally centered on hate crime allegations that involve photogenic POC victims and thus provide the maximum opportunity for virtue-signaling. However, the media's taste for sensationalism has also occasionally inspired global publicity for hate hoaxes involving white or conservative victims. Cue the next case: no book on racial hoaxes could be complete without the horrible story of Susan Smith.

On October 25, 1994, Smith acquired the sort of fame few Nobel Prize laureates ever receive after claiming that a "big Black guy" had stolen her car with most of her family inside it. According to NBC News, she told officers that her Mazda Protegé had been "carjacked" on that date by a Black stranger, who drove away with her two young sons still screaming inside the vehicle.[37] After the alleged attack, the media made Smith a truly national figure. She appeared on multiple national television platforms to make dramatic pleas for her children's lives. Most famously, on the *Today* show, she pouted her lips, stared directly into the camera, and said, "I would like to say to whoever has my children that...I prayed every day that you are taking care of them!"[38] Race was obviously a subtext of media and popular analyses of the Smith case. While accounts differ as to whether Smith ever said that she was attacked *because* she was white, an NPR special on the case, "Racial Hoaxes: Black Men and Imaginary Crimes," accurately identifies fear of "the criminal black man" as the defining feature of Smith's own account and of most coverage of the case.[39]

Inevitably, Susan Smith ended up being revealed as a liar, to the horror of many. Local South Carolina police detectives, who had probably doubted her story from the very beginning, launched an intensive and competent investigation into the disappearance of the Smith children. Police began to dredge "the nearby lakes and ponds," looking for Smith's stolen vehicle. It was finally discovered, at least 120 feet from the shore, under the dark waters of the state's John D. Long Lake, with the drowned bodies of both of Smith's children inside. Michael Smith was three years of age when he was killed, and little Alexander Smith fourteen months old.

As "in the middle of a lake" struck law enforcement officers as an odd place for a car thief to leave a decently nice vehicle, suspicious officers conducted an in-depth interrogation of Smith. She cracked. On November 3, 1994, she confessed to letting her car roll "down the access ramp of John D. Long Lake" from an elevated area of ground, drowning the kids inside.[40] Smith's motivation was apparently to be child-free in order to begin a relationship with a wealthy local man, although that gentleman has since come forward to say that he never intended anything serious with Smith and he was unaware of her mental state or her plans.

As the murderer of her own children, Smith became a member of that small tribe of racial hoaxers to do prison time. At trial she claimed to be mentally ill, a common tactic, as we shall see, among Caucasian hate hoaxers. Her defense attorneys David Bruck and Judy Clarke arguing that she was "psychologically destabilized by a lifetime of betrayals: a father who killed himself, a stepfather who molested her, a husband who cheated on her and a boyfriend who toyed with her affections."[41] But the presiding judge in the case wasn't buying it. Apparently viewing these claims with little sympathy, he sentenced Smith to thirty years to life inside the Palmetto State's Graham Correctional Institution.[42] Rather remarkably, however, the Susan Smith case did not end there. The convicted murderess continued to be treated as a celebrity and receive mainstream media attention for her various antics.

Most notably, Smith turned out to have her own unique take on the old convict's slogan "Fuck the Police." While she was an inmate at Graham Correctional Institution during the 1990s, *two* ranking correctional officers at the facility, Lieutenant Houston Cage and Captain Alfred Rowe, were dismissed and subsequently charged after having sex with her.[43] Apparently still looking for male companionship, Smith placed a lengthy personal ad on the website writeaprisoner.com in 2003.[44]

Her fake hate crime (and real murder) has very much remained part of the American zeitgeist. In addition to dozens of lurid true-crime stories, it inspired the Blind Melon song "Car Seats (God's Presents)" and the anthem "When This Is Over" from the 1995 alternative album *Everything I Long For*. Smith even made a brief appearance in left-wing filmmaker Michael Moore's early-2000s opus *Bowling for Columbine*, with her case intended as a cameo-length illustration of the fact that America can be racist.[45] Most Americans are familiar with Smith's story even today. She was at least arguably America's first truly famous white hate hoaxer since the accusers of the Scottsboro Boys. But she was not to be the last. Race relations in the U.S. have improved immeasurably between when those young Black men were convicted of raping white women on false testimony in 1931 and the Susan Smith case sixty years later. Since the 1990s, hate crime hoaxes on both sides have exaggerated the extent of racism in America and, as we have seen, inspired actual racial violence.

Times have changed since 1994, and not always for the better.

Chapter Eight

WHITE HOT: CAUCASIAN HATE HOAXERS

Today, a new wave of hate crime hoaxes is being perpetrated by white Americans. There have always been white hate hoaxers, such as student radicals and insurance fraudsters. But over the past seven to ten years an increasing number of Caucasians have falsely represented that they were attacked by one or more members of minority or activist groups simply for *being* white (or conservative).

Within the Fake Hate Crimes data set of hoax crimes I have cited throughout this book, eighty-one cases (30.1 percent) involved Caucasians as the sole or primary false reporters. Of those cases, twenty-four (29.6 percent of the white hoaxes) involved white individuals who claimed to have been attacked because they were gay, twenty (24.7 percent) involved white individuals who claimed to have been attacked because of Jewish faith or appearance, nineteen (23.5 percent) involved individuals who claimed to have been attacked because of their support for *minority* causes, and just eighteen (22.2 percent) involved whites who claimed to have been attacked because they were white or conservative.[1]

Tellingly, almost all of the cases in this last Identitarian category were quite recent. A quick glance over the dates for those reports lists the years 2008, 2010, 2013, 2014, 2016, and 2017.[2] In the past three years alone, a white military veteran claimed that the Black Lives Matter movement destroyed his truck, a Bosnian-American woman in St. Louis reported that she was beaten senseless by three Black gang members, and a blonde Texas woman lied about being gang-raped in the woods by three Black men. Cases like these are, essentially, full-blown "Klan Springs Eternal" hoaxes, only with the races reversed.

It is probably no coincidence that this upsurge in white hate hoaxes, often with Black men as the alleged attackers, has occurred at the same time as a broader general swell of white racial identification within the U.S. The last ten years have witnessed the election of (and backlash to) the nation's first Black president (2008), the rise of the sometimes white-identified Tea Party movement (2009–13), the publication of Jared Taylor's *White Identity* (2011) and Vox Day's *SJWs Always Lie* (2015), and the near-normalization of the white-nationalist alt-right as a faction within young America (2014–17). Signs saying "It's OK to Be White" and "Diversity Equals White Genocide" are popping up around college campuses and business parks. In an environment where at least some whites are beginning to act on the basis of in-group identification as white, one of those actions is falsifying hate crimes.

As a brown-skinned American patriot, I have no sympathy for white Identitarianism. But it is important to note that the primary motivation for this new movement is not, as the activist Left seems to think, simply that all whites are evil racists at their core. Instead, it appears to be a predictable, if deeply disturbing, response to real events. Simply put, since 1960, the United States has transitioned from a 90 percent white country to a 60 percent white country. Almost all serious demographers see the "tipping point year" in which whites will become an actual minority as falling around 2045. Meanwhile, in these changing times, many middle-income whites see themselves—with some justification—as constantly being called "racist" or "privileged," while in fact they are the victims of social trends such as affirmative action, illegal immigration, Black-on-white crime, and the outsourcing of heartland blue-collar jobs.

Not a few people in this position view themselves not as members of a dominant national ruling class, as the contemporary Left invariably paints them, but as part of one beleaguered group competing for space with many others in the new America. A recent Harvard study found that 55 percent of whites believe that "significant" discrimination against whites exists in the modern United States in arenas such as hiring, and that this bias can be as damaging as prejudice against racial minorities.[3] In this environment, some Caucasians appear to be faking hate crimes out of a perverse sense of "team"—to show racial pride and rally the side to a sympathetic figure.

The increase in white hate hoaxes—with seven of my most serious fourteen cases occurring within the past year—may be the most troubling phenomenon addressed in this book. It would be one thing for a small minority group such as Asian Americans to become full of racially identified zealots frequently complicit in the staging of fake bias crimes, but it is a wholly different sort of problem if two-thirds of the country decides to start behaving in this way.[4] This may seem naïve, but massive, intentional emphasis of our shared *American* identity is needed right now as the threat of Balkanization looms. Without a sense of that unity, our great nation runs the risk of collapsing into a chaotic, perhaps even violent, Babel of hostile ethnic and identity groups.

In other words, if we do not hang together, we will surely all hang separately.

WHITE LIES MATTER: BLM DONE BURNT MY TRUCK

Ironically, pro-white hate hoaxers often attempt to use contemporary Black Identitarian movements as foils for their crimes. In one of the most notable cases, a forty-five-year-old conservative Texas man was arrested after claiming that Black Lives Matter activists came to his house and destroyed his pickup truck.

On September 8, 2015, this case showed up on the regional (and then almost immediately the national) radar screen when disabled veteran Scott Lattin claimed that "members of the movement against police brutality" had defaced his white pickup truck because it "displayed pro-police messages and symbols."[5] According to the *Daily News*, he accused Black radicals of having caused more than $5,000 in damage to the late-model domestic vehicle by tearing out the truck's glove box, slashing up the seats with a sharp object, and stealing all the electronics that were not nailed down. To add insult to injury, the politically woke vandals had allegedly spray-painted the phrase "Fuck your flag, your family, your feelings, and your faith," in one curving sentence around the outside of the truck.[6]

This case seems to have attracted 15 to 20 percent less attention than the typical white-on-Black hate crime accusation, but otherwise to have been treated exactly the same by observers and the mainstream media.[7] The *Daily News*, Fox 4 television, local ABC, and The Root all reported on the matter. The inevitable GoFundMe page went up, with "Big Daddy" Lattin raising nearly $6,000 between September 8 and September 19, 2015. His case also attracted considerable attention from the law enforcement and police-supporting communities. Blue Lives Matter mentioned it briefly on social media. Police officers sent Lattin donations, and multiple blue-collar Texas businesses, including body shops, offered to repair his damaged truck for free. This upswelling of support for a soldier apparently attacked by radicals was American, and it was real.[8]

But then it happened. The cops—let's be honest—may have taken a special interest in an apparent anti-police hate crime involving a veteran, and they investigated the matter thoroughly. Multiple inconsistencies in Lattin's story became apparent almost immediately. According to The Root, police first noticed discrepancies among the multiple "video records of Lattin talking about the incident." When first speaking about the alleged vandalism to law enforcement officers, some of whom were apparently using body cameras, he stated that there was little or no damage to the inside of his truck. But talking to TV news crews not long afterward, one of his main points of complaint was the fact that "the glove box cover had been ripped off and the seats slashed."

In addition to this contradiction, the accounts of witnesses turned out to not support Lattin's story. Neighbor Levonda Bradshaw told Fox in mid-September that she was suspicious of his claims and had been from the start, noting that "the Lattins had a fenced property with dogs that bark at anyone who comes near."[9] It struck Bradshaw as fantastically unlikely that someone could spend an hour vandalizing a truck parked in front of a house occupied by a war veteran, his eighteen-year-old son, and multiple vicious dogs, and not be noticed and engaged. Police began to move toward Bradshaw's view of events after conducting a with-consent search of the Lattin residence and discovering used cans of black spray paint inside the house.

Finally, after being confronted with this, "Scott admitted to doing all the damage to the truck." According to the Daily News, he was arrested Friday, September 18, 2015, and charged with the usual single misdemeanor count of false report. He has long since been released from jail. According to police and the News, Lattin may have been partly motivated by a desire to discredit Black Lives Matter, but his primary goal was more tawdry: "collecting insurance money."[10]

An interesting postscript to *le affaire Lattin* is that it seems to have been a bit of a family matter. Later in 2015, Lattin's wife Cindy and son Jason were also both arrested and charged with making a false report. Police Chief Chris Bentley said simply that "Cindy and Jason lied to support Scott," after he "vandalized the truck in a scheme." The hoax appears to have been the elder Lattin's idea, with police describing the other two defendants as "very sorry and remorseful." Nevertheless, both lied on multiple occasions; as Bentley said, "the media showed up and they were making statements...and they were being recorded." The Lattin family's GoFundMe was suspended by the platform and the donations returned. While none of the criminal charges filed were especially serious, several very prominent individuals weighed in in weary disgust, with the lieutenant governor of Texas saying on the record, "We are disappointed to learn of the latest developments ... (we) believed the original news."

In an ironic twist, by the way, Fox 4's article on this second layer of the Lattin fraud notes that young Jason Lattin's ambition was to become a police officer.[11] Remember to be scrupulously honest on the application, kid! You are clearly not a good liar.

A REAL MASS MURDER ATTEMPT (AND A POSSIBLE HOAX HATE CRIME): ENDICOTT, NEW YORK

A darker version of Scott Lattin's money-grubbing frame-up of Black Lives Matter took place in New York in 2016, when a firefighter was apprehended and charged with attempting to set his house on fire and blame Black Lives Matter. The investigation was speedy and my summary of the case is short. But if this arson attempt—whoever perpetrated it—had succeeded, accounts of the crime would have been pages long, and composed mostly of biographies of the dead.

On an otherwise uneventful night in late August, the home of Endicott city firefighter Jason Stokes was set on fire with his family in it. According to Mediaite, Stokes's wife and all of his children "were upstairs sleeping" when the blaze, a roaring gasoline fire that took other professional firemen hours to extinguish, started. On top of starting the fire, the arsonist had set up a series of deadly booby traps for the first responders who would arrive on the scene, including canisters arranged near the back door filled with "flammable objects and gasoline." A combination of professional skill and pure luck—they chose to enter through the *front* door—apparently saved the lives of many firemen and law enforcement officers.

The words "Lie with Pigs, fry like bacon" were also painted on one outside wall of Stokes's home. The phrase, a reference to the charming Black Lives Matter rally chant, "Pigs in a blanket: fry 'em like bacon," suggested that the Stokeses were being targeted because Stokes was a firefighter who supported the police. In initial interviews with the police, Stokes tried to drive this point home, arguing that his house had been attacked because of his police advocacy. He flew a Blue Lives Matter flag outside his house.[12]

But, as *Vibe* reported, investigating officers quickly began to suspect that Stokes himself was the firebug. He had insurance on the house, and he was a fireman with expertise in how fires are stopped, started, and spread. Law enforcement soon began to ask questions about the multiple gas cans and apparent traps set for firefighters found in and around his home. At some point during what became a very hostile investigation, police and the county district attorney decided to proceed with criminal charges against Stokes, and he was arrested on a count of second degree felony arson on December 6, 2016. Bond was set at $100,000, and the first steps of the criminal trial process set for April 2017. Broome County District Attorney Steve Cornwell stated bluntly that Stokes had vandalized his own home.[13]

New York's first responders and law enforcement community reacted to felony charges being filed against one of their own with weary disgust. Cops and firefighters talk a lot of half-serious trash to one another, but they expect professional courtesy—at least at the level of not-trying-to-kill-me-with-a-gasoline-bomb. District Attorney Cornwall probably summed up the feelings of many in-the-line New Yorkers when describing the "bacon" message written on Stokes's wall: "That...to me is absolutely despicable. It fuels a false narrative when it comes to the work police officers do." Fact check: True.

At Stokes's trial for arson, jurors spent seven hours in deliberations and were initially deadlocked. The firefighter was ultimately found not guilty, and the district attorney commented, "While we respectfully disagree with the verdict of the jury, we respect their decision."[14] Whether the jury or the DA was right about who attempted this murder-by-arson, it is a disturbing sign of the deterioration in race relations in the age of fake hate crimes. If it is indeed true that persons angered by Stokes' pro-police stand tried to kill his family, a real, horrifically violent hate crime was aimed at the people who keep us safe from crime and fires. If Stokes himself staged a fake hate crime, he must have been willing to risk burning his own family alive to frame BLM—and, perhaps not inconsequentially, collect insurance money. Either way, this crime demonstrates how the increasing racial hostility fomented by hate crime hoaxes—which are often said to "draw attention to" racism in America, but which in fact exacerbate it—can lead to horribly violent racial incidents.

THE BALKANIZATION OF AMERICA: AN ANTI-BLACK, PRO-BOSNIAN HOAX IN ST. LOUIS

A recent St. Louis hoax, the veracity of which there remains no doubt whatsoever, involved an accuser who identified as both white and Bosnian. Seherzada Dzanic falsely claimed that three young Black men threatened to kill her in the city's Bevo Mill neighborhood.

The case began on December 5, 2014, when the twenty-six-year-old Bosnian immigrant told St. Louis police that "three Black men in their late teens or early twenties" had walked out in front of a vehicle she was driving on the city's busy Lansdowne Avenue at about 5:30 a.m. According to Dzanic, one of the men pulled a handgun on her when she tried to drive past them and—with her car stopped—the group of males opened her passenger door, threatened her, and went through her purse.

Dzanic described the men as behaving in an openly racist manner, asking her about her ethnicity and "where she was from" before pushing and kicking her. The group appeared to feel strong animus not merely toward whites but specifically against Eastern European immigrants. When she told the trio that she was "European," they purportedly said, "You're a fucking liar. You're *Bosnian*. [We] should just kill you right now." According to Dzanic, the physical manhandling and mental trauma caused her to lose consciousness shortly after this threat was made. She woke up more than a minute later to find the men and some of her valuables gone, although she opted to refuse "treatment at the scene."

Dzanic's story caused an absolute uproar. There had been a number of violent conflicts between Bosnian immigrants and St. Louis Blacks in the days leading up to the alleged attack on her. As the *St. Louis Post-Dispatch* pointed out, Dzanic's report occurred roughly one week after a group of Black teenagers had beat Bosnian-American man Zemir Begic to death with a hammer during a street fight. That case had been widely reported in regional media and had already resulted in the arrests of seventeen-year-old Robert Joseph Mitchell and two other juvenile males by the time of Dzanic's accusations.

Only a few days after that bloody encounter, police had taken a report from "a Bosnian woman, 34," claiming that two Black men had tried to rob her in the Lemay Ferry area and called her a "fucking Bosnian bitch." Multiple other reports of minor incidents surrounded these two serious allegations, with Bosnians by no means always looking like the innocent victims. Dzanic's report hit this charged atmosphere with the impact of a bombshell, leading to a major meeting of city power players at the Bosnian-American Chamber of Commerce.

St. Louis police launched an all-out investigation into the Dzanic case, with multiple detectives requesting surveillance footage from the time of the alleged attack from every business along Lansdowne. And then it happened. What police saw on those tapes surprised and angered them. In the images from the primary surveillance videos analyzed by police, Dzanic is seen "driving along the street in the opposite direction [from what] she told police, then doing a U-turn, stopping, and getting out and lying in the street until a passing motorist finds her."[15] From my reading of the police report, Dzanic never encountered any other people, Black or white, during the time she claimed that she was assaulted, and of course she was never attacked. A St. Louis media source somewhat sardonically described Dzanic as "just getting out of her car and [lying down] in the street."[16]

Law enforcement understandably did not see the Dzanic case as funny at all. Referring to the atmosphere of racial tension that had already prevailed in working-class areas of St. Louis before her false accusations, city Police Chief Sam Dotson said bluntly, "It doesn't help the current climate when people use race as the basis to report crime. It further divides our community. It's important to send a strong message that when people manipulate the system, there are consequences." The circuit attorney for the county, Ed Postawko, agreed, noting that the time spent investigating Dzanic's accusations was "a good seven to ten days that could have been spent investigating real crimes."

Once the alleged victim's duplicity was exposed, the Dzanic case was quickly resolved. Only eleven days after her initial false police report, Dzanic had been charged with the usual single misdemeanor count of making a false report to the police. She seems to have avoided any real jail time. However, the massive regional coverage of the case, which included a front-and-center picture of Dzanic's mugshot on the STL Today website and mockery by the right-wing Daily Caller, is unlikely to have had a positive impact on the Bosnian immigrant's prospects for future employment.[17]

So far, par for the course. But far more interesting than the question of what happened to Dzanic after her comeuppance is the question of what motivated her to act as she did in the first place. The police described her motivation as "emotional issues," but this term seems at once insufficient and excessively broad.[18] It seems almost indisputable that Dzanic was motivated to action by what political scientists call linked fate—a feeling of in-group racial identification during a time of perceived ethnic competition or conflict. Blacks and Bosnians were quarreling in St. Louis during 2014, and there had been complaints on both sides. Dzanic acted essentially to strike a blow for her "team," adding a count to the Bosnian side of the ledger by depicting young Black men as feral street criminals.

This provides another example of the increasing racial polarization to which hate crime hoaxes contribute. Many hate hoaxes by POC, such as Yasmin Seweid, are very specifically designed to paint whites as racist and to do so in a fashion likely to result in benefits being given to minorities. But it has become indisputable that Caucasians are now doing the exact same thing.

FIRST THEY CAME FOR THE CONSERVATIVE MORMONS: THE PRINCETON JUMPING THAT WASN'T

One of the earliest fake hate crimes specifically associated with the "white right" occurred on Princeton University's campus in early winter 2007, when a white Hispanic Mormon traditionalist conservative—I certainly hope I got all that in the correct order—named Francisco Nava accused two hooded men of beating him bloody with a bottle of Orangina.

This case was fully as bizarre as it sounds. It began on December 15 when Nava, the president of Princeton's pro-abstinence Anscombe Society, placed an emergency call to police and claimed that he had been violently attacked by two cloaked men wearing stocking caps. According to *The Nation*, which ran a nine-page account of this case that quoted the original police report extensively, Nava alleged that these men had repeatedly "slammed him into a wall" before smacking him around with the aforementioned bottle of orange soda. "Shut the fuck up," they yelled at him over and over. After contacting the police, Nava was apparently taken to a hospital where doctors confirmed that he had ugly "cuts and bruises covering his face."

Nava explicitly connected his beating to his conservative campus activism, and his case rapidly became a rallying cry for the national activist Right. A Mormon chastity advocate who opposes all premarital sex, the young man argued that he had been targeted for violence because of a guest column he had penned for the *Daily Princetonian*. In that piece, titled "Princeton's Latex Lies," Nava argued passionately against Princeton's policy of free condom distribution to students via the campus health center. To Nava, this common university practice constituted "an infectious threat," given the Princeton culture of casual dating and sexual hookups, and it demonstrated "tacit support for hookup sex." Nava claimed that he had been "bombarded with death threats" in the wake of this article, and that his being jumped was a physical extension of this campaign of harassment.

Conservative campus activists and national media stars rallied to Nava's banner, seeing in his case a counter-weight to mushrooming, if mostly fake, leftist charges of bias crime and racial-political harassment at American universities. Harvey Mansfield, the famous neo-conservative writer and author of *Manliness*, called for a "manly" response to the cowardly attack on Nava, saying, "I hope Princeton comes down on them like a ton of bricks."[19] Fox News anchor Brit Hume personally authored a post published on the cable news channel's website headlined, "Little Outrage Over Student Beating at Princeton University."[20] Perhaps most notably, witty right-of-Charlemagne bomb thrower David Horowitz said that Nava had been beaten up for his traditionalist views and accused Princeton of failing to protect conservatives from physical and verbal violence. His website Front Page Mag ran a graphic account of the Nava beating under the header "Student Beaten Unconscious for Conservative Views."[21]

And then, as the groundswell of interest around this case began to morph into a legitimate national conversation, it happened. Activists on the gun-and-eagle side of American politics may not lie as often as SJWs, but fanatics of any stripe tend to have a flexible relationship with the truth. Princeton police soon began to "suspect the veracity" of Nava's account. Several officers have noted that signs of "an elaborate hoax" were present in the Nava matter from its very beginning—including the "cinematic" way in which the allegedly traumatized victim told his fight story and the similarity of his account to several situations already uncovered as hoaxes on other American campuses.

In addition to these warning signs, Nava turned out to have a personal history of fabricating death threats. When he was in boarding school, he had on one occasion sent a threatening letter containing phrases such as "Die, Fags!" to himself and his roommate, who was the president of the Gay-Straight Alliance. On December 17, 2007, after detectives confronted him with these facts, Nava confessed to making up the entire story. While I haven't seen any discussion of this in news reports, it would seem logical to conclude that Nava likely inflicted the damage to his own face, perhaps hitting himself repeatedly or slicing himself with a sharp implement. Not a well man.

Following Nava's confession, he faced the usual lack of any serious consequences. A week after the first report of the attack, *The Nation* noted that Nava might "face expulsion," but had not yet been thrown out of school.[22] He does not seem to have ever faced criminal charges. It is to be sincerely hoped that at some point Nava sought out a therapist and figured out why the hell he had been acting as he did. Whatever the possible explanations for his behavior, however, it seems fair to say that the police and other power players involved with the Nava situation treated his case much as they would have a fake hate crime accusation from a left-winger or any other student. Such equivalence would seem to be the norm; typically, white hate hoaxes are not treated notably more harshly than Black ones, or vice versa.

There was, however, one major difference between the aftermath of the Nava matter and the aftermath of most major left-wing hate hoaxes: when the young conservative activist was exposed as a hoaxer, his allies immediately deserted him. Even the decidedly left-wing *Nation* admitted that "his defenders disappeared almost as quickly as they had mobilized."[23] David Horowitz scrubbed all accounts of the bogus attack from his website, while Brit Hume left his article up but added a written addendum.[24] Princeton professor Robert George, a well-known conservative critical of the far-left climate on most college campuses, went so far as to praise both campus and local law enforcement, saying, "Princeton...had the good sense to hold their fire, get the facts first, before drawing conclusions."[25]

It seems highly unlikely that the same thing would have happened on the other side of the political spectrum. It is worth contrasting reasonable behavior like George's with the actions of some left-wing activists after hate crime allegations are proven false, which have often included outright refusal to believe the new revelations (such as at the University at Albany) and frenzied claims that the fake charges reflect some "deeper climate" of bigotry and thus remain meaningful. Both liberals and right-wing activists certainly fake hate crimes, but conservatives seem less likely to keep the story going *after* a hoaxer has been exposed. At least so far.

THE MOST INFLUENTIAL HATE HOAX OF ALL TIME?

Somewhat surprisingly, Francisco Nava does not hold the title for most bizarre liberal-on-conservative hate hoax faked this decade. How quickly glory doth fade! That honor was taken from him by the John McCain presidential campaign's Ashley Todd, barely a year after Nava made up his story.

The Todd case was a strange one, and it deservedly received national media attention. It began on October 22, 2008, when Ashley Todd, a campaign operative for presidential candidate John McCain, claimed to have been robbed and beaten by a supporter of McCain's Democratic rival, Barack Obama. Todd was a field representative for the College Republican National Committee who had traveled to Pennsylvania to recruit conservative college students.

While there she contacted the Pittsburgh police and claimed that she had been robbed at knifepoint in that city's Bloomfield neighborhood.

Todd's description of her attacker, like Nava's, was remarkably precise: "a six foot four African American of medium build, dressed in dark clothes [and] wearing shiny shoes."[26] Todd claimed that this man's attack on her was both racial and political. After initially assaulting her, her robber had seen a pro-McCain bumper sticker on Todd's car, and told her, "You are going to be a Barack supporter today!" He then allegedly sliced a reversed letter "B" into her cheek with a knife or other hand weapon. Todd's stated assumption was that this single scarlet letter was intended as shorthand for "Barack."[27] This also seems to have been the general first-take assumption of conservative media, although some voices speculated that it might have stood for "[white] bitch."

This alleged attack occurred less than two weeks before the 2008 presidential election, a genuinely historic race pitting the man who became our first Black president against one of the nation's most recognized war heroes. Unsurprisingly, the level of press coverage was through the roof. One lengthy account of the Todd matter noted that her story had "spread around the world," "becoming political fodder on the internet," and received massive coverage from conservative media outlets including Fox News and the Drudge Report.[28] The story became so big on the right that Fox News Executive Vice President John Moody weighed in on it personally, saying on the Fox website, "This incident could become a watershed in the 11 days before the election."[29]

Cue the foreshadowing music. Moody's words turned out to be amazingly prescient, although probably not in the sense that he intended or hoped. Unsurprisingly, given the context, Todd's narrative came under intense scrutiny within hours of her report. Several acute observers of the national scene, including right-wing Filipina

American columnist Michelle Malkin—a dogged exposer of hate hoaxers of all stripes—noted that the "B" on Todd's face had been carved in reverse. This fact suggested that she had cut it into her own skin, using a mirror for guidance. Apparently after talking to Pittsburgh officers, the columnist pointed out that Todd had refused any medical treatment after reporting her attack to the police. Malkin asked, "Why on earth would she do that?"[30]

As the internet sleuths stepped up their efforts, it was also soon revealed that Todd had engaged in a previous hate crime hoax when she had a different political job. In February of 2008, while working for Ron Paul, Todd complained to police that her car's tires had been slashed and campaign materials had been stolen from the vehicle because of her support for Paul. While this allegation was apparently not true, this level of partisan dishonesty seems to have been viewed by other Paul staffers as tolerable, at least at first. However, Todd was subsequently asked to leave the Paul campaign by regional boss Dustan Costine, after yet another incident in which she "posed as a Mike Huckabee supporter and called the local Republican committee seeking information about [other candidates'] campaign strategies."

Around this time, Todd confessed. Following a polygraph administered to her by the Pittsburgh police department and their announcement that they planned to review surveillance footage of the scene of the crime, Todd admitted to making up her entire story. She still did not confess, though, to carving the giant backwards "B" into her own face, saying only that "she did not remember how it got there," but that she might have done the harm to herself given "incidents of memory loss in the past."[31] But the rest of her tale was admitted to be a straight-up lie. Officers say she never gave an explanation for the motivation behind her false story. No big deal; I think we can all probably figure that one out.

Showing a great degree of mercy (surely unrelated to Todd's being a cute female defendant), Pennsylvania police and prosecutors decided to treat her as mentally ill rather than as a scheming political operative who had almost completed the mission. Good of them. Charged with the usual single misdemeanor count of false filing, Todd was released from jail on October 30, 2008 to "undergo psychiatric counseling." This release turned out to be permanent. During her formal sentencing a few months later, in January of 2009, she was assigned to a special probation program for first-time offenders, at the end of which her criminal files would be fully expunged if she committed no further crimes. (She didn't, and it was.) Throughout this process Todd was never required to enter a formal plea. This courtesy left her without a guilty plea or conventional conviction on her record. She has apparently moved on with her life.[32]

There is at least an outside chance that Todd's fake hate crime was the most influential hate hoax of all time. We will never know. But Obama won the presidency by a margin of less than 7 percent nationally, and his margin even in traditionally liberal Pennsylvania was only 10 percent. It is worth recalling the last line of Fox executive Moody's post: "If the incident turns out to be a hoax, Senator McCain's quest for the presidency is over, forever linked to race-baiting."[33]

THE JUNIOR LEAGUE: A WHITE RACIAL HATE HOAX IN MIDDLE SCHOOL

The next politically and racially motivated hate hoax by a white conservative comes to us from the youth division. In early 2008, perky blonde middle-schooler "Melody Beaver" attracted nationwide attention after claiming that she had been threatened with murder and rape by a group of Hispanic boys as retaliation for a class project critical of illegal immigration.[34] But, you see, she was simply lying.

This case began with an assignment in Melody's eighth grade history class. The teacher asked students to make a protest sign "for or against any issue." Although the instructor's honest expectation may well have been different varieties of CultMarx fluff, Beaver chose opposition to illegal immigration as her topic. She drew up a sign reading "If You Love Our Nation, Stop Illegal Immigration," and brought it to class on the day the assignment was due. She received a grade for the project, did a bit of discussion and defense of it in the school hallways, and brought the thing to lunch with her.

At that point things got weird. According to the blog WizBang, Beaver claimed that her sign had been taken from her at lunch, was "passed around," and ended up angering a group of Latino students. After the meal, they jumped her. She described the beating as brutal. She said that it began when "one young man jumped on her back and put her in a choke-hold." And things only got worse from there: "We have brick walls in the middle school, and he slammed my face into the bricks."

Throughout all of this, other members of the same pack of boys threatened to rape and kill her, yelling vile insults as the scuffle went on. Perhaps even worse, when Beaver attempted to report her attack to school authorities, they showed her no sympathy as the white victim of a hate crime. Some notes were taken, but she was "ordered back to class and told she could not call her parents." Family member "J.R. Beaver" summed up the apparent situation in a sentence: "They handled this wrong, you know. They put a child back in danger."[35]

When Beaver's story leaked out of the Athens Independent School District, many members of the press seemed to agree with J.R., and an almost immediate media feeding frenzy began. A young, blonde white girl threatened with rape in middle school? Send in the cameras! Major local television station KLTV, Michelle Malkin, and many other outlets ran major stories on the case.[36] Most of these observers were initially disgusted with the school system and asked similar sets of obvious questions. To quote WizBang: "How was it there was no one there to defend her? Second, if a girl has just been attacked by a bunch of teenage boys—and goes and reports it to school officials—why in the hell was she sent back to class? Why were her parents not immediately notified? Why would they put her in more risk?"

Good questions, to which there turned out to be a very simple answer: Beaver was never attacked. She had made the whole tawdry incident up.[37] After her account went public, school administrators ordered a review of all surveillance videotape. The tape proved instructive. Instead of showing a violent fight, much less a group of students attacking and pummeling Beaver, the video revealed the young woman "scratching herself on her arms, face, and neck and [then] walking through the halls of the school calmly." When Beaver was confronted with this video evidence, she confessed to making up her story. She faced the juvenile version of the mandatory single misdemeanor count of false report a few days later, on April 9, 2008, after the Henderson County DA reviewed the situation and opted to bring charges.[38]

Melody Beaver's parents had probably the best response to a hate crime hoax that I came across in my research for this book. While stating unequivocally that they still loved their daughter, both absolutely refused to make excuses for her behavior. In a formal apology to the school system, Beaver's father said that he had to reluctantly agree with all charges against her: "I have reviewed the recording and agree...[they] will need to be filed." Beaver's mother released an official statement reading in part, "I see my daughter was not assaulted, and put the marks on her body. No gang violence was witnessed. She filed a false report." Both Texans spoke unsmilingly.[39] One suspects that Melody was sitting down very carefully for a week or so after her parents' "she-a culpas." Imagine how much saner the

American university campus would be if the same blend of affection, pattern recognition, and actual discipline were dealt out to other perpetrators of hate crime hoaxes.

It is also worth mentioning that Beaver's hate hoax, almost uniquely, was partly a response to a real and immediate provocation. While she was never beaten, choked, or threatened with rape, KLTV reporters pointed out that her protest sign project had in fact been taken from her by other students and apparently torn apart and thrown away. At least "three students involved in taking Melody's project" were identified by the school district and suspended.[40] The censorship of speech seen as offensive, especially by the political Left, is a feature of young American life, and an attempt to censor speech did occur in this case. Beaver's allegations seem to have had a rebellious component, coming after she saw her work destroyed for political reasons.

But there are no excuses for hate crime hoaxes. Being offended does not justify anyone, Right or Left, to make up fake battery allegations. Remember that in college, snowflake!

ABOUT-FACE: THE BETHANY STORRO ACID HOAX

One of the most gruesome Caucasian hate hoaxes involved a Washington woman who threw hydrochloric acid onto her own face and then blamed the attack on Black people.

In September of 2010, Pacific Northwest resident Bethany Storro garnered international media attention after telling Vancouver police that she had been attacked in the street with a cup of acid. According to a lengthy account published in the *Daily News*, Storro reported that a complete stranger, "whom she described as a Black girl in her 20s," approached her carrying a cup of suspicious-looking liquid. The young African American woman allegedly asked "Hey, pretty girl:

do you want to drink this[?]" and threw the mixture into Storro's face when she said "No." The liquid turned out to be a potent industrial acid. As a result, the entire front of Storro's face was, and is, covered with a "red bloom" of serious chemical burns.

When Storro's horrific story was reported to them, police launched an extensive search for the alleged attacker. But the manhunt didn't last long. Within days, actual eyewitnesses had informed both police and the *Vancouver Voice* newspaper that the alleged hate crime victim had been alone when she "fell to the ground and started screaming" on the day of the hoax.[41] She had in fact been splashed in the face with a heavy-duty acid, but she had done the deed herself. On September 17, Ana Hunter of CBS had penned a follow-up story headlined, "Acid Attack Hoax: Why Did She Say Attacker Was Black?"[42]

But the discovery of her dishonesty did not end the case. Astonishingly Storro, who is still photogenic even after having injured herself in this horrifying way, has kept herself relevant in the media. After her confession, she first stayed in the headlines by claiming to have body dysmorphic disorder, a recently popularized psychological condition involving individuals who perceive their physical bodies as something other than what they are.[43] During a TV appearance, Storro described her case of the condition as a severe one: "In the mirror, I saw a distorted monster. It was, like, my eyes were gouging out, my face was just, it was just terrible." The cleansing splash of acid apparently fixed her belief that she was remarkably ugly—or possibly just made her as ugly as she already believed she was. Storro went on, "I could feel it burning through my skin, like melting into my face...I was so happy."

It is tempting to view Storro as what a less enlightened and politically correct age would have called "a harmless lunatic"—an essentially sympathetic figure in need of serious therapeutic care. But it has to be said that there is evidence against that conclusion. After her hoax was uncovered, Storro apparently faced no charges of making a false report, but she was charged with three distinct counts of theft—for taking and spending the considerable amount of money donated by horrified friends for her medical care. She pled guilty and spent a year in custody, although most of this period consisted of "undergoing mental health treatment" at a Washington involuntary care facility.[44]

An eminent psychologist, Manhattan practitioner Samuelle Klein-Von Reiche, has gone on the record to say that she does not necessarily see Storro as a sympathetic victim suffering from body dysmorphic disorder. Klein-Von Reiche has described Storro as a potentially dangerous narcissist: "We shouldn't minimize the fact that she got enormous notoriety from this, and any sort of attention, positive or negative, is gold for an extreme narcissist." Klein-Von Reiche also found it fascinating that Storro chose to specifically blame a Black woman for her fake attack, particularly given that she resided in a region of the U.S. that is less than 10 percent Black. "Of course," this choice could imply racism or "racial issues," Klein-Von Reiche noted. Perhaps more disturbing, blackness could represent a hidden and seductive dark side of herself over which Storro "has little control."[45]

Whatever her actual psychological profile and moral character, Storro has only become more prominent during the last few years, almost half a decade after her alleged attack. She appeared on *Good Morning America* midway through 2013, telling the host team that she was "starting to feel comfortable in her skin," three years after the acid incident. She has since published a full-length book, *Facing the Truth*, which she co-authored with writer Monica Krueger. It is currently one of the top seven hundred sellers among all books on fitness, health, and dieting. Throughout all of this, Storro has had one consistent message: "I hope that people forgive me and give me a chance. Because I'm, I'm a good person. I promise."[46]

Only God, I suppose, can judge her. But you lot should feel free to write your own opinions in the margins.

GONE WITH THE WIND: A SOUTHERN BLACK-ON-WHITE RAPE HOAX

Our next Caucasian hate hoax comes from Denison, Texas, and strongly invokes shades of the Old South. Teen Breana Harmon, a nineteen-year-old blonde, gained fame after she charged into a conservative church and claimed she had been raped by three Black men.

This particular saga began on March 8, 2017. During an otherwise uneventful spring night, Harmon entered a church located along the South Eisenhower Parkway wearing only a ripped shirt, bra, and panties, with "visible cuts and scratches" covering her body. She had a horrifying story to tell. According to witnesses at the church and law enforcement interviewers who came later, she claimed that she had been kidnapped at her apartment complex by three Black males wearing ski masks. These men, according to the *Daily Mail*, then took Harmon to a "wooded area" behind the church where she would later make her dramatic appearance. In the woods, two of the men took turns raping her "while the third suspect pinned her down." Before allowing Harmon to run off, half-naked and filthy, these men allegedly told the young woman they would assault her again if she reported the incident to anyone.

When she did report it, the feeding frenzy was immediate. Shocked but stalwart parishioners dressed the shivering Harmon and turned her over to the police, who immediately opened an investigation. As word of the incident got out, feature stories detailing the case ran across local media, in the New York newspapers, and across the pond in London.[47] Even BET ran an article, although this admittedly occurred after major questions about the case had arisen.[48] On the less respectable fringe of journalism, many alt-right websites, which I will not dignify by naming here, pulled the story off the wires and ran with it. Although, to be scrupulously fair, Harmon seems never to have actually said this, there was considerable speculation that she had been raped *because* she was a white blonde, in an archetypal hate crime scenario. Texans of all races tend to be scrappy types willing to defend their own, and racial tensions in Denison apparently sky-rocketed following Harmon's allegations.[49]

By this point, you know what was bound to happen next. Harmon's comeuppance occurred on March 22, 2017, when articles in both the New York City press and local Texas papers reported that she had confessed to making it all up. According to the *Daily News*, "A Texas teenager has admitted that her claims she was kidnapped and gang-raped by 'three black males' were a hoax."[50] As the *Daily Mail* reported in a longer account that ran a few months later, Texas detectives became suspicious of Harmon almost immediately after launching the investigation, when doctors who examined her "found she did not suffer injuries consistent with her claims." When law enforcement officers confronted Harmon with these inconsistencies, "she admitted to staging…her own injuries when she walked into the church."

Because of the racially charged nature of her allegations and the tensions they had caused in an integrated Southern city, Harmon was hit fairly hard by the local DA when exposed as a hoaxer. She was originally arrested only for the standard-issue single count of misdemeanor false report. But after reviewing the case—and almost certainly, after hearing the loud plaints of Denison's Blacks, church-goers, and law enforcement—Grayson County District Attorney Joe Brown took the unusual step of tacking on multiple more serious criminal counts.

Harmon faced two charges of tampering with physical evidence and two charges of tampering with an official government record. These are very serious criminal counts. Three of the charges are felonies carrying a maximum sentence of ten years in prison, while the fourth is also a felony but carries only a sentence of two years in state jail and a $10,000 fine. Explaining his decision to up the ante against Harmon, Brown said, "The more we have looked at what happened in this case, and considered the harm it caused and certainly could have caused, we believe what she did fits the elements of these higher charges. What she did was very serious, and we believe it was felony conduct."[51] Even a Texas lawman is not going to say, "These Black and redneck boys was about to knock each other's heads in," at a formal press conference. What Brown did say was harsh but fair. The local police force, which includes multiple decorated Black officers, agreed, calling the hoax "insulting to our community, and especially insulting to [our] African American community."[52] Ultimately, Harmon was found guilty of tampering with evidence and government records. She did not have to serve time behind bars, but she was sentenced to eight years of probation and required to pay more than $10,000 in fines and restitution.[53] Karma is a female dog.

VIRTUE-SIGNALING ARSON

Most hate crime hoaxes, whether carried out by whites or by POC, involve allegations that a member of the targeted group was attacked because he or she is white, Black, brown, or whatever. But as we saw in the Brexit case on the University of Michigan campus, white radicals sometimes engage in a different variety of hoax, alleging that they were targeted for their liberalism or for supporting minority rights too strongly. One of the most bizarre and extreme examples of this phenomenon took place in the Dallas–Forth Worth metroplex in late 2016.

On December 12, 2016, Denton, Texas, resident David Williams told police that he and his wife Jenny had woken up to find the family pickup truck set on fire, David's motorcycle burned, and the words "Nigger Lover" painted across the family's garage door. Perhaps most frightening, a fire had been lit but burned itself out while the young couple's four children were sleeping in the house with them. One unlucky spark and the kids easily could have been killed. Williams—who, like his wife and children, is white—told the local paper that he suspected "punk kids" with alt-right leanings were behind the attacks.

As usual, David and Jenny were the beneficiaries of sympathetic media coverage and local support. Denton police opened arson and hate crime investigations into the incident, and the regional *Denton Record-Chronicle* newspaper ran a major story on the attack.[54] A GoFundMe page went up, apparently launched by Jenny Williams and a personal friend, asking for donations to help pay for the family's Christmas, because the Williams's insurance would not cover the majority of the damage.

The pitch on the GoFundMe page read, in part: "The kids won't be able to have anything under the Christmas tree due to this horrible act. Please find it in your heart, please donate what you can, to help this family of six out." The page attracted more than a hundred donors, who gave well over $5,000, and the Williamses became minor celebrities within the anti-racist community. Even the right-wing website Breitbart quoted Jenny Williams, who said that the family was attacked "because it just so happens that we aren't as racist as someone would like us to be."[55]

And then it happened. By December 28, 2016, (just after his family's crowd-funded Christmas, a cynic might note) multiple sources were reporting that David Williams had confessed to starting the fire and painting the graffiti himself. None of it had been the work of racist vandals; "Williams...admitted he was responsible for the whole thing." Interestingly, his confession seems to have been spontaneous. Williams was being treated with sympathy rather than any serious suspicion by the police, and he may have 'fessed up out of pure seasonal guilt. His wife was certainly dumbfounded by the unexpected admission, telling the local newspaper, "He confessed, and, that entire conversation, I just don't even know how to wrap my head around it all." She added, "It was clear to me...that his head was definitely not in the right place." The rest of the family reacted similarly, with a relative describing the Williams children in a Facebook post as being in "a state of shock, and sadness."[56]

David Williams attempted to explain and partly excuse his actions by claiming to be mentally ill, saying he had been diagnosed with bipolar disorder and borderline personality disorder back in 2012. While countless Americans truly and bravely struggle with real diseases of the mind, it is remarkable how common it is among Caucasian hate hoaxers to claim to be to be suffering from fairly rare mental health conditions such as body dysmorphic disorder. There is a much smaller percentage of minority hate hoaxers who attribute their behavior to mental illness.

Perhaps all of the white Americans who use insanity as a defense for their hate crime hoaxes are indeed mentally ill. It may even be the case that, as some have argued, mental illness is under-diagnosed among minorities, and an equivalent percentage of the POC who stage hate crimes are unknowingly suffering from mental afflictions. Certainly, psychiatric treatment needs to be an option available to prosecutors and judges confronted with the bizarre reality of elaborate hate crime hoaxes.

However, it could also be the case that the widely reported phe-nomenon of over-diagnosis of bunkum "mental illnesses" among middle-class Americans, which is responsible for the U.S.A.'s current consumption of "88 percent of the world's legal Ritalin-type drugs," provides people who are basically criminals with excuses for their actions.[57] This particular excuse is simply more readily available to higher-income whites. Denton fire and police spokesman David Hedges certainly seemed to plump for the latter explanation; he told the area media that Williams might have been experiencing mental issues when he committed his crimes, but that he would nonetheless "be charged at minimum with arson." The lawman added that police officials were also certainly still "exploring other possible charges."[58]

David Williams went to ground in a mental institution, presum-ably seeking to avoid the felony charges. Meanwhile, his wife Jenny, in many ways the hero of this story, seems to be doing her best to keep her family stable and intact. More than a year ago, she announced via Facebook that she and the co-creator of the Williams's GoFundMe account had "started the process" of contacting each of the hundred-plus benefactors and returning all of their money to them.[59] This task was apparently completed in early 2017. Around the same time, Jenny Williams was quoted in SplinterNews, sounding extremely frazzled but determined: "There are so many things up in the air, and I just don't know where to begin. But I know I have four kids who need a parent, and I have to do what's right."[60]

Chapter Nine

SOLUTION SETS: HOW TO DEAL WITH THE EPIDEMIC OF HOAX HATE CRIMES

When I decided to write this book, I dedicated myself to comprehensively exploring the phenomenon of fake hate crimes in modern America. Thus far I have provided rough estimates of the number of highly reported hate crime hoaxes that occurred during the past few decades; outlined the background context—the Continuing Oppression Narrative—against which the wave of hate hoaxes is occurring; explored the astonishing prevalence of hoaxes on American college campuses; examined the "Klan Springs Eternal" sub-set of hate fakes involving POC who falsely claim to have been attacked by white racist gangs; debunked a number of "Trump hate crime" incidents that were falsely reported during and after the 2016 election; outlined a series of hoaxes involving gay Americans and religious minorities, reviewed the long and bizarre history of media complicity with the publication of hate crime hoaxes; and finally addressed, perhaps for the first time in a book from a major publisher, the surge of hate hoaxes committed by the alt-right and other white-identifying whites. With those tasks completed, one question remains: what can we *do* about the epidemic problem of hoax hate incidents?

To me, speaking both as a law school graduate with extensive criminal legal training and as a social scientist, there are four steps that law enforcement, campus judicial systems, and perhaps especially media organizations need to take in order to mitigate the current epidemic of fake hate accusations.

First, stakeholders need to recognize that between 15 and 50 percent of hate crime accusations are flatly false. Every government and school authority, every reporter and editor should treat accusers respectfully. But none of them should greet each new claim with instant and total credulity.

Second, colleges and police departments need to *actually punish* individuals discovered to have falsified hate crime allegations. No more two-week suspensions from school, no more short periods of probation. Every hour that detectives spend chasing hate crime fakers is one hour less they have to catch real rapists, and the reality of this lost time should be taken seriously.

There are multiple serious charges that could be brought in the wake of a hoax hate incident: tampering with physical evidence, tampering with a government record, impeding an ongoing investigation, falsifying a police report, and plain fraud. These counts should usually be brought, and the normal sentences for them should be sought by the authorities at trial. The Overton window of what is tolerated needs to shift, so that falsely reporting a potential campaign of racial murder and costing the government $89,000 in investigative costs—as student activists did at Kean College—is treated as a serious crime.

Some have suggested going further. In a paper for the Independence Institute, academic David Kopel proposed a minor legal revision that would impose stricter penalties for hate crime hoaxers, equivalent to those given for actual hate crimes. Kopel argues, "To the extent that arguments in favor of special hate crimes laws are persuasive, the arguments for special anti-hate-crime-hoax laws are at least as persuasive. Hate crime laws are promoted under the theory that they send a message…that such crimes are especially heinous. Precisely the same can be said about hate crime hoaxes—which are often treated quite offhandedly by the authorities."[1]

I endorse Kopel's proposal. It might well be worth enhancing the sentence for hate hoaxers so that it is closer to what currently exists for the perpetrators of real hate crimes. Punishments for the generally Misdemeanor C offense of falsifying a police report could be made more serious for those individuals who fake a bias crime.

Third, the culture of making excuses for bias crime hoaxers should be dismantled, certainly among law enforcement professionals and to the greatest extent possible among members of the media and college officials. The insidious idea that hate hoaxers are well-meaning anti-racists who commit their crimes to "draw attention" to the horrific real racism in America should be debunked, opposed, and ridiculed wherever it rears its ugly head. Hoaxes and their perpetrators are deliberately exaggerating the degree of racial animosity and violence in the United States and in the process actually *making it worse*. We should quit treating them like noble crusaders for civil rights.

It is currently common to argue that hoaxers such as the Albany bus beating hoax perpetrators must have experienced *some* kind of victimization—a persistent battle with mental illness or ubiquitous low-key racism—that caused their behavior. Tenured professor Sami Schalk argued that the three women involved in that case must have encountered "prejudice and 'racialized language'" on the University at Albany's campus "on or before that bus ride," and that this probably "played a role in provoking the fight."[2] Even the long-since-exposed

Tawana Brawley and Sabrina Collins hoaxes continue to be excused with weasel words like *Someone did something to her, something happened to that girl.*

In most hate crime hoaxes, however, there is literally no evidence that this theory is true. As we have seen in case after case, hoaxes are often perpetrated for simpler and much less creditable reasons: to collect on the insurance, to win an election, to cover up the perpetrator's own crimes or disobedience to her parents, to get attention, or in a deliberate attempt to bolster the Continuing Oppression Narrative. People who attempt to damage American race and class relations for such reasons are not heroes but criminals, and they should be prosecuted.

Fourth, any benefits awarded by government entities or colleges because of a bias crime—or a "wave" of them—should be revoked immediately if those crimes are shown to be fakes. If a university agrees to build, say, an "Afro-Centric Dialogue Center" in response to a wave of hate crimes, that commitment should be rescinded when the crimes are revealed as fake. Otherwise the university is only incentivizing hate hoaxes.

In reality, it almost *never* happens today that initiatives inspired by hate hoaxes are cancelled, even when they are revealed as fakes. For example, the perpetrator of a series of disgusting racist graffiti incidents that rocked Eastern Michigan University during 2016 was recently discovered to be a Black man named Eddie Curlin, and he did in fact receive a fairly serious punishment from the university— although this turned out to be irrelevant given that he was already incarcerated on an unrelated charge.

But Eastern Michigan University president James Smith definitively refused to end any of the campus-wide initiatives that had been adopted specifically in response to the "racism" panic triggered by Curlin. These included "increased lighting and added cameras on campus, the creation of a Presidential Commission on Diversity and Inclusion, and [mandatory] diversity and inclusion training for all employees."[3] According to Smith, "The many initiatives put in place as a result of the incident are vitally important and will continue regardless."[4]

That's crazy. Whatever the objective merits of mandatory diversity training, it would be difficult to think of a better way to inspire more hate hoaxers. Campus and area radicals now know that if they falsify a hate incident, they will receive benefits like major campus improvements and presidential commissions, *and that these benefits will continue even after the incident itself is exposed as a fake*. To prevent the operation of perverse incentives of this kind, benefits linked to incidents of racial or other inter-group conflict that are later exposed as fakes should, if possible, be taken away once the hoaxes are debunked.

Obviously, no campus can un-build a $15,000,000 "Post-Modern Social Justice Center" that has already been built. But institutional leaders certainly could decide not to spend the $15,000,000 if it turns out that no major recent incidents of bigotry actually occurred on their premises. It might, again, be protested that this policy is harsh—that even in the absence of a few high-profile felonies, bigotry is everywhere and the general climate in most communities easily justifies the benefits that usually follow a hate crime hoax. But there is little empirical evidence that this is true. In multiple settings in which hate crime hoaxes have occurred, such as the campus of an integrated upper-middle class college in Minnesota, literally the only "hate" incidents to make the police blotter during the past decade or so were those falsified by radicals.

Of my four rules, the first is the simplest and would be the easiest to implement. Sophisticated players such as police sergeants and university deans of discipline should be keenly aware that a very large percentage of hate crimes are hoaxes. This fact is indisputable. I personally put together a set of 409 hate crime hoaxes during a period when probably fewer than 3,500 widely reported hate crime allegations occurred—meaning a fake rate of 12 percent.[5] The University of Wisconsin, in a well-done small study, similarly concluded that roughly 15 percent of campus hate crimes are fakes—though they coded things such as "a blog post about life as a white student" as legitimate hate incidents.[6] Going the other route and tossing such ambiguous incidents into the "didn't happen" pile, conservative writers including Ann Coulter have argued that the actual numerical majority of reported hate crime allegations never happened. I would not go that far myself, but my strong suspicion is that at least half of college campus hate incident reports are fakes.[7]

In this context, authorities who come in contact with individuals reporting hate crimes must be aware that they are dealing with accusations unusually likely to be untrue. People who report hate crimes should be treated by law enforcement and university officials with utmost respect, like all other self-proclaimed victims of crime. But immediate and dramatic steps based upon the assumed accuracy of a claim should generally not be taken—except in situations that involve plausible threats of *future* violent harm. To give two examples: university officials should wait until an investigation has turned up factual support for an allegation before telling their students that a "wave of hate" is underway, and members of the media should ideally take the same precaution before reporting stories. Many hoax hate crime cases collapse within a week or so. In a large number of situations, ranging from the Matthew Schultz case to the "You'll be white today!" shoe polish incident, public frenzies could have been prevented with a bit of patience. Stakeholders should say, "We are still investigating," instead of publicizing the gory details of a story that could very easily turn out to be fictional.

Another aspect of the "trust, but verify" approach is that hate crime accusations should in every case by treated as law enforcement matters. This prescription is especially relevant for hate crime cases on college campuses. If, say, black tape is found covering the eyes of a series of portraits depicting every minority legal scholar at Harvard, university officials should not tweet despairingly, but rather call in the police. Can the portraits be finger-printed? Forensic technology could clear up many of these cases. A DNA test, a simple procedure these days, could easily identify the race and possibly the identity of the duct tape bandit.

Then, when campus cases *have* been reported to the police—as in the case of the San Diego State and Villanova allegations of Trump-inspired beatings and car-jackings—students making the accusations should not be allowed to simply stop cooperating with law enforcement. An actual hate criminal is a serious threat to any community, especially one made up of vulnerable young people. Both to catch such individuals where they exist and to expose hoaxers, officers should ask polite but tough questions from the moment of the initial report, and threats of potential disciplinary action should be used when needed to keep students involved in the investigative process— except perhaps in cases of reported rape and sexual assault.

When accusers are definitively shown to have faked hate crimes, they must be punished. Very often this simply does not occur. Again, colleges and universities are the worst offenders. To give several examples: Sabrina Collins, who claimed to have been the target of weeks of sustained criminal abuse at Emory, does not seem to have been punished at all. Francisco Nava, the white Hispanic conservative hate hoaxer who ran a pro-abstinence organization and turned Princeton on its head for weeks, was apparently merely kicked out of school. The University at Buffalo student who placed "Whites Only" and "Blacks Only" signs above the water fountains on campus got away scot-free as an "artist." And so on. In many cases, the name of the student perpetrator of an internationally famous probable hoax—such as the Muslim SDSU student who claimed to have been car-jacked by Donald Trump supporters—is never even revealed to the public.

To boil principles down to essentials, this is what we need to do to fight the hate crime hoaxes that are dangerously undermining relations between Americans of different races: (1) understand that many hate crimes are hoaxes, (2) actively and aggressively punish individuals discovered to have faked bias crimes, (3) stop making excuses for these criminals, and (4) stop the flow of benefits with which we currently reward these crimes. Hate crime hoaxes only feed the cynical false narrative of ethnic conflict and oppression that is destabilizing our society. Widespread implementation of this four-point program would represent at least the end of the beginning. There is no race war in the USA in 2018. Let's stop letting liars tell us there is...or we might actually get one.

God bless America.

Acknowledgments

Authors often say that their books could not have been written without the help of others. In my case, by George, this is not true! I am a notably cocky person, I have written dozens of peer-reviewed research articles, blogs, and speeches by myself, and I strongly suspect I would have gotten some kind of dubious monograph which no one out there would read written with no help whatsoever. But that said, the fact that this book is coming out as a major press hardcover obviously involved the physical and intellectual labor of many persons other than myself.

Thanks first to my excellent editor at Regnery, Elizabeth Kantor, who worked closely with me through the entire process of providing final edits to *Hoax*, showed infinite patience during the exchange of literally almost one hundred technical e-mails, and managed to incorporate improved versions of nearly all my "suggestions" and technical tweaks into the book. Thanks also to Tom Spence, my original editor on the project, who provided a very great deal of useful input about the book whilst it was still being written.

Any flaws which may remain in the finished product are to my demerit, and none of theirs. Closer to home, great thanks to Jane Lingle—my life partner and dear friend—who got a reminder of her law school days, and some practice for her upcoming M.L.S. degree, when I proved foolish enough to try writing a 256-page book and bold enough to ask her for assistance researching it. The second pair of hands, and of reviewing eyes, was invaluable!

These people do not stand alone. I also owe a considerable amount of gratitude to the more than half dozen writers, soldiers, and social scientists who agreed to read *Hoax* and provide official blurbs for the book or reviews of it. That list includes: Jonathan Bean (Southern Illinois University), Jimmy Cobb (Snake Oil Salesmen: lead singer), Kaiter Enless (Logos Club), Scott McConnell (*The American Conservative*), Darryl Pinto (U.S. Special Forces, Ret.), and Jonathon Sharp (Kentucky State University). Thanks also to the senior figures in the human sciences— most, but by no means all, of whom write from a conservative perspective—who agreed simply to analyze the book and provide commentary on it: John McWhorter, Alan Charles Kors, Richard Sander, Marc Siegel, Amy Wax, and many others.

Finally, I owe a far from insignificant debt to the great number of my personal friends who did essentially the same work as the scholars just cited—reading *Hoax*, and talking about it with me. In no particular order, thanks to Jairus Liner, Joe Pate, Sara Hines, Tim and Ariel Miller, Kristen Wheatley (aka "Lil' Wheat"), Evan Veremakis, Kamden Summers, Alex "Cat Yoder" Fox, Jessica Salgado, Steven Gilchrist, Dagan Bora, Meredith Wilson, Ken Suzuki, Ramadan Sulejmani, Jonnie Walker, Joel Eledesma, and Commander David Lyons of the Lexington Police Department. Mark Spiro ("Mark England") would have reviewed the thing, but he had to hop on a plane.

Perhaps most important, kudos to my mother, Jean Marie Ward, and my teachers as such "urban" schools as St. Mary's

Chicago, K.D. Waldo Middle, and East Aurora High School—who taught me how to read, write, and think.

W—

Notes

INTRODUCTION

1. It is probable that at least 15 percent of all reported hate crimes and hate incidents are hoaxes. A quantitative report put together by the Bias Response Team at the University of Wisconsin La-Crosse found that 28 of 192 hate incident reports from the campus and surrounding area were "either completely fake or not a bias…incident." This was the case despite the fact that the investigators counted things like the posting of a Campus Crusade for Christ poster and a blog post about life as a white student as "legitimate" incidents. Anthony Gockowski, "Crucifix, Trump chalkings reported as 'hate incidents' at UW-L," CampusReform, September 27, 2016, http://www.campusreform.org/?ID=8080. My own data support a similar conclusion. Despite the fact only five to six thousand hate crimes are reported nationwide in a typical year (see the FBI's Uniform Crime Reports at https://ucr.fbi.gov/hate-crime), and that perhaps 10 percent of these cases receive the level of media coverage that would make them easily accessible to researchers, I was able to put together a database of 409 confirmed and widely reported hate hoaxes concentrated during the years

2010–17. The website www.fakehatecrimes.org has published a substantially different list of 341 incidents. The most widely discussed nationally publicized hate incidents seem most likely to be revealed as fakes as we saw during the "Eastern Michigan," "Air Force Academy," "U.S. Navy," and "Burnt Black Churches" cases in 2017 alone.

2. Barry Glassner, *The Culture of Fear: Why Americans Are Afraid of the Wrong Things* (New York: Basic Books, 1999).

3. The entire platform of BLM umbrella organization "The Movement for Black Lives" can be found at https://policy.m4bl. org/platform/.

4. Heather Mac Donald, *The War on Cops: How the New Attack on Law and Order Makes Everyone Less Safe* (New York: Encounter Books, 2016).

5. www.fakehatecrimes.org.

6. Laird Wilcox, *Crying Wolf: Hate Crime Hoaxes in America* (Olathe, Kansas: Editorial Research Service, 1994), 1–2.

7. Darryl Fears, "Study: Many Blacks Cite AIDS Conspiracy," *Washington Post*, January 25, 2005, http://www.washingtonpost. com/wp-dyn/articles/A33695-2005Jan24.html.

8. I will note here that I use the standard FBI/Hate Crime Statistics Act Definition of a "hate crime" throughout this work: a felony or misdemeanor offense based on or caused by bias against the victim's "race, color, religion, national origin, gender/sex, sexual orientation (real or perceived), gender identity, or disability."

9. KC Johnson and Stuart Taylor Jr,, *The Campus Rape Frenzy: The Attack on Due Process at America's Universities* (New York: Encounter Books, 2017).

10. Ashe Schow, "Even If False Rape Reports Are Rare, They Shouldn't Be Ignored," *Washington Examiner*, July 14, 2015, https://www.washingtonexaminer.com/even-if-false-rape-reports-are-rare-they-shouldnt-be-ignored.

11. This is my own estimate, based on nationwide rates of reporting and media coverage for all crimes. This estimate likely errs, if at all, on the *high* side; it is very doubtful that the national media extensively covers 585 hate incidents in a typical year.

12. Anthony Gockowski, "Crucifix, Trump chalkings reported as 'hate incidents' at UW-L," CampusReform, September 27, 2016, http://www.campusreform.org/?ID=8080.

CHAPTER ONE: LANCING A BOIL

1. The Southern Poverty Law Center, "Financial Information: The Southern Poverty Law Center's latest financial information and annual report," https://www.splcenter.org/about/financial-information.

2. KPMG LLP, "Anti-Defamation League and Anti-Defamation League Foundation Consolidated Financial Statements and Schedules," December 31, 2016 and 2015, https://www.adl.org/media/10267/download.

3. "Black Lives Matter," Facebook, https://www.facebook.com/BlackLivesMatter/.

4. Laird Wilcox, *Crying Wolf: Hate Crime Hoaxes in America* (New York: Feral House, 1993).

5. The Movement for Black Lives, "Platform," https://policy.m4bl.org/platform/.

6. J.M. Berger, "How White Nationalists Learned to Love Donald Trump," *Politico*, October 25, 2016, https://www.politico.com/magazine/story/2016/10/donald-trump-2016-white-nationalists-alt-right-214388.

7. Adi Robertson, "Hillary Clinton Exposing Pepe the Frog Is the Death of Explainers," The Verge, September 15, 2016, https://www.theverge.com/2016/9/15/12926976/hillary-clinton-trump-pepe-the-frog-alt-right-explainer.

8. Sarah Posner and David Neiwert, "How Trump Took Hate Groups Mainstream," *Mother Jones*, October 14, 2016, https://www.motherjones.com/politics/2016/10/donald-trump-hate-groups-neo-nazi-white-supremacist-racism/.

9. Brian Beutler, "Trump Promised White Supremacy, Now He's Delivering It," *New Republic*, February 3, 2017, https://newrepublic.com/article/140377/trump-promised-white-supremacy-now-hes-delivering-it.

10. Darryl Fears, "Study: Many Blacks Cite AIDS Conspiracy," *Washington Post,* January 25, 2005, http://www.washingtonpost. com/wp-dyn/articles/A33695-2005Jan24.html?noredirect=on.

11. Richard H. Sander and Stuart Taylor Jr., *Mismatch: How Affirmative Action Hurts Students It's Intended to Help, and Why Universities Won't Admit It* (New York: Basic Books, 2012), 192.

12. Thomas J. Espenshade and Alexandria Walton Radford, *No Longer Separate, Not Yet Equal: Race and Class in Elite College Admission and Campus Life* (Princeton, NJ: Princeton University Press, 2009).

13. Sander and Taylor, *Mismatch,* 4–6, 35–36.

14. Wilcox, *Crying Wolf,* 2.

15. Thomas Sowell, *Affirmative Action around the World: An Empirical Study* (New Haven, CT: Yale University Press, 2004).

16. Aftab Ali, "Kean University's Kayla-Simone McKelvey pleads guilty to sending anonymous racial threats on Twitter," Independent, April 19, 2016, https://www.independent.co.uk/ student/news/kean-university-s-kayla-simone-mckelvey-pleads-guilty-to-sending-anonymous-racial-threats-on-twitter-a6991841. html.

17. Jessica Chasmar, "Black activist charged in race hoax at Kean University in N.J.," *Washington Times,* December 2, 2015, https:// www.washingtontimes.com/news/2015/dec/2/kayla-simone-mckelvey-black-activist-charged-in-ra/.

18. Sharita Erves and Henry Rosoff, "21-year-old UW-Parkside junior created hit list," Fox6Now, February 6, 2012, https://fox6now. com/2012/02/06/student-on-uw-parkside-hit-list-admits-to-hoax/.

19. Ben Axelson, "University of Buffalo 'White Only' sign sparks outrage; student calls it art," Syracuse Online, September 18, 2015, https://www.syracuse.com/state/index.ssf/2015/09/university_at_ buffalo_whites_only_sign_controversy.html.

20. Greg Hadley, "A diversity council at one small college admits to posting racist flyers on campus," *Star-Telegram,* March 24, 2017, https://www.star-telegram.com/news/nation-world/national/ article140695168.html.

21. John Agar, "'Poster boy for white hatred:' Michigan Tech misled students about racial threats, suit says," MLive, September 8, 2016, https://www.mlive.com/news/grand-rapids/index. ssf/2016/09/poster_boy_for_white_hatred_mi.html.

22. Vivian Yee, "Racism Charges in Bus Incident, and Their Unraveling, Upset University at Albany," *New York Times*, March 1, 2016, https://www.nytimes.com/2016/03/02/nyregion/racism-charges-in-bus-incident-and-their-unraveling-upset-u-of-albany. html.

23. Katie Mettler, "Miss. black church fire was called a hate crime. Now parishioner has been arrested for it," *Washington Post*, December 22, 2016, https://www.washingtonpost.com/news/ morning-mix/wp/2016/12/22/miss-black-church-fire-another-highly-publicized-suspected-hate-crime-debunked-police-say/?noredirect=on&utm_term=.2f4a1725e3e4.

24. Madeline Buckley, "'Heil Trump' church graffiti was 'false flag,'" *IndyStar*, May 3, 2017, https://www.indystar.com/story/news/ crime/2017/05/03/why-heil-trump-spray-painted-church/101240824/.

25. Stephanie Allen, "Cops: Man faked 'KKK' hate crime, own kidnapping after lighting car on fire," *Orlando Sentinel*, December 12, 2016, https://www.orlandosentinel.com/news/ breaking-news/os-fake-hate-crime-arson-20161212-story.html.

26. Dorkys Ramos, "Update: Police Say Alleged Racist Attack Is a Hoax," BET, October 23, 2012, https://www.bet.com/news/ national/2012/10/23/woman-allegedly-set-on-fire-in-possible-hate-crime.html.

27. Rocco Parascandola and Leonard Greene, "Muslim college student made up Trump supporter subway attack story to avoid punishment for missing curfew," *Daily News*, December 15, 2016, https://www.nydailynews.com/new-york/muslim-woman-reported-trump-supporter-attack-made-story-article-1.2910944?barcprox=true.

28. Jessica Chasmar, "North Park University student fabricated anti-gay 'Trump' notes, school says," *Washington Times*, November

25, 2016, https://www.washingtontimes.com/news/2016/nov/25/
taylor-volk-north-park-university-student-fabricat/.

29. Brigette Burnett, "BG police say student lied about politically driven attack," 13ABC News, November 17, 2016, https://www.13abc.com/content/news/BG-police-say-student-lied-about-politically-driven-attack-401814426.html.

30. John Counts, "Ann Arbor woman pleads guilty to making up hate crime," MLive, March 7, 2017, https://www.mlive.com/news/ann-arbor/index.ssf/2017/03/ann_arbor_woman_pleads_guilty_1.html.

31. Coalition Against Insurance Fraud, "Arson at Illinois gay bar likely a fake hate crime by owner," Insurance Fraud News, November 2, 2013, http://www.insurancefraud.org/IFNS-detail.htm?key=17559.

32. Caitlin Ryan and Ian Rivers, "Lesbian, gay, bisexual and transgender youth: Victimization and its correlates in the USA and UK," *Culture, Health, & Sexuality* 5, No. 2 (2003): 103–19.

33. "Owner of Oak Park's torched Velvet Rope gay night spot charged with arson, insurance fraud," November 2, 2013, https://www.oakpark.com/News/Articles/11-2-2013/Owner-of-Oak-Park%27s-torched-Velvet-Rope-gay-night-spot-charged-with-arson,-insurance-fraud/.

34. HuffPost, "Joe Williams, Tennessee Health Food Store Owner, Beaten in Alleged Anti-Gay Hate Crime," December 29, 2013, https://www.huffingtonpost.com/2013/11/25/tennessee-healthy-thyme-hate-crime-_n_4337809.html.

35. Julie Zauzmer, "Gay pastor admits he faked homophobic slur on Whole Foods cake," *Washington Post*, May 16, 2016, https://www.washingtonpost.com/news/acts-of-faith/wp/2016/05/16/gay-pastor-admits-he-faked-homophobic-slur-on-whole-foods-cake/?utm_term=.c3e72d3e3873.

36. Bil Browning, "Donations Will Be Returned by Woman with 'Relentlessly Gay' Yard Decorations," *The Advocate*, August 20, 2015, https://www.advocate.com/breaking/2015/08/20/relentlessly-gay-yard-donations-be-returned-after-hoax-allegations.

37. "Bias Incidents at Vassar Were a Hoax As One of the Culprits Was 'the Transgender Student Leading the Investigations into the Offensive Graffiti,'" *Daily Mail*, December 5, 2013, https://www.

dailymail.co.uk/news/article-2518748/Vassar-graffiti-hoax-culprit-transgender-student-leading-investigations.html.

38. Eytan Halon, "American-Israeli Teen Hacker Behind JCC Bomb Threats Found Guilty," *Jerusalem Post*, June 28, 2018, https://www.jpost.com/Israel-News/American-Israeli-teen-hacker-behind-JCC-bomb-threats-found-guilty-561073.

39. Many centrist and right-wing writers have discussed the Brawley Hoax at some length. One of the best accounts is in Ann Coulter's book, *Mugged: Racial Demagoguery from the Seventies to Obama* (New York: Sentinel, 2013).

40. For a less edgy but equally critical review of the mainstream media's Jena Six narrative, containing most of the facts given above, see Craig Franklin, "Media Myths about the Jena Six," *Christian Science Monitor*, October 24, 2007, https://www.csmonitor.com/2007/1024/p09s01-coop.html.

41. Latifah Muhammad, "Firefighter Charged with Arson After Blaming BLM Members for Burning His House Down," *Vibe*, December 11, 2016, https://www.vibe.com/2016/12/firefighter-blames-black-lives-matter.

42. "Police: Mom, Son Charged in Truck Vandalism Hoax," Fox4News, September 21, 2015, http://www.fox4news.com/news/police-mom-son-charged-in-truck-vandalism-hoax.

43. Christine Byers, "St. Louis Bosnian woman who claimed hate crime is charged with making false report," *St. Louis Post-Dispatch*, December 16, 2014, https://www.stltoday.com/news/local/crime-and-courts/st-louis-bosnian-woman-who-claimed-hate-crime-is-charged/article_2d835f8c-5385-5c5d-9496-de7b6559070f.html.

44. Aina Hunter, "Acid Attack Hoax: Why Did She Say Attacker Was Black?," CBS News, September 17, 2010, https://www.cbsnews.com/news/acid-attack-hoax-why-did-she-say-attacker-was-black/.

CHAPTER TWO: A CONFLICT OF VISIONS: THE "CONTINUING OPPRESSION" NARRATIVE VERSUS REALITY

1. The Movement for Black Lives, "Platform," https://policy.m4bl. org/platform/.

2. Wesley Lowery, "Aren't more white people than black people killed by police? Yes, but no," *Washington Post*, July 11, 2016, https:// www.washingtonpost.com/news/post-nation/wp/2016/07/11/arent-more-white-people-than-black-people-killed-by-police-yes-but-no/?utm_term=.07ce900225aa.

3. Wesley Lowery, "Study finds police fatally shoot unarmed black men at disproportionate rates," *Washington Post*, April 7, 2016, https://www.washingtonpost.com/national/study-finds-police-fatally-shoot-unarmed-black-men-at-disproportionate-rates/2016/04/06/e494563e-fa74-11e5-80e4-c381214de1a3_story. html?utm_term=.2900938f609d.

4. Justin Hansford, "Body cameras won't stop police brutality. Eric Garner is only one of several reasons why," *Washington Post*, December 4, 2014, https://www.washingtonpost.com/posteverything/wp/2014/12/04/body-cameras-wont-stop-police-brutality-eric-garner-is-only-one-of-several-reasons-why/?utm_term=.1ec7333e4eeb.

5. Jennifer R. Halladay, *White Anti-Racist Activism: A Personal Roadmap* (Roselle, NJ: Crandall, Dostie, & Douglass, 2000).

6. Andrew Hacker, *Two Nations: Black and White, Separate, Hostile, Unequal* (New York: Ballantine, 1995), 36.

7. Gina Crosley-Corcoran, "Explaining White Privilege to a Broke White Person," HuffPost, May 8, 2014, https://www. huffingtonpost.com/gina-crosleycorcoran/explaining-white-privilege-to-a-broke-white-person_b_5269255.html.

8. Karen Yuan and Lucy Price, "Teen's 'White Boy Privilege' slam poetry goes viral," CNN, July 14, 2016, https://www.cnn. com/2016/07/13/us/teen-slam-poet-white-privilege-hln/index.html.

9. Susan Scarfidi, *Who Owns Culture?* (New Brunswick, NJ: Rutgers University Press, 2005).

10. Nadra Kareem Nittle, "A Guide to Understanding and Avoiding Cultural Appropriation," ThoughtCo., June 1, 2018, https://www.

thoughtco.com/cultural-appropriation-and-why-iits-wrong-2834561.

11. Susan Scarfidi, *Who Owns Culture?* (New Brunswick, NJ: Rutgers University Press, 2005).

12. Maisha Z. Johnson, "What's Wrong with Cultural Appropriation? These 9 Answers Reveal Its Harm," Everyday Feminism, June 14, 2015, https://everydayfeminism.com/2015/06/cultural-appropriation-wrong/.

13. Several of the articles discussed in this chapter assume that minorities who identify as mainstream Americans are *de facto* whites, no longer possess "authentic" minority voices, and thus can commit sins such as cultural appropriation.

14. Johnson, "What's Wrong with Cultural Appropriation?"

15. Kenan Malik, "In Defense of Cultural Appropriation," *New York Times*, June 14, 2017, https://www.nytimes.com/2017/06/14/opinion/in-defense-of-cultural-appropriation.html.

16. Roger Clegg, "Latest Statistics on Illegitimate Births," *National Review*, October 4, 2012, https://www.nationalreview.com/corner/latest-statistics-illegitimate-births-roger-clegg/.

17. Jason Riley, *Please Stop Helping Us: How Liberals Make It Harder for Blacks to Succeed*, (New York: Encounter, 2016).

18. Riley, *Please Stop Helping Us*, 158–59.

19. Niall McCarthy, "Income Inequality Between White and Black Americans Is Worse Today Than in 1979," *Forbes*, September 21, 2016, https://www.forbes.com/sites/niallmccarthy/2016/09/21/income-inequality-between-white-black-americans-is-worse-today-than-in-1979-infographic/#603b68413740.

20. Bruce Drake, "Incarceration gap widens between whites and blacks," Pew Research Center, September 6, 2013, http://www.pewresearch.org/fact-tank/2013/09/06/incarceration-gap-between-whites-and-blacks-widens/.

21. Walter E. Williams, "The True Black Tragedy: Illegitimacy Rate of Nearly 75%," CNS News, May 19, 2015, https://www.cnsnews.com/commentary/walter-e-williams/true-black-tragedy-illegitimacy-rate-nearly-75.

22. Suzanne Model, *West Indian Immigrants: A Black Success Story?* (New York: Russell Sage, 2008).

23. Nicholas Eberstadt, "White Families Are in Trouble, Too," Dallas News, August 21, 2005, http://www.aei.org/publication/white-families-are-in-trouble-too/.

24. Dennis Prager, "The Fallacy of 'White Privilege,'" *National Review*, February 16, 2016, https://www.nationalreview.com/2016/02/white-privilege-myth-reality/.

25. Riley, *Please Stop Helping Us.*

26. Drake, "Incarceration Gap."

27. Patrick A. Langan, "Race of Prisoners Admitted to State and Federal Institutions, 1926–1986," U.S. Department of Justice Office of Justice Programs Bureau of Justice Statistics, May 1991, https://www.ncjrs.gov/pdffiles1/nij/125618.pdf.

28. For comprehensive data on American lynchings broken down by race and year, see "Lynching, Whites and Negroes, 1882–1968," Tuskegee University, http://192.203.127.197/archive/bitstream/handle/123456789/511/Lyching%201882%201968.pdf.

29. Matthew Cella and Alan Neuhauser, "Race and Homicide In America, by the Numbers," U.S. News and World Report, September 29, 2016, https://www.usnews.com/news/articles/2016-09-29/race-and-homicide-in-america-by-the-numbers.

30. Dinesh D'Souza, *The End of Racism* (New York: Free Press, 1995).

31. John McWhorter, *Losing the Race: Self-Sabotage in Black America* (New York: Free Press, 2000).

32. The 2.5:1 ratio of Black-to-white crime, as well as some interesting conclusions about interracial crime, can be drawn directly from the tables appearing in this article: Heather Mac Donald, "The Shameful Liberal Exploitation of the Charleston Massacre," *National Review*, July 1, 2015, https://www.nationalreview.com/2015/07/charleston-shooting-obama-race-crime/.

33. Van Jones, "Are Blacks a Criminal Race? Surprising Statistics," HuffPost, October 5, 2005, https://www.huffingtonpost.com/van-jones/are-blacks-a-criminal-rac_b_8398.html.

34. For decades of Uniform Crime Report data from the Federal Bureau of Investigation, see "Uniform Crime Reporting," FBI, https://www.fbi.gov/services/cjis/ucr.

35. For data dating back to 1973, see "Data Collection: National Crime Victimization Survey (NCVS)," Bureau of Justice Statistics, https://www.bjs.gov/index.cfm?ty=dcdetail&iid=245.

36. Heather Mac Donald, *The War on Cops* (New York: Encounter, 2016).

37. Milo Yiannopoulos, *Dangerous* (London: Dangerous Books, 2017).

38. Erik Wemple, "Dear Mainstream Media: Why so Liberal?," *Washington Post*, January 27, 2017, https://www.washingtonpost.com/blogs/erik-wemple/wp/2017/01/27/dear-mainstream-media-why-so-liberal/?noredirect=on&utm_term=.ad58ff87bf67.

39. For good summary of the full "Lichter-Rothman Study" this statistic comes from, see American Life League, "Chapter 124—The Source and Nature of the Media's Biases," EWTN, http://www.ewtn.com/library/prolenc/encyc124.htm.

40. "Fatal Police Shootings: England and Wales 2008–2017, INQUEST, April 26, 2018, https://www.inquest.org.uk/fatal-police-shootings.

41. Tim Wise, "Nazis Can't Do Math: Reflections on Racism, Crime and the Illiteracy of Right-Wing Statistical Analysis, August 25, 2013, http://www.timwise.org/2013/08/nazis-cant-do-math-reflections-on-racism-crime-and-the-illiteracy-of-right-wing-statistical-analysis/; Jared Taylor, *Paved with Good Intentions* (New York: Carroll and Graf, 1993).

42. Tim Wise, "Race, Crime, and Statistical Malpractice: How the Right Manipulates White Fear with Bogus Data," August 22, 2013, http://www.timwise.org/2013/08/race-crime-and-statistical-malpractice-how-the-right-manipulates-white-fear-with-bogus-data/.

43. Jared Taylor, "The Mind of the Killer: How Can We Prevent Future Dylann Roofs?," The Unz Review, July 27, 2015, http://www.unz.com/article/the-mind-of-the-killer/.

44. John J. Dilulio, Jr., "My Black Crime Problem, and Ours," *City Journal*, Spring 1996, https://www.city-journal.org/html/my-black-crime-problem-and-ours-11773.html.

45. Kelly Bauer and Mark Konkol, "Chicago Police Stops Down by 90 Percent as Violence Skyrockets," DNA Info, March 31, 2016, https://www.dnainfo.com/chicago/20160331/bronzeville/chicago-police-stops-down-by-90-percent-as-gun-violence-skyrockets/.

46. Mac Donald, *The War on Cops*, 1–2.

47. Cella and Neuhauser, "Race and Homicide in America."

48. Nicholas Stix, "The Knoxville Horror: The Crime and the Cover-Up," American Renaissance, May 14, 2007, https://www.amren.com/news/2007/05/the_knoxville_h/. To be completely transparent, a second search on November 8, 2018, with all cookies on the author's computer deleted, did also turn up stories from the alt-right VDare website and a single mention from hard-Right The Blaze. But the point here stands.

49. Andrew Knapp, "Man once named suspect Ii Brittanee Drexel case is jailed, accused of violating jail release rules," *Post and Courier*, October 31, 2017, https://www.postandcourier.com/news/man-once-named-suspect-in-brittanee-drexel-case-is-jailed/article_ba0aced6-be7a-11e7-860f-6f5ca3660b5f.html.

50. Clark Howard, *Zebra* (New York: Richard Marek Pubs, 1979).

51. John McWhorter, "Stop Obsessing Over Race and IQ," *National Review*, July 5, 2017, https://www.nationalreview.com/2017/07/race-iq-debate-serves-no-purpose/.

52. See Twitter user @hbdchick discuss the unexpected suspension(s) of her account at https://twitter.com/hbdchick/status/1046381839160610816?lang=en.

53. Christopher Jencks and Meredith Phillips, *The Black-White Test Score Gap* (Washington, D.C: Brookings Institution, 1998).

54. Roland Fryer and Steven Leavitt, "Understanding the Black-White Test Score Gap in the First Two Years of School," *Review of Economics and Statistics* 86, no. 2 (May 2004): 447–64. See also William T. Dickens and James R. Flynn, "Black Americans Reduce the Racial IQ Gap: Evidence from Standardization Samples," *Psychological Science* 17, no. 10 (October 2006): 913–20, showing

how the Black-white IQ gap shrank by roughly half (7 points) between 1972 and 2002. Both these pieces are must-reads for anyone interested in discussions of genetics and IQ from a non–alt-right perspective.

55. McWhorter, *Losing the Race.*

CHAPTER THREE: BIG FAKE ON CAMPUS: FAKE HATE CRIMES IN AMERICAN ACADEMIA

1. Mitchell Langbert, Anthony J. Quain, and Daniel B. Klein, "Faculty Voter Registration in Economics, History, Journalism, Law, and Psychology," *Econ Journal Watch* 13, no. 3 (September 2016): 422–51; Bradford Richardson, "Liberal professors outnumber conservatives nearly 12 to 1, survey finds," *Washington Times*, October 6, 2016, https://www. washingtontimes.com/news/2016/oct/6/liberal-professors-outnumber-conservatives-12-1/; Kevin Eagan et al., "Undergraduate Teaching Faculty: The 2013–2014 HERI Faculty Survey," Higher Education Research Institute, University of California at Los Angeles, 2014, https://www.heri.ucla.edu/ monographs/HERI-FAC2014-monograph.pdf, 39.

2. "What Are Speech Codes?" Foundation for Individual Rights in Education, https://www.thefire.org/spotlight/what-are-speech-codes/.

3. Kassy Dillon, "After protests and riots, free speech is MIA on college campuses," *The Hill*, February 3, 2017, https://thehill.com/ blogs/pundits-blog/education/317719-after-protests-and-riots-free-speech-is-mia-on-college-campuses.

4. Tara Hoffman, "UW-Parkside students charged following 'hate crime' hoax," *Badger Herald*, March 18, 2012, https:// badgerherald.com/news/2012/03/18/uwparkside-students.

5. Christine Won, "Parkside reports hate crimes in residence hall, third incident reported Thursday evening," *Journal Times*, February 2, 2012, https://journaltimes.com/article_54bc8282-4de6-11e1-85d2-0019bb2963f4.html.

6. Eric Owens, "Justice: Judge Sends Black Activist to Jail for Hoax Death Threats to Black Students, Faculty," The Daily Caller, June 19, 2016, https://dailycaller.com/2016/06/19/justice-judge-sends-black-activist-to-jail-for-hoax-death-threats-to-black-students-faculty/.

7. Jessica Remo, "Twitter threats to black Kean students made by black alum, police say," December 14, 2015, https://www.nj.com/union/index.ssf/2015/12/arrest_made_in_kean_twitter_threat.html.

8. Jazz Shaw, "Kean University Racist Death Threats Turn Out to Have Come from One of the Protesters," Hot Air, December 2, 2015, https://hotair.com/archives/2015/12/02/kean-university-racist-death-threats-turn-out-to-have-come-from-one-of-the-protesters/.

9. Khaleda Rahman, "Black woman who tweeted anonymous racist threats to fellow black students is jailed," Daily Mail, June 17, 2016, https://www.dailymail.co.uk/news/article-3647516/Black-woman-tweeted-anonymous-racist-threats-fellow-BLACK-students-jailed.html.

10. Owens, "Justice: Judge Sends Black Activist to Jail."

11. Amber Athey, "'Poster boy for white hatred' sues Michigan Tech for scapegoating him," Campus Reform, September 9, 2016, https://www.campusreform.org/?ID=8116.

12. Kat Stafford, "Man accused of threatening black Michigan Tech students sues school," Detroit Free Press, September 8, 2016, https://www.freep.com/story/news/local/michigan/2016/09/08/man-accused-threatening-black-michigan-tech-students-sues-school/89996710/.

13. Justin P. Hicks, "Former Michigan Tech student refunded $42K in lawsuit settlement," MLive, August 9, 2017, https://www.mlive.com/news/grand-rapids/index.ssf/2017/08/expelled_michigan_tech_student.html.

14. John Agar, "'Poster boy for white hatred:' Michigan Tech misled students about racial threats, suit says," MLive, September 9, 2016, https://www.mlive.com/news/grand-rapids/index.ssf/2016/09/poster_boy_for_white_hatred_mi.html.

15. Heather Barr, "Campus police determine reported hate crimes were fabricated, student shares truth," The Chimes, February 9, 2017, http://cuchimes.com/02/2017/campus-police-determine-reported-hate-crimes-fabricated/.

16. "Hate crime hoax alert: Capital University student admits to fabricating several incidents," The College Fix, February 24, 2017, https://www.thecollegefix.com/hate-crime-hoax-alert-capital-university-student-admits-fabricating-several-incidents/.

17. Barr, "Campus Police Determine Reported Hate Crimes Were Fabricated."

18. "Hate crime hoax alert," The College Fix.

19. Barr, "Campus Police Determine Reported Hate Crimes Were Fabricated."

20. Megan Crepeau, "U of C—Feds investigate threatening Facebook hack," Chicago Tribune, November 20, 2014, https://www.chicagotribune.com/news/local/breaking/race-petition-u-chicago-20141119-story.html.

21. Matt Lamb, "Racially charged hacking incident was just a hoax to push diversity agenda," The College Fix, December 1, 2014, https://www.thecollegefix.com/racially-charged-hacking-incident-was-just-a-hoax-to-push-diversity-agenda/.

22. Crepeau, "U. of C."

23. Lamb, "Racially Charged Hacking Incident Was Just a Hoax."

24. Maroon Editorial Board, "Eyes on the prize: controversy on Facebook should not distract from students' legitimate grievances," Chicago Maroon, November 25, 2014, https://www.chicagomaroon.com/2014/11/25/eyes-on-the-prize/.

25. Lamb, "Racially Charged Hacking Incident Was Just a Hoax."

26. Gabriela Julia and Marlee Tuskes, "UB art student admits to hanging 'White Only' and 'Black Only' signs on campus," Spectrum, September 16, 2015, https://www.ubspectrum.com/article/2015/09/ub-student-admits-to-hanging-white-only-and-black-only-signs-for-art-project.

27. Eileen Buckley, "UB art student admits posting controversial signs," WBFO 88.7 Buffalo, September 18, 2015, http://news.wbfo.org/post/ub-art-student-admits-posting-controversial-signs.

28. Ashley Powell, "Letter to the editor: UB student sends statement to The Spectrum about 'White Only' and 'Black Only' signs," *Spectrum*, September 18, 2015, https://www.ubspectrum.com/article/2015/09/white-only-and-black-only-letter-to-editor.

29. Julia and Tuskes, "UB art student admits to hanging 'White Only' and 'Black Only' signs."

30. It is worth noting that these are separate and distinct organizations, some presumably with paid employees, that exist— along with the previously mentioned Campus Bias Response Team—to promote diversity at Gustavus Adolphus College. Gustavus Adolphus has 2,450 students, 1.9 percent of whom are Black. There must be one diversity bureaucrat for every brother on the campus!

31. Anthony Gockowski, "College 'diversity council' posts FAKE racist flyers," Campus Reform, March 23, 2017, https://www.campusreform.org/?ID=8965.

32. So are seven of the first ten results for the search "Gustavus Adolphus diversity." This incident got press.

33. CJ Siewert, "St. Peter Police investigating possible hate crime at Gustavus Adolphus College," *St. Peter Herald*, October 8, 2013, https://www.southernminn.com/st_peter_herald/news/article_9743677e-2645-529f-a7d7-74cff3bef6f2.html.

34. Michelle Malkin, "The left fakes the hate at GWU," October 9, 2007, http://michellemalkin.com/2007/10/09/the-left-fakes-the-hate-at-gwu/.

35. Lisa Rab, "The Edge of Reason," *Cleveland Scene*, May 16, 2007, https://www.clevescene.com/cleveland/the-edge-of-reason/Content?oid=1498563.

36. University Diaries, "Depillation," Inside Higher Ed, November 17, 2007, https://www.insidehighered.com/blogs/university-diaries/depillation.

37. John C. Kuehner, "Case prof gets prison for reporting fake hate mail to FBI," *Plain Dealer*, November 16, 2007, http://blog.cleveland.com/metro/2007/11/case_prof_gets_prison_for_repo.html.

38. Rab, "The Edge of Reason."

39. Michealangelo Conte, "Jersey City high school candidate for student gov't sent racist texts to himself," *Jersey Journal*, August 26, 2013, https://www.nj.com/hudson/index.ssf/2013/08/the_black_st_peters_prep_student_who_received_racist_text_during_his_run_for_student_council_sent_th.html.

40. Michaelangelo Conte, "Racist text messages sent to St. Peter's Prep student running in school election: cops," *Jersey Journal*, May 17, 2013, https://www.nj.com/hudson/index.ssf/2013/05/racist_text_messages_sent_to_s.html; Michaelangelo Conte, "Probe into racist texts sent student at Jersey City high school is ongoing," *Jersey Journal*, May 30, 2013, https://www.nj.com/hudson/index.ssf/2013/05/probe_into_racist_texts_sent_s.html.

41. Conte, "Jersey City High School Candidate."

42. Megan Brockett and Cindy Huang, "Police charge teenager with sending threatening tweet to Arundel High," *The Capital*, January 11, 2017, https://www.capitalgazette.com/news/for_the_record/ph-ac-cn-suspect-kkklan-0112-20170111-story.html.

43. Michael Pearson, "A timeline of the University of Missouri protests," CNN, November 10, 2015, https://www.cnn.com/2015/11/09/us/missouri-protest-timeline/index.html.

44. Michael Miller, "Black grad student on hunger strike in Mo. after swastika drawn with human feces," *Washington Post*, November 6, 2015, https://www.washingtonpost.com/news/morning-mix/wp/2015/11/06/black-grad-student-on-hunger-strike-in-mo-after-swastika-drawn-with-human-feces/?noredirect=on&utm_term=.14717cef2bbf.

45. Pearson, "A timeline of the University of Missouri protests."

46. Clay Travis, "Is the Entire Mizzou Protest Based on Lies?," November 11, 2015, https://www.outkickthecoverage.com/is-the-entire-mizzou-protest-based-on-lies-111115/.

47. Andrew McCarthy, "Hey Mizzou, Where's the Poop?," *National Review*, November 10, 2015, https://www.nationalreview.com/corner/hey-mizzou-wheres-poop-andrew-c-mccarthy/.

48. The Federalist has pursued this story with rather remarkable aggression. See Sean Davis, "Was the Poop Swastika Incident at Mizzou a Giant Hoax?," The Federalist, November 10, 2015,

http://thefederalist.com/2015/11/10/was-the-poop-swastika-incident-at-mizzou-a-giant-hoax/; Sean Davis, "Mizzou Finally Releases Poop Swastika Police Report," The Federalist, November 11, 2015, http://thefederalist.com/2015/11/11/mizzou-finally-releases-poop-swastika-police-report/.

49. McCarthy, "Hey Mizzou, Where's the Poop?"; Davis, "Was the Poop Swastika Incident at Mizzou a Giant Hoax?"

50. David French, "Mizzou after the Meltdown," *National Review*, October 25, 2018, https://www.nationalreview.com/magazine/2018/11/12/university-of-missouri-meltdown-aftermath/; Anemona Hartocollis, "Long After Protests, Students Shun the University of Missouri," *New York Times*, July 9, 2017, https://www.nytimes.com/2017/07/09/us/university-of-missouri-enrollment-protests-fallout.html.

CHAPTER FOUR: THE KLAN SPRINGS ETERNAL! HOAX HATE GROUP ATTACKS AND THE REAL CRIMES THEY COVER UP

1. Pew Research Center Staff, "Values and the Press," Pew Research Center, May 23, 2004, http://www.people-press.org/2004/05/23/iv-values-and-the-press/.

2. The key findings of the *L.A. Times* study, along with a number of other empirical studies that come to similar conclusions, can be found here at "Media Bias Basics," Media Research Center, http://archive.mrc.org/biasbasics/biasbasics.asp.

3. S. Robert Lichter, Stanley Rothman, and Linda Lichter, *The Media Elite: America's New Powerbrokers* (New York: Adler, 1986).

4. Dave Levinthal and Michael Beckel, "Journalists Shower Hillary Clinton with Campaign Cash," The Center for Public Integrity, October 17, 2016, https://www.publicintegrity.org/2016/10/17/20330/journalists-shower-hillary-clinton-campaign-cash.

5. "Media Bias Basics," Media Research Center.

6. Heather Mac Donald, *The War on Cops* (New York: Encounter, 2016). I will note that, while the exact figures vary from year to year, the basic point that the huge majority of people shot by

American police officers are white or Hispanic, rather than Black, is not disputed by any serious social scientist. Raw data for 2017 and 2018 can be found at "Number of people shot to death by the police in the United States in 2017–2018, as of October, by Race," Statista, 2018, https://www.statista.com/statistics/585152/people-shot-to-death-by-us-police-by-race/.

7. A crude but effective way to gauge levels of media coverage is simply to Google the name of the victim or accused perpetrator in a particular legal case and see what results return. A search for "Trayvon Martin" returned fourteen links to major national mass media outlets—the *New York Times*, CNN, and so forth—within the first two pages of Google search results. "Mike Brown" yielded fourteen results as well, and "Freddie Gray" twelve. In contrast, a search for "Dylan Noble," who is easily the most widely known white victim of police violence, yielded only one national media hit, for the *Los Angeles Times*. A search for "Knoxville Horror" returned none, for "Brittanee Drexel" returned one (ABC News), and "Dillon Taylor" two (the *Washington Times* and HuffPo: the Huffington Post's headline began "Shooting of Dillon Taylor Was Justified"). With the sole exception of outlier Kate Steinle, white victims of police shootings and similar dramatic homicides received roughly one tenth as much coverage as Black victims. Jane Lingle, formerly of Southern Illinois University-Carbondale, assisted me with this analysis.

8. Wilfred Reilly, "Hearts All A-Twitter? A Quantitative Examination of Potential Correlations between New (and Old) Media and the American Culture of Fear," Academia, 2016, http://www.academia.edu/33785163/Hearts_All_A-Twitter_A_Quantitative_Examination_of_Potential_Correlations_between_New_and_Old_Media_and_the_American_Culture_of_Fear.

9. Lydia DePillis, "Lots of Americans fear flying. But not because of plane crashes," *Washington Post*, December 31, 2014, https://www.washingtonpost.com/news/storyline/wp/2014/12/31/lots-of-americans-fear-flying-but-not-because-of-plane-crashes/?utm_term=.1ff1c3d454b2.

10. Barry Glassner, *The Culture of Fear* (New York: Basic Books, 1999).

11. Hillary Clinton's claim that she "keeps hot sauce in her purse," like Beyonce, struck many Black voters as one of the more absurd examples of racial pandering on record. Jeva Lange, "Clinton Stirs Anger by Claiming That She Keeps Hot Sauce in Her Bag," The Week, April 18, 2016, https://theweek.com/speedreads/619127/clinton-stirs-anger-by-claiming-carries-hot-sauce-bag-like-beyonc.

12. Vivian Yee, "Racism Charges in Bus Incident, and Their Unraveling, Upset University at Albany," *New York Times*, March 1, 2016, https://www.nytimes.com/2016/03/02/nyregion/racism-charges-in-bus-incident-and-their-unraveling-upset-u-of-albany.html.

13. Ibid.

14. Cleve Wootson, "A man set his ex's car on fire for revenge, then blamed it on the KKK, police say," *Washington Post*, December 14, 2016, https://www.washingtonpost.com/news/true-crime/wp/2016/12/14/a-man-set-his-exs-car-on-fire-for-revenge-then-blamed-it-on-the-kkk-police-say/?noredirect=on&utm_term=.4f1ec4545a66.

15. Mark Bowes, "Court records: Ex-Petersburg city attorney made phony call to himself claiming racial threats to city leaders," *Richmond Times-Dispatch*, June 29, 2017, https://www.richmond.com/news/local/central-virginia/tri-cities/petersburg/court-records-ex-petersburg-city-attorney-made-phony-call-to/article_08a33542-2a0c-5ea3-a59c-614b31a735f7.html.

16. Mark Bowes, "Ex-Petersburg city attorney convicted for calling in fake racist threats to cancel council meeting," *Richmond Times-Dispatch*, September 1, 2017, https://www.richmond.com/news/local/crime/ex-petersburg-city-attorney-convicted-for-calling-in-fake-racist/article_3f1e814f-d60a-5373-a729-0e582202aa6c.html.

17. Mark Bowes, "Minister sentenced to 2 years for setting fire," *Richmond Times-Dispatch*, November 1, 2013, https://www.richmond.com/news/local/crime/minister-sentenced-to-years-for-setting-fire/article_75c0c600-423b-11e3-bcf1-0019bb30f31a.html.

18. Bowes, "Minister Sentenced to Two Years."

19. "Man Accused of Writing 'N*****' on receipt given to black Red Lobster waitress sues restaurant," *Daily Mail*, May 24, 2014, https://www.dailymail.co.uk/news/article-2637914/Man-accused-writing-N-receipt-given-black-Red-Lobster-waitress-sues-restaurant-waitress-handwriting-experts-finds-DIDNT-write-racial-slur.html.

20. Susan Kuczka and Lisa Black, "Racial threat called hoax of unhappy black student," *Chicago Tribune*, April 27, 2005, https://www.chicagotribune.com/news/ct-xpm-2005-04-27-0504270153-story.html.

21. J.P. Travis, "Alicia Hardin takes a gun to chapel," Bogus Hate Crimes, April 21, 2005, http://www.bogushatecrimes.com/050421_AliciaHardinsGun.php.

22. See Barbara Bell, "Ex-Student at Trinity convicted for threats," *Chicago Tribune*, April 14, 2006, https://www.chicagotribune.com/news/ct-xpm-2006-04-14-0604140250-story.html http://www.chicagotribune.com/news/ct-xpm-2006-04-14-0604140250-story.html.

23. Kuczka and Black, "Racial threat called hoax."

24. Carolyn Roy, "Charges filed in Winnsboro burning hoax," KSLA News, March 18, 2013, http://www.ksla.com/story/21671602/charges-filed-in-winnsboro-burning-hoax/.

25. Associated Press, "Louisiana woman says 3 racist men set her on fire," *USA Today*, October 22, 2012, https://www.usatoday.com/story/news/nation/2012/10/22/louisiana-hate-crime/1650645/.

26. "Update: Police Say Alleged Racist Attack Is a Hoax," BET, October 23, 2012, https://www.bet.com/news/national/2012/10/23/woman-allegedly-set-on-fire-in-possible-hate-crime.html.

27. Associated Press, "Louisiana woman, 20, set on fire in possible hate crime attack," *Daily News*, October 23, 2012, http://www.nydailynews.com/news/crime/la-woman-set-fire-hate-crime-article-1.1189946.

28. "Update: Police Say Alleged Racist Attack Is a Hoax," BET.

29. "Sharmeka Moffitt, Louisiana Woman, May Have Set Herself on Fire In Dubious Race-Related Attack: Police," HuffPost, October

24, 2012, https://www.huffingtonpost.com/2012/10/23/sharmeka-moffitt-louisiana-woman-set-on-fire-kkk-race-related-attack-_n_2005232.html.

30. "Update: Police Say Alleged Racist Attack Is a Hoax.," BET.

31. Jenna Lyons, "Man charged with making false hate crime report in Palo Alto," SF Gate, January 12, 2016, https://www.sfgate.com/crime/article/Man-charged-with-making-false-hate-crime-report-6754335.php.

32. "Jesus Francisco Cabrera Stabbed by Imaginary Xenophobes," MoonBattery, January 15, 2016, https://moonbattery.com/jesus-francisco-cabrera-stabbed-by-imaginary-xenophobes/.

33. Michelle Roberts, "East Palo Alto Man Arrested for Falsely Reporting Hate Crime," NBC Bay Area, January 12, 2016, https://www.nbcbayarea.com/news/local/East-Palo-Alto-Man-Arrested-for-Falsely-Reporting-Hate-Crime-365063461.html.

34. Come on. You *knew* Palo Alto had to have a human relations commission.

35. Lyons, "Man charged with making false hate crime report."

36. "Jesus Francisco Cabrera Stabbed by Imaginary Xenophobes."

37. Alison Boggs, "Rights educator finds noose on porch of Spokane home," *Spokesman-Review*, September 24, 2009, http://www.spokesman.com/stories/2009/sep/24/rights-educator-finds-noose-on-porch-of-spokane/.

38. "Human rights activist finds noose on porch," KHQ-Q6, September 23, 2009, http://www.khq.com/story/11187090/human-rights-activist-finds-noose-on-porch.

39. The original article cited here appears to have been taken down by the source, but the exact quotation can be found in Nicolas Medina Mora, "Just Two Months Ago, Rachel Dolezal Did an Interview About Passing For Another Race," Buzzfeed News, June 12, 2015, https://www.buzzfeednews.com/article/nicolasmedinamora/heres-what-rachel-dolezal-said-about-passing-two-months-ago.

40. George Prentice, "An Ugly Reminder…," *Boise Weekly*, June 21, 2010, https://www.boiseweekly.com/CityDesk/archives/2010/06/21/an-ugly-reminder.

41. Boggs, "Rights educator finds noose on porch of Spokane home."

42. Rachel Dolezal, *In Full Color* (Dallas, TX: Benbella Books, 2017). The same quotation can also be found in Bill Chappell, "'I Identify as Black,' Rachel Dolezal Says In TV Interview," WBUR News, June 16, 2015, http://www.wbur.org/npr/414863516/-i-identify-as-black-rachel-dolezal-says-in-tv-interview.

43. For an interesting analysis of the majority-white composition of BLM's marchers and fighters in most cities, see Marcus Harrison Green, "What White Marchers Mean for Black Lives Matter," *Seattle Weekly*, December 27, 2017, http://www.seattleweekly.com/opinion/what-white-marchers-mean-for-black-lives-matter/.

44. For a complete breakdown of military service rates by race, see "Distribution of active-duty enlisted women and men in the U.S. Military in 2016, by race and ethnicity," Statista, 2018, https://www.statista.com/statistics/214869/share-of-active-duty-enlisted-women-and-men-in-the-us-military/.

CHAPTER FIVE: THE TRUMP HATE CRIMES: DONALD TRUMP'S ELECTION AND THE RESULTING WAVE OF HOAXES

1. Samantha Schmidt, "This Is CNN Tonight. I'm Don Lemon. The President of the United States Is Racist," *Washington Post*, January 12, 2018, https://www.washingtonpost.com/news/morning-mix/wp/2018/01/12/this-is-cnn-tonight-im-don-lemon-the-president-of-the-united-states-is-racist/.

2. In the interest of fairness, I will note that there have been two serious discrimination claims brought against Trump over the years. In 1973, at the age of 27, he was one of a group of real estate players sued by the U.S. Justice Department for allegedly refusing to rent some high-end units to African Americans. Trump counter-sued for $100,000,000, and the case was eventually settled. In 1989, *after* a group of minority teenagers that became known as the Central Park Five had confessed to raping and brutalizing a white jogger, Trump paid to run full-page ads in the New York papers mentioning them obliquely and calling for the return of the death penalty. He took considerable heat for this later, when issues

arose with the teens' confessions. I personally am not horrified by either incident, but you be the judge.

3. Rocco Parascandola and Leonard Greene, "Muslim college student made up Trump supporter subway attack story to avoid punishment for missing curfew," *Daily News*, December 15, 2016, http://www.nydailynews.com/new-york/muslim-woman-reported-trump-supporter-attack-made-story-article-1.2910944.

4. Valerie Richardson, "Hoax: N.Y. police say Muslim teen made up story about being harassed by Trump supporters," *Washington Times*, December 14, 2016, https://www.washingtontimes.com/news/2016/dec/14/yasmin-seweid-made-up-story-about-being-harassed-b/.

5. Parascandola and Greene, "Muslim College Student Made Up Trump Supporter Subway Attack Story."

6. Notably, in addition to the piece just cited, the *Daily News* ran this lead editorial: "The damage done by Yasmin Seweid's hijab hate hoax," *Daily News*, December 15, 2016, http://www.nydailynews.com/opinion/damage-yasmin-seweid-hijab-hate-hoax-article-1.2911776.

7. Richardson, "Hoax."

8. Mickey White, "Hoax or a Cry for Help? Yasmin Seweid and 'Honor' Crimes," RedState, December 16, 2016, https://www.redstate.com/mickeywhite2/2016/12/16/hoax-cry-help-yasmin-seweid-honor-crimes/.

9. Associated Press, "Arrest made in 'Vote Trump' burning of Mississippi black church," Memphis WREG, December 21, 2016, https://wreg.com/2016/12/21/mississippi-authorities-make-arrest-in-burning-of-african-american-church-spray-painted-with-vote-trump/.

10. Emily Wagster Pettus, "Suspect in 'Vote Trump' vandalism and burning of black Mississippi church reportedly a member of the congregation," Business Insider, December 21, 2016, https://www.businessinsider.com/suspect-in-vote-trump-vandalism-and-burning-of-black-mississippi-church-reportedly-a-member-of-the-congregation-2016-12.

11. In addition to Mississippi Department of Corrections records themselves, a full breakdown of McClinton's record can be found here: Associated Press, "Black congregation member tagged Mississippi church with 'Vote Trump' graffiti," *Daily Mail*, December 21, 2016, https://www.dailymail.co.uk/news/article-4056406/Arrest-Vote-Trump-burning-Mississippi-black-church.html.

12. "Black Suspect Arrested After Racist Message Discovered Outside Predominantly Black Church," CBS4Denver, June 30, 2015, https://denver.cbslocal.com/2015/06/30/suspect-arrested-after-racist-message-discovered-outside-church/.

13. Sarah Larimer, "This Indiana church was defaced with 'HEIL TRUMP' graffiti—and is keeping it," *Washington Post*, November 15, 2016, https://www.washingtonpost.com/news/acts-of-faith/wp/2016/11/15/this-indiana-church-was-defaced-with-heil-trump-graffiti-and-is-keeping-it/?utm_term=.e808366b9106.

14. Alanna Durkin Richer and Sarah Rankin, "Muslims question whether girl's killing was road rage," *Daily Herald*, June 20, 2017, https://www.dailyherald.com/article/20170620/news/306209815.

15. This language appears to have been changed, but searching for it immediately returns Burton's article, which still claims that Hassanen's killing "functions like" a hate crime. Tara Isabella Burton, "Nabra Hassanen's murder may not be a hate crime. It's still a tragedy for Muslim Americans," Vox, June 22, 2017, https://www.vox.com/identities/2017/6/22/15841650/nabra-hassanen-murder-islamophobia-hate-crime.

16. Richer and Rankin, "Muslims question whether girl's killing was road rage."

17. Burton, "Nabra Hassanen's murder may not be a hate crime."

18. Richer and Rankin, "Muslims question whether girl's killing was road rage."

19. "Nabra Hassanen: spectre of hate crime hangs over teenager's funeral," *Guardian*, June 21, 2017, https://www.theguardian.com/us-news/2017/jun/22/nabra-hassanen-spectre-of-hate-hangs-over-teenagers-funeral.

20. Petula Dvorak, "Nabra Hassanen's death may not legally be a hate crime, but it sure feels hateful," *Washington Post,* June 19, 2017, https://www.washingtonpost.com/local/nabra-hassanens-death-may-not-legally-be-a-hate-crime-but-it-sure-feels-hateful/2017/06/19/19454a8e-552b-11e7-a204-ad706461fa4f_story.html?utm_term=.35d8c54af70d.

21. Michael Tanenbaum, "Video: Suspect wanted for racist Trump vandalism in South Philly," PhillyVoice, November 9, 2016, https://www.phillyvoice.com/more-racist-donald-trump-vandalism-found-south-philly/.

22. Julie Shaw, "S. Jersey man arrested in 'Pro-Trump,' racist post-election vandalism in South Philly," *Philadelphia Inquirer,* December 1, 2016, http://www2.philly.com/philly/blogs/real-time/S-Jersey-man-arrested-in-post-election-vandalism-in-South-Philly.html.

23. Brigette Burnett, "BG police say student lied about politically driven attack," 13 ABC News, November 17, 2016, https://www.13abc.com/content/news/BG-police-say-student-lied-about-politically-driven-attack-401814426.html.

24. "BGSU student charged after reporting fake assault," WTOL 11 News, November 17, 2016, http://www.wtol.com/story/33736486/bgsu-student-charged-after-reporting-fake-assault/.

25. Burnett, "BG police say student lied."

26. Burnett, "BG police say student lied."

27. "Fabricating an assault nets woman $200 fine," *The Blade,* January 31, 2017, https://www.toledoblade.com/local/courts/2017/01/31/Fabricating-an-assault-nets-woman-200-fine/stories/20170130255?abnpageversion=evoke.

28. Burnett, "BG police say student lied."

29. Dick Johnson and Richard Ray, "I Just Want Them to Stop': Chicago Student Says Threatening 'Trump' Note Taped to Her Door," NBC Chicago, November 15, 2016, https://www.nbcchicago.com/news/local/north-park-harassment-trump-note-401408916.html.

30. Richard Ray, "Hateful 'Trump' Notes Allegedly Aimed at Student Were Fabricated, University Says," NBC Chicago, November 22,

2016, https://www.nbcchicago.com/news/local/north-park-fabricated-notes-402556366.html.

31. Johnson and Ray, "'I Just Want Them to Stop.'"

32. For example, see: Jessica Chasmar, "North Park University student fabricated anti-gay 'Trump' notes, school says," *Washington Times*, November 25, 2016, https://www.washingtontimes.com/news/2016/nov/25/taylor-volk-north-park-university-student-fabricat/; Johnson and Ray, "'I Just Want Them to Stop,'"; Maureen Sullivan, "Are There Really More Hate Crimes at Schools Following Donald Trump's Election?," *Forbes*, November 29, 2016, https://www.forbes.com/sites/maureensullivan/2016/11/29/are-there-really-more-hate-crimes-at-schools-following-donald-trumps-election/#68f494479795.

33. Ray, "Hateful 'Trump' Notes."

34. Ibid.

35. As I recall, the full note of the text was, "Come on—suck it up, you pussies!"

36. Tyler Arnold, "Another pro-Trump 'hate crime' deemed a hoax," Campus Reform, November 24, 2016, https://www.campusreform.org/?ID=8445.

37. The full list of sources supporting this estimate can be found in Chapter 1.

38. John Counts, "Ann Arbor woman pleads guilty to making up hate crime," MLive, March 7, 2017, https://www.mlive.com/news/ann-arbor/index.ssf/2017/03/ann_arbor_woman_pleads_guilty_1.html.

39. Austin Yack, "University of Michigan Student Fabricates Hate Crime, Claimed Man Threatened to Set Her on FIre," *National Review*, December 22, 2016, https://www.nationalreview.com/corner/university-michigan-muslim-students-hate-crime-hoax-hijab-fire/.

40. Recall that my first hate crime related data set consisted simply of recent reported hate crimes, many of which turned out to be false, while my second data set consisted of 409 definitely fake hate crimes.

41. However suspicious her behavior, this woman has never been formally accused of faking a hate crime and ethically should not be "shamed" here, so I will not give her name.

42. Will Fritz, "Campus police investigate robbery as hate crime," *Daily Aztec*, November 9, 2016, http://thedailyaztec.com/80136/news/hate-crime-on-campus-by-parking-structure-12/.

43. R. Stickney, "SDSU Police: No Suspect in Attack on Muslim Student," NBC San Diego, January 10, 2017, https://www.nbcsandiego.com/news/local/SDSU-Police-Attack-on-Muslim-Student-Unfounded-410296485.html.

44. Susan Snyder, "Villanova U. ends probe into reports of post election incident," *Philadelphia Inquirer*, December 2, 2016, http://www.philly.com/philly/education/20161203_Villanova_U__ends_probe_into_report_of_post_election_incident.html.

45. Anthony Gockowski, "Crucifix, Trump chalkings reported as 'hate incidents' at UW-L," Campus Reform, September 27, 2016, https://www.campusreform.org/?ID=8180.

CHAPTER SIX: FAKE RELIGIOUS, ANTI-LGBT, AND GENDER BIAS INCIDENTS

1. Caitlin Ryan and Ian Rivers, "Lesbian, Gay, Bisexual and Transgender Youth: Victimization and Its Correlates in the USA and UK," *Culture, Health, and Sexuality 55*, no. 3 (March–April 2003), 103–19.

2. Kevin Berrill and Gregory Herek, *Hate Crimes: Confronting Violence against Lesbians and Gay Men* (Newbury Park: Sage Publications, 1992).

3. Daniel Pipes, "'Islamophobic Prejudice' and CAIR," FrontPageMagazine, August 25, 2004, http://www.danielpipes.org/2042/islamophobic-prejudice-and-cair.

4. Ibid.

5. Not in this context, at least. The group does do some genuinely useful charitable work, when not race-baiting. Every coin has two faces, and all that.

6. Daniel Pipes, "Islamophobic Prejudice and CAIR."

7. Ambar Espinoza, "St. Cloud school officials say harassment complaints not valid," MPR News, May 13, 2010, https://www.mprnews.org/story/2010/05/13/st-cloud-harassment-complaints.

8. Rachel Browne, "Man charged with terror hoax," Vice News, March 1, 2017, https://news.vice.com/en_ca/article/mb9y48/canadian-university-evacuated-after-bomb-threat-targeting-muslims.

9. "Montreal man charged with terror hoax after bomb threat targeting Muslim university students," CBC News, March 2, 2017, https://www.cbc.ca/news/canada/montreal/montreal-concordia-university-bomb-threats-1.4006151.

10. "Suspect in Concordia bomb threat hoax released on bail," CBC News, March 10, 2017, https://www.cbc.ca/news/canada/montreal/hisham-saadi-concordia-suspect-bail-granted-1.4019908.

11. Paul Cherry, "18-Month jail term for sending bomb threats to Concordia University," *Montreal Gazette*, October 5, 2018, https://montrealgazette.com/news/local-news/18-month-jail-term-for-concordia-university-bomb-threats.

12. Andre Tartar, "Tragic Beating Death of Shaima Alawadi Feeds into Trayvon Martin Race Debate," *New York Magazine*, March 25, 2012, http://nymag.com/intelligencer/2012/03/beating-death-shaima-alawadi-trayvon-martin-race-debate.html?gtm=top&gtm=bottom.

13. Mary Slosson, "Iraqi-American murder highlights anti-Muslim hate crimes," *Chicago Tribune*, March 31, 2012, https://www.chicagotribune.com/living/ct-xpm-2012-03-31-sns-rt-crime-iraqihate-pixl2e8etccy-20120331-story.html.

14. "The Murder of Shaima Alawadi," Wikipedia, https://en.wikipedia.org/wiki/Murder_of_Shaima_Alawadi.

15. Elizabeth Flock, "Trayvon Martin case, Iraqi woman's death spark 'hoodies and hijab' rally," *Washington Post*, March 27, 2012, https://www.washingtonpost.com/blogs/blogpost/post/trayvon-martin-case-iraqi-womans-death-spark-hoodies-and-hijab-rally/2012/03/27/gIQAI6IieS_blog.html?noredirect=on&utm_term=.3b8c67d6b31e.

16. Julia Dahl, "Shaima Alawadi, Iraqi woman killed in her Calif. Home, was planning divorce: documents," CBS News, April 6, 2012, https://www.cbsnews.com/news/shaima-alawadi-iraqi-woman-killed-in-her-calif-home-was-planning-divorce-documents/.

17. "Police: Shaima Alawadi's death was domestic violence not hate crime, arrest husband," NBC News, November 9, 2012, http://usnews.nbcnews.com/_news/2012/11/09/15055001-police-shaima-alawadis-death-was-domestic-violence-not-hate-crime-arrest-husband?lite.

18. Christopher Fried, "10 Egregious Hate Crime Hoaxes," Listverse, March 20, 2015, https://listverse.com/2015/03/20/10-egregious-hate-crime-hoaxes/.

19. This is a very real acronym, popular in college-level American and Canadian sociology courses, which stands for "Lesbian, gay, bi-sexual, pan-sexual, identifying as two or more genders or sexualities, transgender, transsexual, queer, questioning, intersex, intergender, asexual, and allied. Those are, according to the well-known GenderBread Person meme, the "color bars of the rainbow."

20. "Owner of Oak Park's torched Velvet Rope gay night spot charged with arson, insurance fraud," November 2, 2013, http://www.oakpark.com/News/Articles/11-2-2013/Owner-of-Oak-Park%27s-torched-Velvet-Rope-gay-night-spot-charged-with-arson,-insurance-fraud/.

21. "Arson at Illinois gay bar likely a fake hate crime by owner," Insurance Fraud News, November 2, 2013, http://www.insurancefraud.org/IFNS-detail.htm?key=17559.

22. "Owner admits setting fire to gay nightclub in Oak Park," ABC 7News, August 4, 2015, https://abc7chicago.com/news/owner-admits-setting-fire-to-gay-nightclub-in-oak-park-/902837/.

23. "Joe Williams, Tennessee Health Food Store Owner, Beaten In Alleged Anti-Gay Hate Crime," HuffPost, November 25, 2013, https://www.huffingtonpost.com/2013/11/25/tennessee-healthy-thyme-hate-crime-_n_4337809.html.

24. Sunnivie Brydum, "Watch: Gay Owner of Tenn. Health Store Assaulted in Possible Hate Crime," *The Advocate*, November 26, 2013, https://www.advocate.com/crime/2013/11/26/watch-gay-owner-tenn-health-store-assaulted-possible-hate-crime. This article contains Robert Spicer's interview with MSMV and also links to other sources of interest.

25. Robert Stacey McCain and Smitty, "Another Fake Hate Crime? Arrest Discredits Tennessee Anti-Gay Case," The Other McCain, December 28, 2013, http://theothermccain.com/2013/12/28/another-fake-hate-crime-arrest-discredits-tennessee-anti-gay-case/.

26. Robert Stacey McCain and Smitty, "Another Fake Hate Crime? Arrest Discredits Tennessee Anti-Gay Case," The Other McCain, December 28, 2013, http://theothermccain.com/2013/12/28/another-fake-hate-crime-arrest-discredits-tennessee-anti-gay-case/.

27. Hayley Peterson, "Pastor admits he lied about a Whole Foods incident that caused a public outcry," Business Insider, May 16, 2016, https://www.businessinsider.com/pastor-drops-lawsuit-against-whole-foods-2016-5.

28. Julie Zauzmer, "Gay pastor admits he faked homophobic slur on Whole Foods cake," *Washington Post*, May 16, 2016, https://www.washingtonpost.com/news/acts-of-faith/wp/2016/05/16/gay-pastor-admits-he-faked-homophobic-slur-on-whole-foods-cake/?utm_term=.1062493f5e13.

29. For the record, I am describing Julie Baker as bisexual because she identifies as LGBT/ "queer" but has four biological children with men.

30. Bil Browning, "Donations Will Be Returned by Woman with 'Relentlessly Gay' Yard Decorations," *The Advocate*, August 20, 2015, https://www.advocate.com/breaking/2015/08/20/relentlessly-gay-yard-donations-be-returned-after-hoax-allegations.

31. Joel Christie and Kieran Corcoran, "Mom who raised $43,000 claiming her homophobic neighbor was intimidating her over her 'relentlessly gay yard' is accused of FAKING threats herself," *Daily Mail*, July 1, 2015, https://www.dailymail.co.uk/news/article-3146256/Was-relentlessly-gay-yard-campaign-giant-

GoFundMe-hoax-Mom-raised-43-000-claiming-Christian-neighbor-homophobic-accused-FAKING-threats.html.

32. If only I had known! In my old college apartment, the boys and I heard worse than that from neighbor "Mr. Paul,"a no-nonsense Vietnam vet, literally every night. #MeToo

33. This is, unfortunately, not a joke. See Tessa Sheets and J.D. Gallop, "Bacon used in hate crime: Titusville man gets 15 years in mosque vandalism," *Florida Today*, December 5, 2017, https://www.floridatoday.com/story/news/crime/2017/12/05/titusville-man-sentenced-15-years-prison-after-mosque-vandalism/924987001/.

34. Browning, "Donations Will Be Returned."

35. Biological women who identify as male prefer to be referred to as "he," while biological males who identify as females prefer "she." I honor these preferences here.

36. Does a left-leaning Seven Sisters school have a standing rapid-response team devoted *just* to investigating dubious allegations of campus hate crime? You bet your new kiln and best pair of Birkenstocks it does!

37. Robby Soave, "Exclusive: Shocking Discovery in Hoax Bias Incident at Vassar College," The Daily Caller, November 27, 2013, https://dailycaller.com/2013/11/27/exclusive-shocking-discovery-in-hoax-bias-incident-at-vassar-college/.

38. "Bias incidents at Vassar were a hoax as one of the culprits was 'the transgender student leading the investigations into the offensive graffiti,'" *Daily Mail*, December 5, 2013, https://www.dailymail.co.uk/news/article-2518748/Vassar-graffiti-hoax-culprit-transgender-student-leading-investigations.html.

39. Alex Pfeiffer, "Anti-Trump Communist Arrested for Jewish Community Center Bomb Threats," Daily Caller, March 3, 2017, https://dailycaller.com/2017/03/03/anti-trump-communist-arrested-for-jewish-community-center-bomb-threats/. Kudos to The Daily Caller for this headline. This was one of the few occasions where the media header describing a case was so dark and funny that I didn't have to make up my own.

40. Max Kutner, "Ex-Journalist Juan Thompson Allegedly Made Bomb Threats to JCCS, ADL," *Newsweek*, March 3, 2017, https://

www.newsweek.com/juan-thompson-arrest-jcc-bomb-
threats-563435.

41. For the Caller's entertaining account of the situation, see: Alex
    Pfeiffer, "Anti-Trump Communist Arrested for Jewish Community
    Center Bomb Threats," The Daily Caller, March 3, 2017, https://
    dailycaller.com/2017/03/03/anti-trump-communist-arrested-for-
    jewish-community-center-bomb-threats/.

42. Max Kutner, "Ex-Journalist Juan Thompson Allegedly Made
    Bomb Threats to JCCS, ADL."

43. Doyle Murphy, "Juan Thompson Sentenced to 5 Years for Cyber-
    Stalking, Jewish Bomb Threats," The River-Front Times,
    December 20, 2017, https://www.riverfronttimes.com/
    newsblog/2017/12/20/juan-thompson-sentenced-to-5-years-for-
    cyber-stalking-jewish-bomb-threats.

44. Stephen Rex Brown, "Juan Thompson gets five years in prison for
    Jewish Community Center threats, revenge plot againsteEx,"
    Daily News, December 20, 2017, http://www.nydailynews.com/
    new-york/juan-thompson-years-jewish-community-center-threats-
    article-1.3711668.

45. Yonat Friling, "Israeli-American arrested in US Jewish community
    center bomb threats," Fox News, March 23, 2017, https://www.
    foxnews.com/world/israeli-american-arrested-in-us-jewish-
    community-center-bomb-threats.

46. Yonah Jeremy Bob, "Israel Charges Teen Hacker Over JCC Bomb
    Threats, Blackmailing US State Senator," Jerusalem Post, April 24,
    2017, https://www.jpost.com/Israel-News/Politics-And-
    Diplomacy/JCC-Bomb-threat-hacker-indicted-charged-with-
    blackmailing-US-Senator-488803.

47. Friling, "Israeli-American arrested."

48. For normies reading this, the Dark Net is a hidden region of the
    Internet consisting of websites with non-traditional suffixes (e.g.,
    xcccttwferdgtyu.onion vs. cats.com), which can be accessed only
    by downloading specialized anonymized web browsers such as
    TOR. Many of these websites offer unconventional goods such as
    hard drugs, stolen credit cards, extreme pornography, and hacking
    tools for sale.

49. Bob, "Israel Charges Teen Hacker."

50. Andrew Blake, "Michael Kadar, 'JCC hoax bomber,' convicted in Israel over threats against Jewish centers," *Washington Times*, June 28, 2018, https://www.washingtontimes.com/news/2018/jun/28/ michael-kadar-jcc-hoax-bomber-convicted-in-israel-/.

51. "2017 Jewish Community Center Bomb Threats," Wikipedia, https://en.wikipedia.org/wiki/2017_Jewish_Community_Center_ bomb_threats.

52. Bob, "Israel Charges Teen Hacker."

CHAPTER SEVEN: THROWING FUEL ON THE FIRE: MEDIA COMPLICITY WITH HATE CRIME HOAXES

1. Laird Wilcox, *Crying Wolf* (Olathe, KS: Editorial Research Service, 1994).

2. "Tawana Brawley rape allegations," Wikipedia, https:// en.wikipedia.org/wiki/Tawana_Brawley_rape_allegations.

3. Ann Coulter, *Mugged: Racial Demagoguery from the Seventies to Obama* (New York: Sentinel, 2012), 62–63.

4. "Brawley Case: Stubborn Puzzle, Silent Victim," *New York Times*, February 29, 1988, https://www.nytimes.com/1988/02/29/ nyregion/brawley-case-stubborn-puzzle-silent-victim.html.

5. "Tawana Brawley Rape Allegations," Wikipedia.

6. Coulter, *Mugged*, 63.

7. Patricia J. Williams, *The Alchemy of Race and Rights* (Cambridge, MA: Harvard University Press, 1991), 169.

8. As a political scientist, it strikes me that the far-left political bloc often compared to the "alt right" should be called the "ctrl left" rather than the "alt left." In addition to being a funny computer pun, this designation is accurate in political-spectrum terms. Alt-right activists such as like Vox Day and Richard Spencer are in essence provocateurs—offering a sort of fringe-right "alternative" to traditional flag-and-altar conservatism. Their wares are things few modern governments (for good reason!) offer: a volksher understanding of nationalism, monarchism, a return to 1800s gender roles, and so on. In contrast, hard-left activists are almost

all in practice Marxists or Socialists. They do not offer an alternative to welfare state liberalism, but rather an extreme extension of it focused on increasing control over the individual. So, there's that.

9. Ann Coulter, Mugged, 142.

10. Laura Italiano, "Now pay up, Tawana," *New York Post*, December 25, 2012, https://nypost.com/2012/12/25/now-pay-up-tawana/.

11. Dorian Block, "Tawana Brawley's mom seeks amnesty," *Daily News*, November 19, 2007, https://www.nydailynews.com/news/tawana-brawley-mom-seeks-amnesty-article-1.256704.

12. This background detail on the Duke Lacrosse Hoax can be found in "Duke lacrosse case," Wikipedia, https://en.wikipedia.org/wiki/Duke_lacrosse_case.

13. William D. Cohan, *Price of Silence: The Duke Lacrosse Scandal, the Power of the Elite, and the Corruption of Our Great Universities* (New York: Simon and Schuster, 2014), 528–29.

14. "Duke lacrosse case," Wikipedia.

15. KC Johnson, "Closing Comments," Durham-in-Wonderland, July 18, 2014, http://durhamwonderland.blogspot.com/.

16. Associated Press, "Duke lacrosse coach resigns, rest of season canceled," ESPN, April 6, 2006, http://www.espn.com/college-sports/news/story?id=2398409.

17. "Duke Case: Kim Roberts version 6.0," The Johnsville News, October 12, 2006, http://johnsville.blogspot.com/2006/10/duke-case-kim-roberts-version-60.html.

18. "The Duke lacrosse case," Wikipedia.

19. Sasha Goldstein, "Crystal Mangum, Duke lacrosse accuser, arrested and sentenced in boyfriend's stabbing death," *Daily News*, November 22, 2013, https://www.nydailynews.com/news/crime/crystal-mangum-duke-lacrosse-accuser-convicted-boyfriend-stabbing-death-article-1.1526467.

20. KC Johnson, "Checking in with the Group of 88," Durham-in-Wonderland, July 7, 2014, http://durhamwonderland.blogspot.com/2014/07/checking-in-with-group-of-88.html.

21. Peter Applebome, "Woman's Claim of Racial Crime Is Called a Hoax," *New York Times*, June 1, 1990, https://www.nytimes.com/1990/06/01/us/woman-s-claim-of-racial-crime-is-called-a-hoax.html.

22. Ann Coulter, *Mugged*, 59–60.

23. Coulter mentions the genesis of several of these organizations, but for an extensive discussion of BAM I relied on Franchesca Winters, "Stepping up for Awareness," *Emory Magazine*, Spring 2009, http://www.emory.edu/EMORY_MAGAZINE/2009/spring/bam.html.

24. If you don't get that reference, read a book. I drop gems. #WesternCivilization

25. Coulter, *Mugged*, 59–60.

26. Applebome, "Woman's Claim of Racial Crime."

27. Chris Lydgate, "The Perfect Victim: Azalea Cooley, cause célèbre," *Willamette Week*, November 9, 2004, https://www.wweek.com/portland/article-3799-the-perfect-victim.html.

28. Maria Newman, "Officials Pledge Drive to Counter Bias Attack," *New York Times*, January 8, 1992, https://www.nytimes.com/1992/01/08/nyregion/officials-pledge-drive-to-counter-bias-attack.html.

29. Ann Coulter, *Mugged*, 66-67.

30. Lynette Holloway, "Slight Dip in Homicides in New York City in 1992," *New York Times*, January 2, 1993, https://www.nytimes.com/1993/01/02/nyregion/slight-dip-in-homicides-in-new-york-city-in-1992.html.

31. Ann Coulter, *Mugged*, 66.

32. Peter Moses, "Two Sides Clash Over Bias Puzzle," New York Post, February 7, 1992. No current online link to this article appears to exist, but hard copies of it can be obtained, and it is discussed extensively in Coulter, Mugged.

33. Maria Newman, "Police Puzzled by Lack of Leads in Bias Attack on Black Youths," *New York Times*, February 6, 1992, https://www.nytimes.com/1992/02/06/nyregion/police-puzzled-by-lack-of-leads-in-bias-attacks-on-black-youths.html. Coulter notes that this follow-up to the lengthy original story ran "deep within the

newspaper—Section B, page 3, column 5." That is typical, when newspapers even bother to run redactions of hate crime stories that have been exposed as hoaxes.

34. Lynda Richardson, "61 Acts of Bias: One Fuse Lights Manny Different Explosions," *New York Times*, January 28, 1992, https://www.nytimes.com/1992/01/28/nyregion/61-acts-of-bias-one-fuse-lights-many-different-explosions.html.

35. Newman, "Officials Pledge Drive."

36. Ann Coulter, *Mugged*, 66.

37. Elizabeth Chuck, "Susan Smith, Mother Who Killed Kids: 'Something Went Very Wrong That Night,'" NBC News, July 23, 2015, https://www.nbcnews.com/news/us-news/susan-smith-mother-who-killed-kids-something-went-very-wrong-n397051.

38. Keira V. Williams, Gendered Politics in the Modern South: The Susan Smith Case and the Rise of a New Sexism (Baton Rouge, LA: LSU Press, 2012), 40.

39. Michel Martin (host), "Racial Hoaxes: Black Men and Imaginary Crimes," NPR, June 8, 2009, https://www.npr.org/templates/story/story.php?storyId=105096024.

40. Chuck, "Susan Smith, Mother Who Killed Kids."

41. Elizabeth Gleick, "Sex, Betrayal, and Murder," *Time*, June 24, 2001, http://content.time.com/time/magazine/article/0,9171,134423,00.html.

42. Charles Montaldo, "Profile of Child Killer Susan Smith," ThoughtCo., April 1, 2018, https://www.thoughtco.com/susan-smith-profile-of-child-killer-972686.

43. Steve Helling, "Sex, Drugs, and Infractions: Inside Susan Smith's Life in Prison For Drowning Her Two Sons," *People*, September 26, 2017, https://people.com/crime/susan-smith-drowning-sons-inside-life-prison/?utm_campaign=peoplemagazine&utm_source=twitter.com&utm_medium=social&xid=socialflow_twitter_peoplemag.

44. "Susan Smith Apology and Contacts," Write a Prisoner Project, https://writeaprisoner.com/Template.aspx?i=z-221487.

45. "Susan Smith," Wikipedia, https://en.wikipedia.org/wiki/Susan_Smith.

CHAPTER EIGHT: WHITE HOT: CAUCASIAN HATE HOAXERS

1. Interestingly, the phenomenon of falsifying hate hoaxes out of solidarity with *other* racial populations seems to be unique to whites. Throughout all three of my data sets, literally not one Black hoaxer claimed to have been attacked because of his support for white cultural norms, opposition to reverse racism, GOP voting preference, or anything similar.

2. "Fake Hate Crimes, a Database of Hate Hoaxes in the USA," www.fakehatecrimes.org.

3. For an extensive, and generally fair, review of this study, see Don Gonyea, "Majority of White Americans Say They Believe Whites Face Discrimination," National Public Radio, October 24, 2017, https://www.npr.org/2017/10/24/559604836/majority-of-white-americans-think-theyre-discriminated-against.

4. To their credit, I identified exactly one East Asian hoaxer during the entire process of research for this book. So Asian-led hate hoaxes represented 1/260 (.3 percent) of the Fake Hate Crimes data set and 1/409 (.2 percent) of my self-compiled data set. Asians, who currently beat both whites and Blacks in regard to pretty much every positive outcome, seem to have better things to do with their time than fake hate crimes.

5. Why'd the truck have to be WHITE, huh? #racism. Lynette Holloway, "Texas Man Arrested in Hoax Claiming Members of #BlackLivesMatter Vandalized His Truck," The Root, September 19, 2015, https://www.theroot.com/texas-man-arrested-in-hoax-claiming-members-of-blackli-1790861164.

6. Melissa Chan, "Texas Man vandalizes own truck with anti-police messages,blames it on Black Lives Matter activists: cops," *Daily News*, September 19, 2015, https://www.nydailynews.com/news/national/man-vandalizes-truck-blames-black-lives-matter-article-1.2366871.

7. As measured by Google search results.

8. For a detailed discussion of these facts, see: Holloway, "Texas Man Arrested in Hoax." Fox 4 News apparently broke the Lattin story; see "Family's pro-police truck totaled by vandals," Fox 4 News,

September 9, 2015, http://www.fox4news.com/news/familys-pro-police-truck-totaled-by-vandals.

9. Holloway, "Texas Man Arrested in Hoax."

10. Chan, "Texas man vandalizes own truck."

11. "Police: Mom, son charged in truck vandalism hoax," Fox 4 News, September 21, 2015, http://www.fox4news.com/news/police-mom-son-charged-in-truck-vandalism-hoax.

12. Alex Griswold, "Firefighter Accused of Burning Down Home, Framing Black Lives Matter," Mediaite, December 8, 2016, https://www.mediaite.com/online/firefighter-accused-of-burning-down-home-framing-black-lives-matters/.

13. Latifah Muhammad, "Firefighter Charged with Arson after Blaming BLM Members for Burning His House Down," *Vibe*, December 11, 2016, https://www.vibe.com/2016/12/firefighter-blames-black-lives-matter/.

14. Anthony Borrelli, "NOT GUILTY: Ex-firefighter acquitted of arson," *USA Today*, May 15, 2017, https://www.pressconnects.com/story/news/public-safety/2017/05/15/arson-trial-juror-replaced-second-day-deliberations/101703484/.

15. Christine Byers, "St. Louis Bosnian woman who claimed hate crime is charged with making false report," *St. Louis Post Dispatch*, December 16, 2014, https://www.stltoday.com/news/local/crime-and-courts/st-louis-bosnian-woman-who-claimed-hate-crime-is-charged/article_2d835f8c-5385-5c5d-9496-de7b6559070f.html.

16. Chuck Ross, "Hoax: St. Louis Woman Who Claimed She Was Attacked by Black Teens Made It Up," The Daily Caller, December 16, 2014, https://dailycaller.com/2014/12/16/hoax-st-louis-woman-who-claimed-she-was-attacked-by-black-teens-made-it-up/.

17. Byers, "St. Louis Bosnian woman who claimed hate crime is charged"; Ross, "Hoax: St. Louis Woman Who Claimed She Was Attacked."

18. Byers, "St. Louis Bosnian woman who claimed hate crime is charged."

19. Max Blumenthal, "A Hoax Exposed at Princeton," *The Nation*, December 18, 2007, https://www.thenation.com/article/hoax-exposed-princeton/.

20. Brit Hume, "Little Outrage Over Student Beating at Princeton University," Fox News, December 18, 2007, https://www.foxnews.com/story/little-outrage-over-student-beating-at-princeton-university.

21. Max Blumenthal, "The Conservative Persecution Hoax Exposed," HuffPost, December 19, 2007, https://www.huffingtonpost.com/max-blumenthal/the-conservative-persecut_b_77561.html.

22. Blumenthal, "A Hoax Exposed at Princeton."

23. Ibid.

24. Blumenthal, "The Conservative Persecution Hoax Exposed"; Hume, "Little Outrage Over Student Beating."

25. Blumenthal, "A Hoax Exposed at Princeton."

26. "Mugger Attacked Campaign Volunteer in Pittsburgh," KDKA, October 25, 2008, https://web.archive.org/web/20081025075412/http://kdka.com/video?id=47866%40kdka.dayport.com.

27. Hannah Strange, "Republican volunteer charged over false claim of mutilation by Obama supporter," *The Times*, October 25, 2008, https://www.thetimes.co.uk/article/republican-volunteer-charged-over-false-claim-of-mutilation-by-obama-supporter-vfrz03cqgpt.

28. Michael A. Fuoco, Jerome L. Sherman, and Sadie Gurman, "McCain volunteer admits to hoax," *Pittsburgh Post-Gazette*, October 25, 2008, http://www.post-gazette.com/local/neighborhoods/2008/10/25/McCain-volunteer-admits-to-hoax/stories/200810250133.

29. Greg Mitchell, "Fox News VP: If McCain Worker 'Mutilation' Story Is a Hoax, His Campaign Is 'Over,'" HuffPost, November 24, 2008, https://www.huffingtonpost.com/greg-mitchell/fox-news-vp-if-mccain-wor_b_137522.html.

30. Michelle Malkin, "Why That McCain volunteer's 'mutilation' story smells awfully weird," October 23, 2008, http://michellemalkin.com/2008/10/23/why-that-mccain-volunteers-mutilation-story-smells-awfully-weird/.

31. Fuoco, Sherman, and Gurman, "McCain volunteer admits to hoax."

32. Associated Press, "McCain worker reaches deal in hoax assault," NBC, October 30, 2008, http://www.nbcnews.com/id/27456042/ ns/us_news-crime_and_courts/t/mccain-worker-reaches-deal-hoax-assault/#.XArI0hpKhTY.

33. Mitchell, "Fox News VP: If McCain Worker 'Mutilation' Story Is a Hoax."

34. "Melody Beaver" is a fictional name, because the perpetrator-defendant in this case was, after all, just a kid.

35. Cassy Fiano, "Student attacked for anti-illegal immigration stance," WizBang, April 9, 2008, https://wizbangblog.com/ content/2008/04/09/student-attacked-for-antiillegal-immigration-stance.php.

36. "East Texas Teenager Attacked Over History Project," KLTV, April 8, 2008, http://www.kltv.com/story/8132283/east-texas-teenager-attacked-over-history-project/; Michelle Malkin, "Update: False claim by anti-illegal immigration student," Michelle Malkin, April 9, 2008, http://michellemalkin. com/2008/04/09/update-false-claim-by-anti-illegal-immigration-student/.

37. Fiano, "Student attacked for anti-illegal immigration stance."

38. "Athens School 'Attack' Proven to Be False, Girl to Be Charged," KLTV, April 9, 2008, http://www.kltv.com/story/8142322/athens-school-attack-proven-to-be-false-girl-to-be-charged/.

39. Casey Fiano, "Student attacked for anti-illegal immigration stance."

40. Ibid.

41. Christine Roberts, "In the mirror, I saw a distorted monster," Daily News, February 18, 2013, https://www.nydailynews.com/ news/national/woman-threw-acid-face-speaks-gma-article-1.1267001.

42. Ana Hunter, "Acid Attack Hoax: Why Did She Say Attacker Was Black?", CBS News, September 17, 2010, https://www.cbsnews. com/news/acid-attack-hoax-why-did-she-say-attacker-was-black/.

43. The range of claims made by individuals who have this condition is extremely broad. Severe anorexics, who see themselves as obese while quite skinny, represent a "lower bound" example of BDD that is fairly common, and obviously can be ameliorated by conventional and drug-based psychotherapeutic treatments. At the other extreme of the condition, however, are "Otherkin"—people who insist with varying degrees of seriousness that they are non-human animals such as wolves or cats. Transgender people used to almost universally be diagnosed with BDD, but several medical and psychiatric organizations (notably the American Medical Association) have insisted since the early Obama years that it is inaccurate to classify trans people as mentally ill at all.

44. Roberts, "In the mirror, I saw a distorted monster."

45. Hunter, "Acid Attack Hoax."

46. Roberts, "In the mirror, I saw a distorted monster."

47. Among multiple stories about this case published by the U.K.'s the *Daily Mail*, my account relies on Jessica Chia, "Teenager who ran into a Texas church half naked covered in blood…admitted it was a hoax," *Daily Mail*, July 26, 2017, https://www.dailymail.co.uk/news/article-4734016/Teenager-claiming-raped-charged-lying.html. It is worth noting that many stories which initially presented Harmon as the legitimate victim of a hate crime or sexual assault have since been updated to reflect the fact that her claim was a hoax.

48. "Outrage After White Teen Admits She Lied about Being Abducted and Gang-Raped by Three Black Men," BET, March 23, 2017, https://www.bet.com/news/national/2017/03/23/texas-teen-lies-about-getting-raped-by-three-black-men.html.

49. The BET story cited above contains many quotations and re-tweets from both Blacks and alt-right whites describing their extreme anger about the Harmon case. Extensive quotes from a police statement about the damage done by the hoax to the Denison "African American community" can be found in: Christopher Brennan, "Texas teen admits she made up hoax claims about abduction," *Daily News*, March 22, 2017, https://www.

nydailynews.com/news/national/teen-admits-hoax-abduction-black-males-article-1.3006108.

50. Ibid.

51. Chia, "Teenager who ran into a Texas church half naked covered in blood."

52. "Denison Police: Sexual assault case unfounded," KXII-TV, March 22, 2017, https://www.kxii.com/content/news/Denison-Police-Sexual-assault-case-unfounded-416834783.html.

53. K. Querry, "Woman sentenced to probation for making up sexual assault, kidnapping story," KFOR Oklahoma News 4, March 21, 2018, https://kfor.com/2018/03/21/woman-sentenced-to-probation-for-making-up-sexual-assault-kidnapping-story/.

54. Rafi Schwartz, "Texas father confesses to terrible hate crime hoax," Splinter, December 28, 2016, https://splinternews.com/texas-father-confesses-to-terrible-hate-crime-hoax-1793864420.

55. John Binder, "Hate Hoax: Texan Tags Racial Slur on Own Home," Breitbart, December 26, 2016, https://www.breitbart.com/border/2016/12/26/hate-hoax-texan-tags-racial-slur-home/.

56. Schwartz, "Texas father confesses."

57. Lawrence Diller, "The Ritalin Wars: Understanding America's Adderall Obsession," *Huffington Post*, September 19, 2011, https://www.huffpost.com/entry/the-adderall-wars-continu_b_967971.

58. Rafi Schwartz, "Texas father confesses."

59. Jennifer Smith, "White husband confesses to wife…in staged 'hate crime,'" *Daily Mail*, December 24, 2016, https://www.dailymail.co.uk/news/article-4064080/White-husband-confesses-wife-setting-cars-fire-painting-racial-slur-garage-door-staged-hate-crime.html.

60. Rafi Schwartz, "Texas father confesses."

CHAPTER NINE: SOLUTION SETS: HOW TO DEAL WITH THE EPIDEMIC OF HOAX HATE CRIMES

1. David Kopel, "Hate Crime Laws: Dangerous and Divisive," The Independence Institute, January 2003, http://www.davekopel.org/CJ/IP/Hate-Crimes.htm.

2. Vivian Yee, "Racism Charges in Bus Incident, and Their Unraveling, Upset University at Albany," *New York Times*, March 1, 2016, https://www.nytimes.com/2016/03/02/nyregion/racism-charges-in-bus-incident-and-their-unraveling-upset-u-of-albany.html.

3. Geoff Larcom, "Suspect arraigned in last year's Vvandalism incidents on the Eastern Michigan University campus," EMU Today , October 23, 2017, https://today.emich.edu/story/news/10479.

4. Martin Slagter, "Eastern Michigan racist graffiti suspect arraigned," M-Live, October 23, 2017, https://www.mlive.com/news/ann-arbor/index.ssf/2017/10/suspect_arraigned_from_eastern.html.

5. I am assuming here that the FBI estimate of roughly 5,000 hate crimes per year is accurate, and that 1/10 of these incidents drew national media attention. If these figures are correct, there were about 3,500 "high-profile hate crimes" between 2010 and 2017. Nit-picking critics may note that I sometimes stray outside that research window, via for example coverage of the Ashley Todd and Tawana Brawley matters—potentially broadening my draw-from pool of data points beyond 3,500. But, in *that* case, sirrah, let me note that Fake Hate Crimes also sourced a different data set of 330 hoax cases within a research window similar to mine, and Laird Wilcox tabbed 400 more just a decade or two ago. My 409/3,500 or 12 percent estimate for hoax frequency is almost certainly an underestimate.

6. Anthony Gockowski, "Crucifix, Trump chalkings reported as 'hate incidents' at UW-L," Campus Reform, September 27, 2016, https://www.campusreform.org/?ID=8180.

7. Coulter's commentary, including her famous "I have read through dozens of SPLC hate crimes, and they are all lies" line, can be

found here: Ann Coulter, "Ann Coulter: The Great Hijab Cover-Up," Breitbart, January 4, 2017, https://www.breitbart. com/the-media/2017/01/04/ann-coulter-great-hijab-cover/. I personally stand by my 15–50 percent figure.

Index